ALEXANDER SCHRECK
CARSTEN M. STAMMEN

WINE ENTREPRENEURS

THE MAKERS OF THE WINE BUSINESS AREA

WINE ENTREPRENEURS

THE MAKERS OF THE WINE BUSINESS AREA

Bibliographical Information of the Deutsche Nationalbibliothek

The Deutsche Nationalbibliothek (German National Library) records this publication in the German National Bibliography; detailed bibliographical information is available on the Internet at dnb.d-nb.de.

Copyright

ISBN 978-3-945870-19-8
edition graafmann & schreck
Wein-Plus Solutions GmbH
Print: tredition, Hamburg
publisher: Alexander Schreck
editors: Carsten M. Stammen,
Alexander Schreck
Cover: Medienagenten,
Bad Dürkheim
Photos: see Credits & Mentions
first edition 2015

WINE ENTREPRENEURS

Brands and trademarks

Cover design

Many agencies come up with a beautiful design. Working out the right design that is based on a consistent communication concept is something else altogether. This is the challenge that Medienagenten, who are responsible for the cover, face every day - time and again.

Medienagenten: a one-stop advertising agency that lives and breathes wine

It was in 2001 when, amid the vineyards of the German region of Vorderpfalz, the Medienagenten advertising agency was set up. Over the years its rhythm started to be increasingly determined by the seasons of vine pruning, the ProWein wine fair and bud break.

Today Medienagenten is considered by the industry as Germany's leading advertising agency for wine. Apart from established and renowned top wineries such as von Othegraven, Egon Müller - Scharzhof, Bassermann-Jordan or Künstler, its clients in Germany and Europe include newcomers, people from outside the industry and those who think outside the box. Its staff consists of approximately 20 permanent employees. Trainees engaged in winery business studies ensure a lively exchange of ideas. Freelancers supplying scripts, photos and film footage provide creative support.

The consulting process starts with a workshop where Medienagenten work directly and intensively with the client in order to develop ideas, products and distill the essence of the company. The design is then based on the focus themes that are targeted to the needs of the client. After all the media have been used, a leitmotiv runs through all areas of communication, and the brand, which is always focused on the individual, can be experienced across all media. The PR team of Medienagenten works closely with editors, journalists and bloggers and advises its clients to ensure consistent and authentic external communication.

Not only vintners but also restaurateurs, sommeliers, journalists and wine merchants appreciate the in-depth consulting and, in particular, the good network offered by the agents. For its stand-alone and strong brand communication, Medienagenten was awarded the Red Dot Award in 2009 (Weingut Diehl) and in 2010 (Weingut von Othegraven); the agency also received the descom Design Award handed out by the Design Forum of the Federal State of Rhineland-Palatinate in 2012 (Weingut Pflüger) and in 2014 (Weingut Hörner).

The events that are organized by Medienagenten, such as „Winerotation" during Pentecost, show that the agency feels genuinely passionate about wine: „What truly matters to us is engaging with the vintners and living a wine culture that consists of more than just wine tastings. There are so many wonderful and different wines to discover. Ideally they should be enjoyed with good music and in the company of relaxed people." This is how Managing Director Christoph Ziegler summarizes the idea behind the event; but equally it could be the agency's mission statement.

www.medienagenten.de

BUERO MEDIENAGENTEN

PARTNERS

VDP.DIE PRÄDIKATSWEINGÜTER

BUERO **MEDIENAGENTEN**

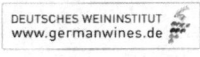

#weinmarketing.

CONTENT

AUTHORS

ALEXANDER SCHRECK

Economist , Author, Speaker
Publisher & Initiator of
WINE ENTREPRENEURS

Alexander Schreck is himself a businessman, and for over 10 years he deals with psychology and communication in the marketing and sales area. The economist and NLP trainer (DVNLP) works for years, with his network, with winemakers, wine dealers and media experts, and among other things, he is the manager of Wein-Plus Solutions GmbH. He manages the Internet site weinmarketing.org and is active as a lecturer for the Deutsches Weininstitut, as well as other organisations and associations. In 2013, Schreck published the book "Weinmarketing – Das Praxishandbuch" (Wine Marketing – the Practical Book), which received the Gourmand Prize "Best Winebook for Professionals".

Contact

Wein-Plus Solutions GmbH
Wetterkreuz 19
D-91058 Erlangen

mail: hello@edition.wein-plus.eu
twitter: @schreckco
facebook: facebook.com/Wein.Marketing.Entrepreneurship

ALEXANDER SCHRECK

WINE
ENTREPRENEURS

Wine Journalist, Writer, Wine Taster
Editor WINE ENTREPRENEURS

Carsten M. Stammen is a specialised journalist (DJFV) and writer concentrating on wine, as well as the hospitality and service industry. After his graduation in restaurant service and tourism business administration, he has been working for over 10 years in the areas of communication, training, and event management. Currently, he is online editor and taster at Vicampo.de, and was previously editorial manager and taster at Wein-Plus. He also blogs on his Internet site vinolog.de and holds lectures, tasting events, and seminars about wine. Stammen has also already participated in "Weinmarketing – Das Praxishandbuch".

He lives near Frankfurt am Main.

Contact

Carsten M. Stammen

mail:	contact@vinolog.de
twitter:	@vinolog
facebook:	facebook.com/Wein.Marketing.Entrepreneurship

CARSTEN M. STAMMEN

WINE
ENTREPRENEURS

FOREWORD

FOREWORD
Prof. Dr. Ruth Fleuchaus
Vice President, Heilbronn University

FOREWORD

Dear readers,

Businesspeople are a special category of people. Even if they all pursue different goals or interpret the concept of "success" in a different way, there are properties which they have in common. To be a businessperson – that means to sniff out opportunities, realise ideas, and enjoy responsibility. However, being a businessperson also means to have diligence, courage, willingness to take risks, perseverance, and stamina. But above all, it also means a lot of passion for your own work.

But what constitutes successful entrepreneurship in the world of wine? A world that is as fascinating as it is heterogeneous. In the first part of this book you'll find out, to a great extent, how people and makers in this world work, what unites them and what connects them. The life circumstances of their livelihoods, and what special features have marked their characters.

Entrepreneurship in the wine business has many facets. Hardly any area is comparable to the wine area, with respect to the diversity of the options of formation. The second part of this book tells about many examples of being successful, but also about quite different livelihoods in the wine business. You'll read about different characters and resumes, about taking over companies and lateral entrants, about successful winemakers and world-renowned personalities whose names are negotiated as brands. You'll also read about merchants and service providers, who create new things with innovative and creative ideas. They all represent an enormous business potential, whose thinking and acting determines our business area. With them, innovations can be advanced, and jobs can be created. They maintain the structures in the area, and ensure forward-looking changes. And they create jobs and preserve cultures and traditions.

However, they also create courage for independence in this wonderful world of wine. The life journeys of these people, about which this book writes, are quite different. Some followed the footsteps of their ancestors and have taken over existing companies, continued developing them or changed them and taken them to success. Others have found the way to independence, and created new livelihoods creatively.

The path to an own livelihood, whether it is taking over a company or founding a new one, is often hard and rocky. It requires careful preparation, to be successful. The statement that you have to be born a businessperson and can't learn it is only partially correct. The required know-how is existential. Successfully founding a livelihood or taking over a company requires knowledge and abilities that can be learned. There is hardly a university at which young people don't deal with the topics of founding livelihoods and taking over companies. Just as at our university, students of all professional disciplines in the Centre for Entrepreneurship can obtain their knowledge and abilities, from the initial idea, passing through the business plan creation up to registering the company, numerous seminars and workshops, some of them outside the universities, are intended to prepare people for their own livelihoods. There are many who appreciate the freedom of self-responsibility; it is worthwhile to promote business thinking and acting. Often there is no lack of courage and ideas, but rather of opportunities, to fulfil them. At the same time, there are more than enough companies, and not just in this area, who don't have successors for the business.

I hope that this book has an interesting readership, and that the readers discover a lot of new and interesting things when browsing through the world of entrepreneurship in the wine area. Enjoy the stories of, and for, businesspeople with a good glass of wine! I thank the authors for compiling this interesting reading material. Hopefully some will get the desire to become independent. There are enough opportunities in the world of wine, which is as challenging as it is fascinating. For those of you who are interested in wine, I hope that the thrilling insights into the world of the makers gives them even more appetite to the topic of wine.

Prof. Dr. Ruth Fleuchaus

FOREWORD

WINE
ENTREPRENEURS

PROLOGUE

PROLOGUE

Motivation and concept of this book

"The makers of the wine business area" is the subtitle of this book. That refers not only to the "wine makers", which work in their own business in a region or as freelancing oenologists anywhere in the world, producing high-quality plants. The book is also about top-level winegrowers. The subtitle, however, refers to business personalities, who shape the wine business area as such – both in Germany and internationally.

As manufacturers, dealers, journalists, multipliers, event organisers or consultants, they move an entire branch of the economy. They are initiators, opinion formers, and creators. Vigour, creativity and assertiveness characterise them. We wanted to know: How was the development of these people who have an influence on other people and on market developments? What makes them successful? What properties do they have in common, what properties differentiate them? How do they tackle new challenges? Thus, this book is about the people behind the wines, behind the media and behind the companies. We show a portrayal of these people based on interviews which we had on them.

Wine Entrepreneurs is aimed at all those who are interested in wine – whether it is as an occasional wine drinker, who appreciate a good glass, as a passionate wine fan, who has acquired a lot of knowledge about wine and always has a well-filled cellar, or as a professional who himself works in wine production, wine commerce, or gastronomy. All those who are interested in people and their stories, in companies and their development, and in economic contexts in a special branch of the economy will also get their money's worth out of this book.

To approach the group of wine businesspeople, we will first investigate the question what a businessperson or an entrepreneur really is, and what entrepreneurship in the wine business area is about. For this purpose we asked experts and researched the relevant literature. Therefore, in the following introduction we analyse the definitions of the concepts entrepreneur, businessperson, and manager, and we take a look at the international wine market – in other words, the environment in which the businesspeople are active and which they themselves help shape. After that, in the main section we let the "wine entrepreneurs" themselves speak, telling their success stories.

We hope that you have a lot of fun and that you acquire knowledge and inspiration while reading this book!

Entrepreneur, businessperson, manager – a delimitation

When we talk about an entrepreneur, we don't simply mean the founder or owner of a company. The word entrepreneur is of French origin; it is made up of the preposition "entre" (among, between) and the verb "prendre" (take). Thus, literally it actually means between-taker. In English, the term entrepreneur was already used at the beginning of the 18th century by the British economist Richard Cantillon, who also worked for several years as a banker in Paris.

But not every businessperson is automatically an entrepreneur; here the English understanding of the concept continues: an entrepreneur is "a personality, willing to bear large responsibility and high risk", defines the Internet portal gruenderszene.de in its dictionary. Thus, the entrepreneur has a special attitude, he has "character, a certain attitude towards life, and the capacity to bring forth ever new innovations", according to the portal. Independence, responsibility, and willpower are essential qualities of the entrepreneur; he has charisma and a special zest. On the basis of the over 20 businesspeople portrayals in this book we will see to what extent this definition applies in each case.

The Gabler Dictionary of Economy describes entrepreneurship as "exploiting business opportunities, as well as the creative and artistic business process in an organization or in a phase of business change". It also says that entrepreneurship is "a scientific sub-discipline of business administration" and "presents itself as an interdisciplinary research area. Apart from business administration theories, in the context of research works methodical approaches from economics, geography, sociology, psychology, and jurisprudence are also used."

A scientifically recognised and standard definition of the concepts entrepreneur and entrepreneurship, however, doesn't exist yet. In current parlance, entrepreneurship is not limited to a single activity – such as founding companies – rather, it comprises numerous, and different, areas such as founding and acquiring companies, obtaining and awarding venture capital, managing large companies as well as small family companies, as well as several others. Science only started hesitantly with entrepreneurship research in the 20th century; the Austrian economist Joseph Schumpeter with his work from the 1930s and 1940s is considered one of the forerunners in this area. According to his theory, a businessperson or entrepreneur is willing and capable to convert new ideas or inventions into successful innovations, and it was Schumpeter who added, to the three production factors soil, labour and capital, entrepreneurial activity as a fourth one.

Entrepreneurship only really became part of the interest of economic research since the 1980s. Today, the discipline is taught at many universities and business schools – for instance the universities in Heilbronn and Geisenheim, which in Germany lead in the area of wine growing and wine business economy. The University of Heilbronn even has a "Competence Centre Entrepreneurship" under the leadership of professor Dr Ruth Fleuchaus which, under the slogan "Promote ideas – promote innovation" regularly invite to competitions about ideas and business plans.

PROLOGUE

For Dr Liv Kirsten Jacobsen, professor at the Freie Universität Berlin, an entrepreneur is somebody who uses intuition and creativity to perceive market chances where others don't find them – or, as strategy consultant Jon Kao formulates it: "The entrepreneur will often say 'Aha!' while others are still scratching their heads." Entrepreneurship specialist Prof Dr Günter Faltin from the Freie Universität Berlin prefers to compare an entrepreneur with an artist, rather than an artisan or manager: "Entrepreneurship is the creative activity of the new design, which requires inspiration, intuition, and empathy – also in social and society contexts." In this sense, the entrepreneur is an innovator – not the routine businessperson from the business administration textbook, whose primary goal is to maximise profit.

The entrepreneur is also clearly quite different from a hired manager chief executive officer. This distinction not only refers to the property situation, where the entrepreneur is usually personally responsible with his property, but also to the framework of action: a manager operates within fixed limits, while an entrepreneur tries to move those limits if necessary.

Entrepreneurs have a high tolerance for frustrations, a high endurance, and they perceive errors as opportunities to learn. They have an extraordinary sense of developments, trends, and business opportunities, even though not every opportunity will result in success; their motto can be expressed in the formula: "Fall down and quickly stand up again". They must be able to cope with an uncertain future – and this also applies specifically in wine-growing: every year, the prosperity and adversity of a winegrower, and therefore also of all downstream market actors, depend to a great extent on climate conditions; a few days or even hours may ruin the work of an entire year. Despite this fact – or precisely because of it, and not just in the wine business – entrepreneurs are willing to bear the consequences of their decisions. "Entrepreneurs believe that in the end, their company will emerge from the crisis as a winner", says Wolfgang Glauner, former director of the auditing company Ernst & Young, in the magazine Harvard Business Manager.

Thus, optimism and confidence are among the attributes of the entrepreneur, and Dr Gergely Szolnoki from the University of Geisenheim names the following additional key qualifications: personality, assertiveness, leadership, and courage, as well as tact and know-how. Dr Edith Rüger-Muck, who teaches as a professor at the University of Ludwigshafen and at the Wine Campus Neustadt, expresses similar opinions, and also adds strategic farsightedness as well as networking and cooperation abilities as entrepreneur qualifications.

In addition, a pronounced willingness to take risks has an important role, as a study of the company consultant McKinsey about executives confirms: The research identifies, as success factors, both perseverance and a strong willingness to take up calculated risks. The entrepreneurs portrayed in this book have indicated that they manage challenges and risks, as much as possible, in a planned and calculated way, but that even so, to a great extent they take their entrepreneurial decisions from a gut feeling.

A decisive criterion that distinguishes businesspeople and entrepreneurs from hired managers is their central desire for self-determination and independence. They reject any type of paternalism, and basically only accept the judgment of the market. Entrepreneurs want to create something, and yet they don't necessarily strive for power. This situation, in turn, distinguishes them from the manager, who gets power lent for a set time and then loses it again when he no longer holds his position. Perhaps for this reason, many managers consider symbols of power and status very important, while businesspeople usually manage capital resources in a planned – and sometimes cautious – way. In most cases, there is a clear corporate culture, characterized by the entrepreneur's personal values. He has internalised these, and doesn't necessarily separate his professional and private life.

The online dictionary of gruenderszene.de notes, however: "Entrepreneurship as a field of action of an entrepreneur is now considered a learnable thought principle, which can also be learned and implemented by 'normal' managers." We also based our selection of the businesspeople portrayed by us on this; some of them are top-managers hired as CEOs, but they still stand out by having the attitudes and qualities of an independent entrepreneur.

Entrepreneurs recognise their social responsibility for their employees, and don't see them as means to an end, but as an essential prerequisite for the company's success. Quite often, they allow their employees considerable freedom, and in turn expect intrapreneurship from them. Intrapreneurship – a portmanteau from "intracorporate" (within the company) and "entrepreneurship" – describes business-oriented thinking and acting by employees within the company. Employees at all levels of the hierarchy and in all functional areas should behave as if they themselves were businesspeople. Responsibility and autonomous acting, foresighted thinking and active shaping of the organization should increase both the company's flexibility and the employees' motivation – both of which are important criteria for success. In their leadership style, entrepreneurs are predominantly cooperative and result-oriented, and they specifically appreciate lateral thinkers, since they can provide new impulses. Businesspeople and entrepreneurs think in the long term, often decades or generations; they want to leave something for their descendants and create something lasting.

The statements of the wine businesspeople portrayed in our book show that all "wine entrepreneurs" are true enthusiasts, or even crazy in a good sense. They love the product wine and consider it to be a central content of life for themselves. This passion distinguishes all of them, fully knowing that entrepreneurship in the wine business area only provides relatively small sales and profit opportunities. Thus, one of the entrepreneurs gave us a jocular, and yet apt, motto: "There are different ways to destroy your fortune: with women it's most fun, gambling is the fastest way – and wine growing the surest one."

PROLOGUE

The wine business area – a special environment for entrepreneurs

The wine business area is a very inhomogeneous branch of the economy. The bandwidth of market participants goes from one-man companies to multinational conglomerates; companies with a highly professional organisation and sometimes chaotic lone fighters live in peaceful coexistence. Editorials, food companies and retail chains enter the wine sector, and in part they complement their portfolio with large purchases. Additionally, ambitious startups try out their luck in the wine business area – especially in Internet commerce – and countless wine blogs are filled with content day after day. It looks as if it is contemporary, or even stylish, to get involved in the wine area.

Many businesspeople in the wine business are lateral beginners. That also affects most of the entrepreneurs portrayed here, as well as the book's authors. Some of the businesspeople are also still engaged in other areas, where they sometimes have considerable economic and social success – as property developers, PR and marketing consultants, musicians, poets, fundraisers or business angels.

So, to what extent is the species "wine entrepreneur" special, and stands out from businesspeople in other business areas? And how important is personality-oriented marketing, when – unlike in other areas of agriculture – the name of a winegrower appears as a brand on the bottle label?

To find this out, on the one hand we looked at the economic framework, and on the other hand – as mentioned before – we asked economy and communication experts, who are quite familiar with the wine area: Dr Gergely Szolnoki, lecturer at the Institut für Betriebswirtschaft und Marktforschung at the Geisenheim University; Dr Edith Rüger-Muck, Professor for Marketing at the University Ludwigshafen and on the wine campus Neustadt an der Weinstraße; Dirk Würtz, manager of the winery Balthasar Ress in Hattenheim as well as wine blogger, author, and lecturer; Dirk Paulus, manager of the full service advertising agency Medienagenten in Bad Dürkheim; Rosamund Barton and Rupert Ponsonby, directors of the PR agency R&R Teamwork in London.

All of them have given us their assessment on entrepreneurship in the wine business area, on the importance of personality for successful marketing, and on the future of the business area, and, with their explanations, they create the background for the statements of the wine entrepreneurs themselves, which we have interviewed for the main part of this book.

PROLOGUE

The Market research company MarketLine estimates the value of the global wine market for 2014 to be 280 billion US-dollars, and expects it to increase to 320 billion dollar until 2017. However, it should be noted that, as mentioned before, the market is very fragmented. According to the Wine economy report 2010 of the Rhineland Palatinate Ministry for Economy, Agriculture, and winegrowing, winegrowing companies in the European Union got an average yearly yield of a bit more than 81,000 euros and a profit of about 30,000 euros; German winegrowers, with a yield of almost 158,000 euros and a profit of ca. 53,000 euros per year are clearly above these values (as of 2007/2008).

According to data from the International Organisation for vine and wine (OIV), the wine market gets increasingly international: the wines sold between countries increased from 25% in the year 2000 to 40% in the year 2013; corresponding to a volume of 9.8 billion litres. The value of the wines traded worldwide, according to the OIV, was 25.7 billion euros in 2013.

According to OIV information, in 2014 a total of 27.1 billion litres of wine were produced; in 2013 it was 28.1 billion litres, and in 2012 – according to an extraordinarily low harvest as a result of the climate – 24.8 billion litres. Basically, about two-thirds of the global amount of wine is produced in the member states of the European Union (EU), and one-third outside the EU. The worldwide area of vines in 2013 was 7519 million hectares, and in 2012 slightly greater, at 7575 million hectares. Within Europe, Spain, France, and Italy have the largest areas of vineyards; outside of Europe these are located in China, Turkey, and the United States of America (USA).

The largest wine producers worldwide in 2014 – according to OIV – were France (4.6 billion litres), Italy (4.4 billion litres), and Spain (3.7 billion litres). In 2013, the ranking for the first three places was changed: Italy was above Spain and France, followed by the USA, Argentina and Chile, as well as Australia, China, South Africa, and Germany. The global wine consumption, according to the OIV, was 24.3 billion litres in 2014, 23.9 billion litres in 2013, and 24.5 billion litres in 2012. The main consumers in 2013 were the USA, France, Italy, Germany, and China; in 2012 France was above the USA. In general, the OIV observed a geographic shift in wine consumption: in 2013, 39% of the wines produced worldwide were consumed outside of Europe; in 2000 it was only 31%.

Especially the smaller winegrowing countries of the southern hemisphere as well as eastern Europe continuously expand the area of their vineyards, increase their wine production, and invest in quality; this includes cooperation and purchase of know-how from the "Old World". In Asian, South American, and Eastern European emerging countries, as a result of economic growth and the corresponding increase in wealth, the wine consumption will continue increasing in the future. Wine businesses from the established winegrowing nations also invest in these markets.

Germany, as the worldwide number one wine importer, is considered among the most attractive, but also most contested, wine markets. Here, wines from virtually all countries on Earth are available, consumption is stable, and during the last few years – as

PROLOGUE

confirmed both by the German Wine Institute (DWI) and the Federal Statistical Office – it even increased slightly. Hardly a country offers a comparable density of retail spaces in all sorts of business models: discount, cash & carry, supermarket, consumer market, hypermarket, independent food retail, and specialised wine shops are side-by-side and sell wines from all over the world – in almost any quality and price class. In addition, there are a growing number of wine dealers on the Internet. The result is an aggressive price competition, and not only in stationary trading.

Prof Dr Dieter Hoffmann and Dr Gergely Szolnoki from the University Geisenheim have written a study with the title "New wine customer segmentation in Germany", in which they classify wine customers into five segments with respect to places of purchase:

- Discount and food retail customers: This group of customers has a simple school education, and clearly a large percentage of lower income groups.
- Supermarket customers: This customer group corresponds to the average of the population and thus of wine drinkers; it has a somewhat higher percentage of higher income groups.
- From-the-farm customers: This customer group has by far the largest percentage of people over 65 years old; customers who mainly purchase the wine directly from the winery; they have an average education and income structure.
- Customers of specialty shops: This customer group has a higher income and lives mainly in urban surroundings.
- Multi-channel customers: This customer group has a strikingly divergent socio-demographic profile, typically middle-aged, a high education level and a high income.

Hoffmann and Szolnoki analyse in their study: "With wine consumption, interest in wine, the use of wine-qualified purchasing places and living under good social conditions, the differentiation of the criteria used to select wine also increases, and the importance of the price diminishes significantly. In contrast, the price as a purchase criteria increases significantly in case of a reduced frequency of consumption, less interest in wine, being anchored in simple social layers, and using discount and food retail as purchasing places." Thus, for marketing high-quality wines two especially interesting groups can be determined: on the one hand, intensive wine consumers, and secondly, the so-called multi-channel customers. "With 24% of wine customers, 62% of the wine consumed and 67% of expenditures for wine, intensive wine drinkers occupy a prime role, and become the core target group of value creation with wine. The multi-channel customers, with 19% of the people and 33% of the value, are the ones who integrate the purchasing places most. Thus, by virtue of their interest in the wine topic and their willingness to pay for good wines, they are the main target of competition among places of sale. They are therefore customers with a high interest for all sales outlets", say the scientists.

Another study – carried out by the market research institute Wine Intelligence and commissioned by the international wine and liquor trade fair ProWein in Düsseldorf – deals with the future of the wine business area; the research is called "The International Wine Industry: Global Experts' Vision 2034". It concludes that the wine economy will continue being characterised by a lot of change; as a result, they say that considerable

WINE
ENTREPRENEURS

changes are to be expected both on the purchasing and on the sales side: "The wine economy will have to adapt more to the needs of the consumer. For communication, this means the end of a 'top-down education of the consumer', and an emphasis on consumer loyalty through experiences and emotions. Over ¾ of the respondents (77%) believe that compared with today, in 20 years consumers will have a shorter concentration span than today, that family and friends will continue to be the main source for reliable information – even though social media are increasingly becoming the transmission channel for such information. Here is a chance for the wine sellers who choose a creative approach in a constantly changing consumer environment, in which mobile technologies and social media will likely dominate the consumer experience."

According to the study's finding, "During the next 20 years, consumers will continue drinking wine", and "will even spend a bit more on it". The knowledge about wine "will be greater in 20 years, because information will be more accessible and structured". In sales, the market researchers expect a greater intensification of the situation: "66% of the respondents believe that supermarkets will dominate the wine business in the year 2034. They expect supermarkets to get more powerful, and many have the impression that the sale of wines will continue getting more polarised. While wines produced for the mass market concentrate on individual retailers, niche and small producers will find a way to sell their products mainly via specialty shops. Even though this polarisation is already evident in some markets, this tendency is expected worldwide; wines that don't fit into any category will be harder and harder to get." Online sales, according to the study, will be expected to "increase significantly in importance", which will have inevitable consequences for stationary wine sales: "Wine specialty shops will have to concentrate on the stories and messages which catch on to the consumer."

Specialty shops try to counteract this development with new concepts and ideas. Projects such as the "wine islands" in Munich and Nuremberg – an initiative to promote small wine sales, wine bars and wine shops managed by their owners – want to reduce the reservations which consumers have about specialty shops. The challenge consists in the fact that wine specialty shops are regarded as expensive, for an elite upper-class. Nicola Neumann, initiator and organiser of the "wine islands", explains: "It's about reducing the inhibitions. Many young people don't dare enter a wine sale or a wine shop, since they don't know what expects them there. Perhaps they are insecure about whether they may look around or have to go ahead and purchase something, or because they think that you have to be a wine connoisseur, to be able to appreciate a special wine enjoyment."

The study commissioned by ProWein about the future wine market, however, even is sceptical about the trade landscape in general, and assumes "that producers will bypass these sales channels in general, and invest in direct sales and marketing to the end customers." A clear positioning and a professional concept, professional marketing knowledge, innovation, and additional services for the customer are therefore the prerequisite for their existence – not just in a few years.

Even today, some of the scenarios foreseen by the ProWein survey have become true. Large importers now bring relatively good qualities at reasonable prices to the food

PROLOGUE

retail and discount markets. And yet – or perhaps precisely for this reason – more and more people want to know more about the products they purchase and the people who are behind those products. Consumers ask more and more often: Where does my wine come from, how was it manufactured, and what is in it? This development should essentially strengthen quality-conscious winegrowers and wine specialty shops.

The higher consumer awareness can also be seen in the increasing demand for bio-wines. The area of ecologically managed vineyards has more than tripled within eight years, as the Forschungsinstitut für Biologischen Landbau (Research Institute for Biological Agriculture – FiBL) informs, and in Germany – according to the Bund Ökologische Lebensmittelwirtschaft (Association for Ecological Food Management, BÖLW), the surface area for biological wine has more than doubled from 2007-2012; according to BÖLW, the market for biological foods remains stronger than the production. In the meantime, also, more and more large wine producers are changing from conventional farming to a biological or biodynamic cultivation. Several aspects are important here: one, the advantages of a sustainable and natural winegrowing for the environment and health, on the other hand, the positive image of biological products among consumers, as well as the fact that purchasers of bio-wines have the tendency of being less price-sensitive. In addition, ecological and economic motivations convene here. The Rhineland-Palatinate wine economy report 2010 summarises the situation of the interests of wine producers succinctly: "The motivations vary. They go from a purely ethically or ecologically characterized attitude, over premium optimization, to a market policies attitude."

PROLOGUE

Entrepreneurship in the wine business area

The environment in which wine businesspeople act, then, is dynamic, heterogeneous, and very fragmented. What type of people are wine entrepreneurs? What do they need in order to be successful in this area? Rosamund Barton from R&R Teamwork in London resumes her observations and experiences – and even finds some parallels between people, grapes, and wines: "Wine entrepreneurs tend to come from different backgrounds/disciplines – ie teaching/hospitality/modelling/sales etc. Invariably they have travelled a lot. I think that the majority of entrepreneurs in the UK are very young start ups, certainly in the tech world but wine entrepreneurs have done something first. They are more mature and have fermented over a longer period than younger entrepreneurs; so they brim with the experience of many worlds, many 'terroirs'; and have inner depths, complexity. Yes, sometimes they are nicely gnarled too, like their vines, and have been known to sparkle."

Dr Gergely Szolnoki from the Geisenheim University also confirms that many wine businesspeople are lateral beginners – and as an illustration, he recounts his own story: "20 years ago, when I started to occupy myself with the wine topic, it was something special for me, and it hasn't lost its charm yet. I still experience the particularities of the wine business area, whether I observe it here in Germany or in some other country. I might compare that with Alice in Wonderland: As a lateral beginner, I really feel like Alice in Wonderland; the Wonderland is the vineyard, and you might say that I am Alice, who just happens to have slipped inside." Szolnoki considers that that which fascinates him are two things: "tradition and innovation, which should normally be separated from one another, get mixed here, and are hand in hand. In the wine business, tradition has been, and continues being, emphasized. Wine as a product of thousands of years of tradition, and innovation, is something that appears over and over in the wine area. The fact that that catches on, I think, is something special in the wine area. This results in a colourful mix."

Szolnoki also occupies himself with the heterogeneity of the wine business – "even though it's a large family, since everybody knows everybody", as he says. "If you visited ProWein once, the number of people that you know is relatively large. However, as in any business area, there are also hardcore investors and business people; then there are generation-long winemakers, many of whom have hundreds of years of tradition; the lateral beginners, the wine lovers, who have simply started to make wine or to sell it. And then there is also the group of mad people – which appear not just in this business area, but in other areas as well. That's how I see the wine area, in other words, my personal impressions. As a scientist, of course, the situation is quite different." As a scientist, you have to "remain factual", clarifies Szolnoki, and on the factual level, he finds it "super interesting, that the wine area covers a complete production chain. If you take a traditional winery, the winemaker is responsible for the wine-growing outside in the vineyard, responsible for the wine in the cellar, responsible in the office for sales, purchases, advertising, events, and taxes; and also for logistics and wine delivery. He is responsible for everything. And that is really something that you don't find in other areas with such a small structure – this complete production chain." Even though he himself deals "more with the consumers", his scientific interest in the wine area is for

PROLOGUE

people "who have to do everything from A to Z", on many facets and details; that's what makes working in this sector "very exciting", says Szolnoki.

Professor Dr Edith Rüger-Muck from the Wine campus Neustadt perceives the wine area as more differentiated: "I think there are many sellers, both national and international, with very different products. I see two tendencies here: one is that innovations are made to continue improving a good massive wine. The other one is rather oriented towards the production of a premium or handmade wine, where fewer machines are used, and the wine product is more likely to be hand-picked at a very high level. Ultimately, I think that the winegrowers are required to act progressively and innovatively – in three disciplines: in winegrowing (that is, the work in the vineyard), in cellar work, and in marketing." Rüger-Muck sees the largest requirement of action in marketing – "so, in the area with which I deal. For I think that in marketing there is still a bit of a lack of strategy, as well as know-how. That starts with the fact that many companies – according to a current survey by me, among others – don't have any software, often don't know their customer base at all, don't evaluate their actions in the area of customer loyalty measures, but they also don't know at all how their market presence is perceived by the consumers." In part, says Rüger-Muck, these deficits are even known to the wineries, "but I believe that the structures of such a classic winery often don't give up such things". Many wineries "are still simply a one-man show", or according to the classic role distribution, the man is "the businessperson", clarifies the professor – responsible for winegrowing and cellar work, while the wife – "often externally" – takes over the marketing area. "So, marketing is often just a small part, and in this area, the fact that marketing can represent a fairly essential distinctive feature is still somewhat unacknowledged. I can only differentiate myself a little bit through a product, but through marketing, perhaps more."

Rüger-Muck has the opinion "that you would have to invest more – more time, but also more staff". Even though there are certain wineries "which take up a large forerunner role in marketing", and Rüger-Muck names the companies from Markus Schneider in the Palatinate or Balthasar Ress in Rheingau as examples. Also, many young wineries unite with innovative concepts, and try to establish markets that way. "But I think, if you take a look at entrepreneurship, a bit more might happen in marketing", considers Rüger-Muck. She considers a comparison with other areas of the economy difficult, "for after all, the wine business is very special". But within the wine business, she sets up international relationships: "During the summer I had a research stay in Australia, in Adelaide, and there I took a look at wine areas. If you take a look at the wineries in Barossa Valley or in Clare Valley, there the subject of marketing has a very essential role; the use of new media is different. There are also many more merchandising articles, and a more professional Internet presence. And I believe that the German wine economy should perhaps develop a bit more in this direction." In this context, Rüger-Muck considers commerce in a critical way, and conjectures that "perhaps it prevents the achievement of a higher price level". Wine dealers "should indeed offer better platforms, to allow individual wineries to present their products there. But ultimately, I consider commerce more of a hurdle; the possibilities to present yourself as an individual brand are simply quite limited."

"Differentiated" and "heterogeneous" are also the attributes with which the winegrower and wine blogger Dirk Würtz describes the area. He speaks harshly of his colleagues: "Quite often, I see only very little entrepreneurship among wineries, if you consider this classic concept of entrepreneurship. Winemakers are usually more farmers, and only businesspeople in the second or third place. This is not as bad as it used to be, but it continues happening that many winegrowers don't think as businesspeople, even if you only think about cost calculations. Much has changed here, not least due to the extremely good training or the extremely good formation status, which we have nowadays. Especially also thanks to Geisenheim and Neustadt a lot happens here." The fact that today entrepreneurial thinking is more pronounced than in the past, according to Würtz, can be noticed by the fact "that somebody might suddenly do a full cost calculation, and say 'I don't work for free', and evaluates that, too, correctly. But here, I think, there are still lots of requirements. The increasing market pressure as well as the increasing cost pressure will slowly but surely force everybody to really do calculations."

Würtz goes into more details: "If I look at entrepreneurship on the basis of innovation and marketing – what is my product, what is my USP – there is still quite a lot to catch up in the winegrowing business." However, here too there is already considerable progress, "once again in part due to cooperation with agencies and young people. In the meantime, I simply must say: The young people are unbelievable! Not least, people such as media agents; it is incredible how much fresh wind they bring, and how they think about the market together with the winegrowers. Well, something happens here as well, but we are still far away from what is classically understood as entrepreneurship or this entire startup scenery. However, what is normal is that we are in agriculture. Farmers think a bit different; not worse, or more stupid, but simply different. Also in very different cycles. Two, three, four years, which is almost an eternity for such a startup, are of course nothing for us. After all, we think in cycles of nature. And sometimes that means that we think over generations. If I set up a vineyard today, I want the next generation after me to continue using it. Thus, we have a quite different approach."

In wine commerce, too, Würtz sees a lot of movement: "Currently a lot is happening there, including all the startups; these come and go like nothing else. Many, I believe, have a completely wrong idea about the wine product and believe that it can be sold just like Zalando shoes. That isn't so – and especially not in Germany. That might perhaps work in other markets, but the German market definitely works differently. We have no relation with the wine product as in other countries, so it's simply more difficult to sell anything. Ultimately, it is sold by the price. If somebody indeed thinks and acts in an entrepreneurial way, in the commercial context – and that should also be applied to the Internet – he can really only think about price categories. So: How do I make a wine attractive? And in Germany that works via the price. That's simply the way it is. The German won't voluntarily generate any other added value, or he will more or less not generate it." The motto is: "People want things cheap and in quantities, that's our mentality."

PROLOGUE

WINE
ENTREPRENEURS

Würtz does recognize "a few great specialty shop concepts which counteract this, people such as Martin Kössler. But even in large concepts, which have commercial success – such as Gerd Rindchen, who goes up and down all the time, because some customers are suddenly not present any more – it boils down to a discount war. I believe that the market for good consulting is simply too small." According to Würtz, nowadays entrepreneurship in wine sales is probably limited to "get a risk capital under the most favourable conditions possible, which doesn't hurt anybody if it is lost and there is no result, and to find a way to offer something five cents cheaper." But a group of actors in the wine market who think and act as entrepreneurs are identified by Würtz: "The wineries as the last great players on the market. Definitely thoroughly entrepreneurs; here everything is calculated to the fourth decimal digit."

The agricultural localisation of the wine area is also taken up by Dirk Paulus from the Medienagenten office; he follows up on Würtz's arguments: "I believe that the wine area is in a radical change right now, that it continues developing, from an area with an agricultural characterisation to an area that acts more like a company." However, with this development, he says, the wine sector is "already relatively late" compared to other areas of the economy. As an example, Paulus cites the carpentry business: "Very few people order a locker or table to be made; rather, they buy it at IKEA or at a furniture store." Therefore he thinks "that other areas are already more advanced and are managed as a business – that also applies to fruits and vegetables, milk, or meat; in other words, other agricultural areas are more advanced in this sense. And the wine area goes more and more in this direction." The reason is that the wine market changes quickly, for less and less customers cover their wine demand with just one provider. "Many winegrowers tell us this, that they have problems in sales for this reason; that the customer who simply buys everything from one dealer no longer exists, but that the customers observe very carefully: What are the products? How are they made? And they get a Riesling from one dealer and a Silvaner from another one, and perhaps even a red wine from the supermarket. The markets change. I even believe that the markets change quickly, very quickly, and many who are involved in the wine area are not able to follow."

In wine sales, too, Paulus diagnoses a radical change, "which is especially due to the Internet's transparency. I believe that the development will go in the direction that there will also be larger online suppliers, but those will again offer a very specialised portfolio. For instance, there might be a provider for young German wine, and another one who only sells Spanish wine, but at a greater depth."

Paulus gets to the bottom of the changes: "On the one hand, the production side results in the fact that the wines – I won't say that they become more comparable, but they are all very, very good. Nowadays bad wine is hardly manufactured at all any more. Therefore – I won't say that it almost doesn't matter, but you can really get very good wine over different channels, for just a small amount of money. But if you want to be successful as a provider, I believe that you have to think about other things and create incentives, to be able to sell your wine."

PROLOGUE

Success factors for wine entrepreneurs

Among the properties that a wine entrepreneur must have to be successful, Ponsonby from R&R Teamwork considers flexibility and farsightedness to be high on the list: "You have to love what you do and draw experience from previous disciplines. And very importantly you need to be able to change your model – for instance the way we do wine pr has changed massively in the last ten years with everything being a lot more immediate. We have an expression in English – you need to 'duck and dive'! And they need to consider how they can be different from their competitors; and be seen to be different; and to have plans in place over a number of years to stay modern and stay ahead, and to address new markets and new ways of selling."

Dr Gergely Szolnoki from the Geisenheim University goes into more depth and explains, based on the example of a young winegrower – "25 years old, just finished his studies, and is now about to take over his parents' business" – what a successful wine business-person must have: "What I think of, spontaneously, is courage; a lot of it. And persever-ance; that you actually carry out what you plan to do. And one thing that is always very important is sensitivity. You need to know how to react, depending on how the market changes. The wine area will continue developing. If you don't keep pace, you still have the possibility to remain a traditionalist, and to serve and sell to a specialised, older segment, but all others simply have to keep pace. Even if you start to apply something new, it is important how well you have this sensitivity." Szolnoki admits that you can't specifically practice this market sensitivity. "But you can gather information, relevant information – of course I am speaking as a market researcher – and fashion everything on the basis of it." The sensitivity also means to decide "whether you gather the infor-mation yourself or get examples from other countries."

As a basis, wine producers "obviously need a well-founded know-how, how to make wine", explains Szolnoki. That is "the alpha and omega, that's how it starts. And when you don't have this sensitivity or feeling for marketing, nowadays there are lots of se-minars or training offers. No master has fallen from the sky so far, we know that, and this also applies to the wine area. If you don't have that from the start, or somehow got it taught from your parents, you can develop it. And fortunately, it isn't the case that if you don't have this strong personality you can't sell any wine. Fortunately you can. Either you do it yourself, in self-education, or you go to a few seminars; in any case it will work then." An encouraging, pragmatic approach. We'll see how the "wine entrepreneurs" interviewed have developed in each case – whether through genetic predisposition, education in the family, targeted training, or perhaps even through a fortunate coincidence.

Prof Dr Edith Rüger-Muck from the Wine Campus Neustadt takes up some of the points mentioned by Szolnoki and adds some more: "A classical businessperson first of all needs a vision, or a strategy. He needs to say: Where do I want to go? With what strategy do I want to position my winery, my products? And of course you also need courage, to take up some money and to say: I'll go along this path. Also a certain perseverance; if you try out something new, don't buckle after the first failure; rather, if you believe in your concept and your strategy, work to implement it. And I think it is very important – but of course that is a business point of view – that you should always evaluate what you do." Often, "in the area of marketing or events, etc., where you try to retain customers and to make them enthusiastic for you" measures are not quantified, reports Rüger-Muck. "And I consider it difficult, precisely that this type of success controlling isn't carried out. I believe that more development could be done in this area."

A good marketing concept, according to Rüger-Muck, is yet another important condition for success for the wine producers: "You need to know: What does my brand stand for? Who are my customers? How many customers do I even have? For what values do I stand, how am I perceived? And you need to make your brand appearance uniform, saying: How do I present myself in the winery, in the salesroom, in a mailing action, on the Internet? There must be a uniform communication and a uniform layout. You can start with that, in any case."

Entrepreneurial farsightedness also includes cooperation along the value chain, as Rüger-Muck explains: "In any case you need to be able to carry out good cooperation and networking, to get your wines known in commerce or gastronomy – for instance in cities which are not in regions that have a wine affinity, that is, not in winegrowing regions, such as Munich, Berlin, or Hamburg." The professor encourages "that you cooperate with gastronomers and get a platform to present your wine. Or in commerce: that you don't just have a standard space on the drawer, but that you develop a sales concept in coordination with commerce, to exhibit a new wine; also perhaps on an uncommon or attractive sales platform that doesn't correspond to the common presentation platform."

Winemaker and wine blogger Dirk Würtz approaches the question of success factors in a less academic way, but he still grazes the topics of brand, emotionality, and image: A winegrower, he says, needs "the capacity to make people enthusiastic for his own product. You need to set up a type of homebase of sympathisers, who are actually convinced of what you do, and don't go on to the next business when it comes along. So, you need sympathisers, you need personality." In the wine business, the success factors, according to Würtz, are just as tangible: "In commerce, of course on the one hand competence is required, but on the other hand, cool business calculation is appropriate."

Dirk Paulus from the Medienagenten office continues with the explanations of Dr Gergely Szolnoki and also emphasises the statements by the other experts: A successful winegrower "must, first of all, know his craft well. And then it gets more and more important that apart from the farm wine lines with classification you also offer innovative products – whether they are brand wines that are somehow related to the winery, to the name, or specific events which you can use to attract customers and get them enthusiastic. You simply have to be able to use different things to achieve an emotional bond to the winery. Here you need to act as a businessperson, be visionary, and be able to anticipate developments."

PROLOGUE

Personality-oriented marketing

Dr Gergely Szolnoki from the Geisenheim University once again builds a bridge from wine manufacture over marketing to businessperson personality, and in doing so, shows the limits of what can be learned in seminars: successful winegrowers must "make good wine" and "know their craft; for me, that's the very first thing that must work." However, nowadays it isn't enough to make good wines, in order to have success. "They know that full well. On the other hand, you also need to market the wines well. Many know how to make good wines. But only a few know how to market the good wines. And for good marketing, in my opinion you really need a face for the wine. That, in my opinion, is one of the most important aspects in the wine world. Therefore I name personality or individuality or character in the first place, for you can learn to make good wine. But personality, for me, is something inborn. Of course you can also train that, etc. But I think that that's what makes up the mix." Thus, Szolnoki's formula for success is: "50% good wine – but that is really the prerequisite, that you make wines that are clean, drinkable, and fit for human consumption. And the other 50% consist in being able to actually market the wines."

Szolnoki lists examples for personality-oriented marketing: "Breuer, Müller, Loosen, Künstler, or at the international level Gaja, Mondavi, etc. – there is always a face, a person behind the brand, and for me that means good marketing. Note that I am talking about the wineries, not the cellars. In cellars that doesn't work; they work on the basis of quantity, personality doesn't play a role there. In the case of cellars personalities might be there, but you might say that they do their work in the background. But in the case of wineries, family properties, in that case the personalities or the people who stand behind the brand are really the most important thing."

Prof Dr Robert Göbel, who teaches strategic management and consulting at the Geisenheim University, is also a follower of personality-oriented business management: "As a result of their focus on personal values and principles, family businesses have the ideal starting conditions to create sustainable competitive advantages", he writes in his book "Wein & Sortiment" (Wine & Assortment). According to Göbel's arguments, the personality of the company or the businessperson must enter even into the product communication: "Limiting yourself too narrowly just on the wine quality doesn't ensure long-term success. For the wine's marketing success, the combination of all relevant quality criteria has a great importance." That is important "because it is possible to a very limited extend to stand out exclusively through flavour and quality characteristics, except for a relatively small consumer layer of specialists. Only when the product in its entirety is convincing will there be a repeat purchase, which can result in a loyal customer."

The key to personality-oriented marketing, according to Dr Gergely Szolnoki, is "to somehow maintain your personality. The point, however – and we can prove this well, now that we have market data – is that not everybody manages to do this. And perhaps not everybody should strive to have such an extraordinary function. That's the top of the wine world; at most 5% can achieve such a good reputation. But not everybody must achieve that." In Szolnoki's opinion, personality-oriented marketing is also an issue of

PROLOGUE

strategy: "First you have to define what you actually want to achieve. Not everybody has the capacity to stand in the forefront and make a big noise and to say: I am a personality, I sell wines via my personality, through my personality. Not anybody can do that. Those who can, do it. Those who can't may possibly try it out, but there are also other marketing strategies. There are all sorts of other options such as rarities, such as addressing special segments, playing with the price, playing with the sales places, or offering events." Szolnoki clarifies: "Personality is not something that you can have or not have. Obviously everybody has personality, but the extent to which this affects a brand depends on how pronounced this personality is, and how assertive it is. So, as I said, not everybody can and not everybody must do that. For if you consider – if in Germany, from the several thousand winemakers everybody would be a personality, if the brand would be so important, had such a good reputation, for instance, as the names I listed previously, we would long ago have lost the overview. So, this personality-powered brand only affects a very small number."

Prof Dr Edith Rüger-Muck from the Wine Campus Neustadt would "not want to specify as a percentage" the portion or the potential of personality-oriented marketing, as she says: "In my studies, the business personality has a very, very important role for the reputation of a winery, but especially for the quality assessment of the wine from the customer's point of view. I have analysed several partial aspects, where many quality factors were investigated, and the winery as a brand, in practical terms the businessperson's personality behind it, almost always came up among the top ten, and usually among the top five of the most important characteristics. Insofar, I think that it is something that must not be underestimated. If a businessperson, a winegrower, places himself skilfully in the foreground, that can have a very good radiance from the point of view of the consumer."

For winegrowers looking for alternatives to personality-oriented marketing, Rüger-Muck also has some recommendations: For example, somebody who as a young business founder or descendant of a founder wants to make his winery advance "can join a concept of young wineries, which appear as a group and perhaps represent the region. That way I experience the topic of authenticity, but also of regionality, which is more and more in demand precisely among the consumers. And I believe that when wineries from a region get together and skilfully market their products jointly, this can also transmit the idea of authenticity." Another option is to develop services, to achieve a stronger personalization: "In E-Commerce, you can of course stand out if you optimise an Internet site or the web shop. Here, too, in my opinion there is still a lot of space to continue improving yourself. Of course, on the one hand there are technical challenges that have to be mastered, but also the entire topic: How do I present my wares on the Internet, on social websites? How easy can I make things for my customer, how many clicks does he require to activate his purchase on the Internet? That, too, is a topic which you can use very well for positioning."

Rupert Ponsonby from R&R Teamwork also talks about the topic of positioning on the Internet, and mentions communicability, required for personality-oriented marketing: "The front person needs to be very outgoing; or to have a team behind them who are being 'out-going' and colourful on their behalf! And even those with minimal resources can now mount a very credible and personal campaign for themselves with colour and pizazz through prolific use of social media." Dirk Würtz is to some extent a proof of this: "The moment that a wine costs over 30 euros, you need your own story, for – as I always say – you can just as well get drunk from 1.99. And then it is all only about emotions and personality; everything else is irrelevant. I, for example, purchase a wine from a winegrower in the Mosel area, because I find him completely likable, and I like what he does on Facebook, etc., etc."

Würtz, however, sets the horizon more widely: "I think that in this structural change, ultimately the number of companies which market themselves will get clearly smaller, and many more wines will be summarised in a single brand via the barrel wine market. If a young winegrower appears now who wants to position himself, he must really have some great idea. He will require a story, but in the meantime, we have an incredible amount of those. Thus, frankly, I am rather pessimistic about this. I believe that it will all be consolidated by the producing providers. Now there won't be a large-scale elimination of wineries, but I expect that at the end, their number will become clearly lower, and that they will focus on a large-area marketing of large brands; those however will not be personality-powered, but will rather be based, for instance, on their origin or the vine variety." Against this background, Würtz sees chances for proper marks of associations and marketing organisations: "There might also be a Riesling generation wine. From 500 people, 1000 litres each, that gives you 500,000 litres. Then you are suddenly an interested partner for the area." Würtz advises young winemakers: "Boy, think what you want. Do you really want to become a winemaker with everything it entails? The personality, which ultimately gives Mr X or Mr Y the bottle of wine that you yourself have produced? If that's what you want, take a large sheet of paper and start calculating, first, whether you can actually afford it, and second whether you want to afford it, and whether you are able to carry out each individual step that is required as professionally as necessary. Otherwise, get some help."

The Medienagenten office of Dirk Paulus and his colleagues has received several renowned design prizes for its brand and communication concepts in the wine area. Paulus explains his approach: "You have to take a look at each individual case, and there you find several starting points. The unique features or focus topics which you find must then be transferred in a very targeted way to text and images. In other words you tell the story in a brief way, so that anybody can quickly grasp it. For every winery, you have to leave the consumer with an anchor point in his head. It doesn't necessarily have to do something with wine. After all, basically, everything we do is an outsourced service, which in the past might have been done by the printing shop with a publishing house label. And now, the point is to tell stories on the label, on the Internet site, and the stories aren't told by the winemakers themselves; rather, we write the stories, which the winemakers then tell."

According to Paulus's point of view, personality is mainly relevant for "luxury goods – at least with our customers. Only a few of them are massive providers; rather, they have more or less premium products. And as far as I know, here in Germany premium starts at eight euros, and most of our customers offer that. Therefore, I think it is quite important to know: Who is behind that? How does he produce the wines? And what sort of person is he?" Paulus assumes that personality "will become more and more important in the future", but he also thinks "that in the past, 50 years ago, people also selected their winemakers, somebody with which they could empathise especially well, about which they could say, oh, he is nice, I'll go to him and get my wine. Nowadays people don't do that any longer – or only very few do it – i.e., going to the winemaker themselves and choosing their wine. But I do believe that if people research on the Internet, they will consider: Who is compatible with me? Who corresponds to my spirit? And in that case, a Lukas Krauß or a Markus Schneider can very well be a person to identify with, about which they say, oh, yes, that's a cool guy; he strikes me as nice, and his wines are also good."

The personality orientation, however, has its limits, as Paulus shows: "If personality provides that, it usually isn't wrong to include it in communication. But in the case of traditional wineries, which have a history of 400 years, this person is only a small building block in the company's long history. In that case, no matter how communicative the person is, the issue will most likely come back to other points."

PROLOGUE

According to Paulus, brands are also a concept of the future for the wine area: "I believe that branding and brand management – in other words, to consider the winery as a brand – will become more and more important than it already is. In general, it will probably become more difficult to get established on the market." Paulus expects that "the development that started 10-15 years ago" will continue, and that "the so-called classic wine drinker will disappear more and more". That, he says, has effects on the sales of wine: "I can imagine that sales will get more and more outsourced, or that winegrowers will join forces and coordinate that together. That already happens; for example, winegrowers make a joint presentation at ProWein, and I believe that that allows them to share staff, if they aren't very big; they might say, we hire somebody who does the sales for us, or cleans doorknobs, and a certain portfolio will then be offered."

Paulus considers Germany to be in a good starting position: "I believe that German wine is certainly a good brand. And I believe that as a result of their climate situation, only a few countries can produce wines as we do. I believe that we are already quite specialised, for instance on Riesling, or on cool climate wines. Probably other countries such as Spain, Italy, or France have more reason to be afraid." Paulus assumes "that German wines will continue getting large sales and large demand, including the international level; that the development will continue being as pleasant as it was during the last few years."

Dirk Würtz, from the Balthasar Ress winery, is also basically optimistic: The German wine market grows. Germans once again drink more wine per person. German cellars are well advised if they recognise that they can also make good business with German wines in the mid-level price segment. What I always advocate: a wine that costs around seven euros on the shelf, pure with respect to vine variety, with an origin that can be assigned clearly. We can do that like nobody else worldwide. Here we are practically unbeatable! And once again, we can only do this together with the wine cellars. A winegrower can't achieve this alone. You need strong partners, to be able to subsist in the area. In this sense, large cellars continue having a future – all those who briefly think, have a future."

Würtz is of the opinion that the German winegrowing world "is at the beginning of a massive, huge structural change. In the long term, we won't be able to attend to the needs of this cheap price segment. Our harvests are too small; our work is too cost-intensive. Even if you rationalise everything to the extent that you can do that alone or with two people, you aren't competitive in comparison with Spaniards or South Americans. That is to say, you won't be able to sell the wine in the barrel so that the large wine cellar later can still place it at the discount store for 2.29 – these times are past. We need to recognise that we must define ourselves on the German wine market through quality. And that takes us back to what I just said: make an artisanal first-class wine, pure with respect to vine variety, with a clear origin, add a nice brand, and sell it for 6.99 in the consumer market, and everything is fine."

PROLOGUE

Würtz is rather sceptical towards commerce platforms for wine on the Internet, and service providers who take over the marketing and the sales logistics from the wineries, if they represent the sole sales channel. "I am certainly a great friend of the idea that everybody does what he knows best how to do, and that all those who know well how to do something get together to do it even better jointly. No question about that. However, I do doubt that this works in our sector, in our segment. It is just too sensitive for that. It might work for a few companies, to sell wines via these channels. But I dare to doubt that this will really happen in quantities that are relevant for the market. I don't think so – not that I don't want this, but I simply can't imagine it. To achieve this, the market, however big it is, is still way too small. You have a platform such as WirWinzer or Vicampo, and ultimately there are 500 articles on it. You are one of the 500 – where is your distinctive characteristic? Why does this customer come now and buy something from me? The network might be a sales channel, but it's part of the entire mix."

Würtz also emphasises, in this context, the importance of the brand for the future: "Logically, the larger the market, the more complicated everything will be. What does Amazon Marketplace provide for you if nobody knows you? So, even in the Marketplace you need somebody that lets you be known on the market X, Y, or Z. I believe that the work of agencies and agents in the positive sense will become more and more important. What is it for you if somebody in Australia can purchase your wine via Amazon? Why should he do that? Really there's no reason to do it. Somehow you have to create the incentive for this." And this incentive, according to Würtz, is the brand: "Everything is about the brand. Even when you tell a story about the origin, ultimately it's all about the brand. You are the brand. And either you have a strong brand or no brand at all. If it is recognisable, you have already advanced a good deal. Or you don't have it; in that case, you need to look around."

Würtz talks once again about the changes in the wine economy: "As I said before, I believe in a serious structural change. I believe that the number of companies that market themselves will get smaller. I might be wrong, but that's my feeling. There will be associations. Within the winegrowers it will also be necessary to set up marketing alliances, to be able to distribute in a way that it still makes sense. And in this case you need to make sure that you strengthen your brand. I notice it here with us." The Balthasar Ress winery has built up a strong brand, he says, and he notes that business with private customer is increasing strongly: "We are on everybody's lips, everybody talks about us. As a result, the business with private customers will also increase." With this background, wine marketing platforms on the Internet don't necessarily make sense and they are not necessarily required, according to Würtz: "As soon as you can notice that the effort that you make with respect to private customers is actually paid back through much larger coverage participations, you say to yourself: Why should I give them 20%, and I still need to ship the wares? Then you calculate 20% of 10 Euros – just an example – so that's 2 euros. Put 2 euros per bottle of wine into a marketing activity, and you will quickly notice: if you do these calculations, you can easily hire somebody. And once that gets firmly established in the heads, I think the situation gets quite difficult for all the 'You-don't-need-to-worry-about-anything' startups."

Still, Würtz thinks that the Internet has brought great advantages for wine marketing. He mentions the "recommendation character via social networks" and the trust in these media: "People google, people read, people use social networks where wine is recommended. There is somebody who I know and who says that the wine tastes good, and I believe him. And then I see the photograph, and I quickly look up what that is. After all, it just takes about ten seconds to google it. And then I am at the winery. That replaces the walk to the specialty shop. Why should I go into a specialty shop and ignorantly say, I need a wine for the evening, I have visitors, when one of my best and most trustworthy friends says on Facebook, drink that, it's good?"

However, Würtz sees no chance for peer-to-peer communities and evaluation portals in the wine area, as it happens for instance in the tourism area: "What result is that expected to provide? We are talking about taste. We aren't talking about whether a hotel room is clean or whether a bathroom has been cleaned, we are talking about taste. For this, you need people who really have a great interest in this sort of thing. Germans love vacations and cars. But how about wine? You would found a peer-to-peer community for the same 300 people whom you also meet in the wine forum or in the Facebook wine group. It won't become anything else. The target group is too small for this. No normal wine drinker would get interested in it; after all, that's all way too complicated. When they go vacationing, that's something different. But wine isn't part of awareness at all." Würtz doesn't have a high opinion of tasting databases: "Who uses them? Perhaps 100 wine freaks. That's about it. Hundreds of thousands of wines tasted, and nobody interested in it. You can find that very quickly. So, if you are interested in wine and google around a bit, you find this tasting database. And what does it help them? Nothing at all. After all, nobody understands it. I mean, if you are looking for a bottle of wine for the evening, what's the point of a tasting note that nobody can retrace? This is about taste. If you say, the loo was dirty in hotel XYZ, that's a statement. When you say, in my opinion the wine tastes too much like pears – sorry, that's ridiculous."

Würtz considers the success of wine guides as provider-driven: "Nobody comes here with a wine guide, nobody. And we have a lot; we make 46% of the turnover with private customers. But nobody comes here with a wine guide. And in any wine guide you will find something good about us in any case." However, Würtz says that there is a considerable market effect when a wine receives a high rating by Robert Parker: "95 Parker points last Saturday, and the shop is full – really full. That, I think, lasted exactly 36 hours. But that is something completely different, that's Parker. In Germany we don't have anybody who gets even close to having the market influence that a Parker has. That is not very dramatic, that's just a fact. And why? Because it actually doesn't interest anybody. If I get 94 points at Falstaff, at Wein Plus or somewhere else, I write that on my homepage, get ten "likes", clean my mouth, and business continues as usual. It all goes around in circles; it isn't really decisive for sales."

Würtz appeals to his colleagues in the wine area: "Dear people, don't spend so much money in absurd startups that nobody needs. Before we think more about platforms, first of all we need to implant, in German brains, the fact that wine can be something different than a drink that gets you drunk. So, we must first of all work in the real implementation of a wine culture, before it gets all the other balderdash." Würtz doesn't consider it pragmatic that such an initiative would or should arise from associations or marketing organizations such as the German Wine Institute (Deutsches Weininstitut, DWI): "Surely this, too, is the task of the DWI, but the DWI must once again represent all interests; that's where it gets complicated and equal and political. No, I believe that the merchants are required, the producers are required; they need to clarify that wine is not just another product such as screws or whatever, that it isn't entirely comparable. But that it is rather about lifestyle and quality, and that wine is a cultural asset. Nobody grasps that wine is a cultural asset. You can't just compare wine with a hotel; that is a very different story."

Dr Gergely Szolnoki from the Geisenheim University is also convinced that the wine economy will have to continue changing: "Every day we have small breakthroughs in the wine area. What we have seen so far in new things mainly came from the new world – whether it is the use of Barriques on a large scale, the old new vine varieties, steel tanks, or social media; all of that came from the new world. I don't know whether it will now continue to be controlled by the new world. But in any case there will be development and innovation." For the following ten years, Szolnoki hopes "that in Germany the small wineries survive. I hope that in Germany the cooperatives survive. And I hope that in Germany the cellars survive, as well. But one thing that is clear about all three of them: They have to continue developing. Nobody knows for sure in what direction. But the other beverage areas have already shown that this can very well happen. The areas of beer and non-alcoholic beverages have already shown that there are possibilities for development and innovation. You simply need to know what the consumers accept, what they don't accept, what the market accepts, and how it continues developing. One thing is sure: super wines from competitors will appear again and again." The overseas markets, China and India, would also continue developing, predicts Szolnoki: "The competition will become even larger."

In this context, Szolnoki considers online marketing, branding, and the use of professional agencies important: "I believe that the new generation might also have quite a bit more affinity with respect to new media or the requirement of advancing e-commerce, or to change something in the area marketing, labels, etc. But I also see that there has to be a stronger cooperation with advertising agencies." But Szolnoki warns against blindly outsourcing business functions. He says it is "dangerous, if there is absolutely no know-how in the company, when marketing is practically outsourced to an agency and the agency develops something that might not match the winery, that simply isn't authentic. You certainly have to see to it that you set up a type of brand personality. But the businessperson must be able to do something with the brand. I consider it dangerous if an agency creates a brand which the winery or the businessperson has trouble embodying."

In commerce, too, changes have already started according to Szolnoki's assessment: "The classic stationary specialty shops currently have a difficult time, and they will continue having a difficult time in the future. On the one hand, there are the discount shops that are really getting off and trying to get a piece of the cake. On the other hand, the normal food retail store doesn't just sit there and waits what happens; rather, they really get off as well – just think about Edeka or similar business companies, which define wine as a real main focus and do great things with 5000 locations or additional events, etc. For laypersons who in the past didn't dare go into specialty shops and buy their wine there, the doors are opening in this case. And people can also buy expensive wines in the supermarket, for example as a gift; we know that people spend quite a bit more money for gifts than for normal consumption. This, of course, makes the situation for the normal stationary specialty shops – the individual shops, not the specialty dealer chains – much more difficult, for they need to add some extra value to their service. And that they can do, by continued development, and by dealing with more innovation. For them, it is more of a service: What can I offer as an extra, so that I may survive? So that people even come to me at all, and my regular customers continue visiting me, and don't buy their expensive products in the food retail or in the discount shop? That's the challenge for specialty shops."

Nevertheless, Szolnoki doesn't consider the situation for specialty shops to be hopeless: "The scissors are there, and year after year, a small part of the turnover of the specialty shops will be cut off. At the same time, however, this development gives them a great chance to reposition themselves and in fact to redefine their function, their tasks and their role. As long as you live comfortably and somehow sell a thousand bottles a year, and you can live off that, nothing happens; at least, nothing that somehow affects innovation. But if you are challenged or accept that as a challenge and don't immediately close the shop, but rather seriously think how you can survive and somehow contribute something positive or innovative, then that means that people are very open and that there can be a chance for them."

Similar to Szolnoki and Würtz, Prof Dr Edith Rüger-Muck from the Wine Campus Neustadt also expects that on the side of the wine producers "during the next few years, there will be an even stronger suppression competition". She expects "fusions or restructuring measures, perhaps towards a stronger professionalization with respect to profitability." With respect to internationalisation, Rüger-Muck considers that "there is still a lot to be done – simply to recognise the relevant markets, to test, perhaps to improve logistics, to have a stronger presence in other countries. That, however, is once more related with the topic of marketing, to practically set up awareness for German wine in other countries." During her research stay in Adelaide, Australia, mentioned previously, she only found German wines in a few stores. "That means that German wines aren't strongly noticed. And I simply believe that it's necessary to emphasise the internationalisation topic more, but of course you also have to decide how you present your wine – with image brochures, or explanations, menu tips, etc. – to achieve international success. After all, there is a tendency towards authenticity and regionality, and I think that it is important that you are aware in what region you work or produce your wine product, and what values and associations go along with this regionality, so as to be able to translate that for your own product, for your own marketing, and to be able to advertise internationally."

PROLOGUE

According to Rüger-Muck, internationalisation and technological development are related: "Ultimately, this goes along, once again, with the topic of e-commerce, for when you are active at the international level, of course you have to make sure that you have a platform. Of course you can do a lot over a dealer, but this is also about the topic of direct sales, and the expansion of your own Internet presence and e-commerce capabilities. And then, of course, you also have to think: How can I be found at all on the Internet? For instance, do I conduct search engine marketing? On what platforms can I be found?"

Rosamund Barton from R & R Teamwork does a bird's-eye overview and considers the wine market globally: "I believe that wine will have no frontiers at all in the future – ie: I think there will be more bottling in the country where it is being sold and that there will be more unusual grape varieties like Carmenere, Albarino or Semillon being planted globally. Europe will no doubt start importing wines from China. And hopefully taste-before-you-buy machines will become more widespread; and this will expand knowledge and make wine fanciers more brave in choosing new wines. And English wines will be taken seriously as the sun is seen in future more than once a month", adds Barton with a wink, referring to climate change.

PROLOGUE

In this book, representatives of virtually all actors who participate in the wine area appear, who are addressed by the experts: owners of German wineries and internationally active wine businesses, owners of independent specialty shops, founders of specialty shop chains and startups in the Internet wine commerce, editors of wine guides and magazines, publishers, wine critics, and several others. The "wine entrepreneurs" that we interviewed come from Germany, Austria, Switzerland, France, Italy, Great Britain, and overseas. They all work in the same area, but each of them expresses himself from the perspective of his corresponding profession – whether it is as a producer, a merchant, a journalist, or a consultant. That way, once more the variety and fragmentation of the wine sector becomes clear, even specifically on the basis of individual statements.

All the businesspeople presented here represent a brand – either that of their wine, that of their company, that of their medium, or for their own person. In this respect, some of the people interviewed – for instance the winegrower legend Angelo Gaja – have created personality-driven branding the sense mentioned above. The concept of brand is related to branding, and according to history, the cowboys – North American herdsmen in the second half of the 19th century – might be the inventors of modern branding: Every evening, they had to laboriously separate the cattle of different owners. Since this task required a lot of time and they wanted to get to their campfire early, they decided to mark the cattle, so that they could recognise more easily what animal belonged to what owner. For this purpose, they provided the cattle with a brand symbol – and the English words "brand" and "branding" for a product brand can be traced back to this.

The economy scientist Prof Dr Heribert Meffert defines the brand as a "usage bundle with specific features, that ensure that this usage bundle is permanently differentiated with respect to other usage bundles, which fulfil the same basic need." This refers to the distinctive characteristics – known in English technical jargon as unique selling position (USP). A brand, then, distinguishes a product from other products of the same type, and it has an emotional value, an image. This applies to the personalities portrayed in this book and their companies.

In the main part of "Wine Entrepreneurs", however, the topic is not entrepreneurship as a scientific or economic discipline, but the entrepreneurs themselves, at most, the so-called entrepreneurial thinking: the topic is entrepreneurial thinking and acting, innovation and values, decisions, leadership, and motivation – not at the academic level, but very pragmatically. This is about getting insights into the founding history and the creation processes of successful businesses, about revolutionary encounters and significant course-setting, about self-realisation and about profound human experiences; also about failure in some situations.

We present outstanding and influential people behind the complex product wine, observe their life journey, their philosophy, and we ask about their recipe for success. As mentioned before, they are people who manufacture wine, market wine, evaluate wine, recommend win, and write about wine. The selection of the interview partners was purely subjective, according to the author's free decision. None of the businesspeople

PROLOGUE

interviewed got money for his or her participation in this book, and – at least as important for us – the authors didn't get money or any other benefits from any of the companies for including a person in the book. Therefore this book doesn't contain advertising presentations of companies; the companies appear exclusively in the context of the corresponding businesspeople, and other companies or persons named are repeated just the way they were freely mentioned in the corresponding conversation.

We made our selection according to different criteria. Not just economic success, but especially also interesting aspects of the business concept, the public perception, and communication on the market were important for us. Obviously such a selection can never be complete; nor does it mean that wine businesspeople who don't appear in this book are less interesting or successful. We would have liked to interview and present many more personalities, but unfortunately that isn't possible in this type of publication – if only because there are limits related to the size. Some of the businesspeople portrayed here will no longer be active in less than ten years. The work of their life will be continued by the next generation or by a hired management. We also want to honour their achievements in our book, and save their stories and the corresponding knowledge.

As already mentioned several times, we have interviewed the selected wine entrepreneurs, mainly in direct conversation. We posed them questions about their personal development, about entrepreneurship in the wine area in general, about their own business activity, and about management and employees, business goals and values, and about the future. Some of the questions are also connected to principles of the so-called neuro-linguistic programming (NLP).

The NLP assumes that virtually all abilities can be learned, if the corresponding knowledge about the underlying behaviour, the way of thinking and the motivation is available. The NLP founders, Dr Richard Bandler and Prof John Grinder, under the guide of the anthropologist and systems theoretician Gregory Bateson, have researched the behaviour patterns of successful businesspeople, top salespeople, communicators, and therapists, to make the effective bases for human changes explicit. This revealing and copying of human top performance is designated "Modelling of Excellence". We have used some essential core questions, required for such a modelling process, in our interviews. In this sense, this book can also be understood as an idea pool and inspiration for other wine businesspeople.

PROLOGUE

We have asked the following 20 questions to all our interview partners:

1. How was your path into the wine area?
2. What professional stations were most important for you in your development, and why?
3. How do you experience entrepreneurship in the wine area? In your opinion, what attributes distinguish wine businesspeople? Do you see differences or parallels with other areas of the economy? If yes,　　which ones?
4. What, in your opinion, are the key qualifications of a successful businessperson in the wine area? How must you think and act, as a businessperson in the wine area, to be successful?
5. What is your drive or motivation, to live as a businessperson? To what extent was this a conscious decision?
6. How do you define business success? How is it measured?
7. What is your personal recipe for business success?
8. How do you take your business decisions?
9. How do you handle business risks?
10. Currently, the digital revolution and social media, among others, provide dynamism and change in the wine area. How do you handle the changes and unforeseen challenges (social, economic, legal, etc.)?
11. How would you describe your leadership style?
12. How is the ideal employee for you?
13. What conditions must employees have, to be successful? What conditions must executives of the middle management level fulfil, to be successful?
14. What conditions can and must a company create for the success of its employees?
15. What values and beliefs are especially important for you, and determine your success?
16. What personal goal do you follow with your business activity? What do you want to achieve?
17. What is your life slogan, personal aphorism or favourite quotation?
18. How do you assess the developments in the wine business for the next ten years?
19. What key qualifications will be decisive for the success of wine businesspeople in the near future?
20. What would you specifically advise a young businessperson if he wants to be successful in the wine area?

PROLOGUE

We also asked all conversation partners to complete the following twelve sentences:

1. For me, success is …
2. am successful because …
3. For me, performance is …
4. For me, motivation is …
5. For me, errors are …
6. For me, lateral thinkers are …
7. For me, contradictions are …
8. For me, education is …
9. For me, design is …
10. For me, wine is …
11. My favourite wine is …
12. If I were able to go back and change something in my professional life, that would be …

In some cases, the portrayals include additional information from biographical material, lectures, or print and online publications. Our interviews with the "wine entrepreneurs" were sometimes very time-consuming and intensive, and took us to exciting, sometimes even comical, places. In any case, they were also very fun. Some of the stories were so exciting, absorbing, and instructive, that they would have deserved their own book about the corresponding people.

We heartily thank all the "wine entrepreneurs" portrayed below, for their willingness to participate and for their involvement. We also thank the experts who have supported us with their contributions, and the hired assistants in secretary offices, communications sections and agencies, who have coordinated the critical contacts and important appointments. We hope that this book provides the benefits that we promise our readers from it. For us, in any case, it was a huge learning project with many interesting meetings, and in the meantime we have already made lasting relationships with some of the businesspeople.

Some of the wine entrepreneurs which we have asked for an interview have answered our questions in a compact form; therefore – to match them with the more detailed portrayals – we will let them talk already here.

PROLOGUE

MICHEL ROLLAND
Oenologist and Flying Winemaker

Michel Rolland (born 1947) is one of the best-known oenological consultants worldwide, and as a so-called flying winemaker he manages over 100 wineries in 13 countries. He comes from a family of winemakers in the Appelation Pomerol in Bordelais and he grew up in the small town of Maillet, where he played with his brother, and wandered through the vineries with his grandfather, as he says. The smells and tastes of his childhood are unforgettable for him, says Rolland, and he remembers "the entire culture of a daily life in a family and rural environment. That was the time of carefreeness. Only my parents were always worried in the course of the seasons: frost, flowering, the heat of summer, the rigour of winter, rot, etc. – all of these worries which were then, as today, common to all winemakers."

Rolland says that all his early youth he was "immersed in nature", and adds: "Perhaps that explains my natural tendency towards Earth in general and winegrowing culture specifically." He says that his father already introduced him to winegrowing in his youth. But after his family moved to the city, he only worked in the vineyard during vacations, informs Rolland. "That was very hard, but very formative. I often participated in the harvest. For me, that was a constant feast, where comrades were invited, people worked all day and had fun at night. All this under my father's vigilant eyes, who supervised everything, but who also – I am sure of that – laughed heartily under his stern expression."

After Rolland completed the agricultural high school, he completed a study at the winegrowing school of Château La Tour Blanche and then studied oenology at the Bordeaux University. There, in 1968 he met Dany who later became his wife; she had also completed the oenology study. One of his teachers at the university was the legendary wine scientist Émile Peynaud, of whom Rolland admits that he was strongly impressed: "His explanations were accessible, illustrated with simple concept, and he was great in expressing strong feelings and delights in simple words. Émile Peynaud knew how to taste, not just swallow three drops, and to give apodictic speeches. He was truly a fascinating man."

In 1973, Michel and Dany Rolland together joined as partners in the analysis laboratory Chevrier in Libourne. "At that time, an oenologist was more of a medic than a consultant – and we were just at the beginning of the great oenological adventure in the last 30 years of the 20th century", emphasises Rolland. The laboratory owner Chevrier aroused their enthusiasm for chemical analysis, while Rolland himself turned more towards vines and wine: "I remember that I tasted all the samples that arrived at the laboratory. At that time, oenologists were more familiar with the pharmacy than with the terrain." At the start of the '70s, Rolland started consulting wineries – "while nobody wanted to listen to my advice, and the cellars were not yet well-equipped. We endured more than we intervened, that was a bit frustrating – but what a learning experience! That was the beginning of modern oenology, when you got together with winery owners who weren't convinced that a bit of a scientific approach would bring them benefits, or with winemakers who thought that you wanted to take away their work." In 1976, Rolland and his wife took over the analysis laboratory; it was then that they started to have "a normal, pleasant life".

In 1979, however, Rolland's father died, and since in the meantime his brother worked as a lawyer, Michel and his mother took over the management of the family winery Château Le Bon Pasteur. Until the mid-80s, he simultaneously managed the laboratory in Libourne and the winery in Pomerol, and initially abandoned the alternative to continue expanding the oenological consulting. "But then, everything changed. I was asked to go to California, and to investigate the possibilities of optimising the potential of the wines in the region there. As all young businesspeople, I was interested in traveling and expanding my knowledge", describes Rolland. "That was the beginning of a life as a consultant, which took me to four continents and over 150 wineries. A course marked with extraordinary encounters, visits to vines and grapes in all sorts of conditions, in all climate conditions and all cultures. An extraordinary professional and human adventure!" However, a large part of the three-digit number of wineries in Europe and overseas that Rolland advises as an oenologist are part of the highly renowned top companies in Bordelais.

Rolland's wife Dany now manages both the analysis laboratory and the family's wineries; apart from Château Le Bon Pasteur (Pomerol), over the years they added Château Bertineau Saint-Vincent (Lalande-de-Pomerol), Château Rolland-Maillet (Saint-Émilion), Château Fontenil (Fronsac) and Château La Grande Clotte (Lussac-Saint-Émilion). Through joint ventures, Rolland is also involved in the wineries Bodega Burdigala in Spain, Remhoogte Estate in South Africa, as well as Mariflor, Val de Flores and Yacochuya in Argentina. The laboratory is currently in Catusseau (between Libourne and Rolland's place of birth, Maillet) and has 14 employees, many of which work there for over 30 years, as Rolland emphasises. The company is "expanded through a new structure, and – gradually – through new, young oenologists", says the busy winemaker; the commercial management is now in charge of his oldest daughter, Stéphanie.

"In the family, everything is organised and harmonised – from wine consulting to marketing, from the vine to the glass. In the family, everything is transferred: respect, sensitivity, culture, openness, passion", explains Rolland, with which he also addresses his personal values. He outlines his business principles as follows: "Work, scrutinising, curiosity, identity, vision, personality, quality, professional knowledge, respect, strictness – those are the top requirements for the success of a vineyard, as well as for a person. Both must achieve a certain degree of prominence, to be recognised. There are no recipes, but there is certainly work. Evidently there are risks; any decision comprises them. Information technology – yes, it should be used for communication, but there is also a danger due to a mix-up and too many unannounced communications..."

Rolland notes: "Oenology has developed considerably, to become a top-notch technology." He says that he spends "an exciting life between the vine and the wine." To do that, he had to learn English and Spanish, can only rarely take vacations, and spends a lot of time in the car and in airports. But he is "completely in the service of the wine, which is my passion – to a degree that I never dared to imagine". And "for all those who believe in luck", Rolland has some advice ready: To get started, you need "a lot of enthusiasm and curiosity, and especially, a lot of work!"

PROLOGUE

PORTRAITS

HEINZ KAMMERER
Founder, Wein & Co
Vösendorf, Austria

Heinz Kammerer is the founder and owner of the chain of wine specialty shops Wein & Co in Vösendorf near Vienna. The company has 24 branch offices all over Austria, seven of them with a wine bar or restaurant; the Wine & Co online shop supplies customers in about 15 countries. His path to the wine area had been "by chance", says Kammerer: "I was interested in wine since the seventies. My father had a production for handicrafts in Waldviertel, and when we drove home, we always bought wine at F. X. Pichler in Wachau – today one of Austria's most famous winegrowers. At first, I just liked to drink wine, but over time I became a manic collector, and over time I had no more place for additional purchases. That's when I got the idea to sell wine, and then, at some moment – in view of the fact that in Austria there was no real wine retail trade – the concept of Wein & Co got started."

> "THERE IS NO DOUBT THAT I ALONE BEAR THE ENTIRE RISK, THEREFORE, ESSENTIALLY, THAT WHICH I BELIEVE IS WHAT MUST HAPPEN."

Kammerer was involved with sales from the beginning – first in a carpet business, as he recounts: "After a year, they sent me to England, where I was supposed to sell Austrian carpets. That was like carrying owls to Athens, for compared to the British carpets, ours were twice as expensive, and ugly. I then turned the tables, and sold English carpets – Tufting floors, printed with tiling patterns, and not known here at that time – in Austria and Switzerland." Kammerer decided early in favour of entrepreneurship: "At the end of my two-year employee career, they blamed me for the devaluation of the Pound, and then I knew: That's not for me. I always went quite automatically from one activity to the next. I always listened a lot, and looked at each deal from the point of view of the purchaser, i.e., the customer. Thus, I was first a carpet salesperson, then I worked in the tiling and sanitary retail, and then I ended up in the wine area, always with the intention of offering products that were not available so far, in a way that was as friendly to the customer as possible."

Kammerer looks back at his entrance into the wine sector: "In 1993, I had collected ca. 10,000 bottles, and I founded Wein & Co, since I had to do something reasonable with the wine." He recognised the optimism in the Austrian wine business after the wine scandal in the mid-80s. "The quality of the wines improved, but the winegrowers had no idea about its marketing", he informs. For his concept, he cooperated with renowned sommeliers, who also motivated the best winegrowers to deliver their wines to Wein & Co. "The project started under the slogan '15 waiters and a speculator'" summarizes Kammerer, self-deprecatingly.

He sees an important stage in the development of the Austrian wine market in 1995, when Austria entered the European Union: "Thanks to Austria joining the EU, Austrians got to know foreign wines, and developed their taste and higher demands", according to Kammerer. "After all, we don't have our sight on drunkards, but on people who deal with wine as a luxury item. Wine is a nice thing; just consider that everywhere where it grows it's nice. Just think about Wachau, Southern Steiermark, the Toscana, or Burgundy."

"INNOVATIVE POWER IS THE MOST IMPORTANT THING. YOU MUST BE ABLE TO CHANGE THINGS OF WHICH YOU YOURSELF WERE NOT FIRMLY CONVINCED A SHORT TIME AGO."

Kammerer considers himself as a climber, both economically and socially: "I have created everything for myself", he emphasises. Success is measured "on your own satisfaction with what you achieved. That's all relative: Bill Gates and I have started at approximately the same time in our 'career' as businesspeople. He would probably not be satisfied with my success, but I am. Success, for me, isn't something volatile. For me, it was always important that my work didn't make up more than 50% of my interests. I managed to do that, and therefore I am satisfied. I am successful, because I have always grabbed happiness."

His business success recipe is "to make more correct than wrong decisions, but to do it quickly", defines Kammerer. "There are decisions that you can take on the basis of numbers – good numbers – but most must come from a gut feeling. It is my experience that I mainly took my best and most important decisions quickly." Kammerer, as he admits with a wink, manages risks "perhaps somewhat too relaxed. Errors for me are opportunities. I want to have a company that is economically independent and that works without existential problems, in which employees work that I find likable, and which deals with a respectable item. And that's exactly what I have."

In 2012, Kammerer retired from the operative work at Wein & Co after almost 20 years, and transferred the company management to Mag. Florian Größwang, who worked previously as a manager in the sport articles area. "I don't think it is necessary that the manager knows anything about wine", comments Kammerer about his decision in favour of the marketing professional. "I have recognised that you must withdraw when things are going well." In the business year 2011/2012, for the first time Wein & Co passed a turnover of 50 million euros. "After 40 years as an independent businessperson, I wanted to make room for new impulses, as well as for concepts that go beyond Austria", explains Kammerer. In the meantime, the implementation of others will "surely be larger" than his own, he thinks. He is of the opinion "that you must treat people well. But in business, that's not always possible, therefore I would like to get out of it. Making others trip, ripping them off, being faster, better, more crafty and brutal, is easier in your youth. I don't want to do that any longer. That way, you can no longer manage a company from your gut feeling."

HEINZ KAMMERER

Originally, Kammerer himself strived to obtain the market leadership in Central Europe with Wein & Co, and then to expand to Eastern Europe and Asia. "I was always looking for the right company size, and didn't find it yet. In the East, we failed due to the prices of real estate; also, they don't have a middle class. Therefore we preferred not to go there, though I asked myself how I should communicate that. After all, people are vain and driven by media. The calculation about effect aesthetics is still part of me. But vanity is also an enormous motivating force. It's really the ugly sister of insecurity: you are insecure, want to 'show them all', or you get depressive. So you react to your insecurity either through expansion – or through depression."

"PEOPLE WILL INCREASINGLY REALISE THAT WINE IS A LUXURY ITEM, AND THAT IT SHOULD BE CONSUMED IN REASONABLE AMOUNTS, THOUGHTFULLY AND CONSCIOUSLY."

Kammerer sees parallels between businesspeople in the wine business and in other areas: "The seller must always consider the same things, no matter what he sells: How is the demand, and how do customers want to cover it? It makes no sense to think something up in view of your own requirements or examples from other markets, and then to stubbornly put it into practice. In this sense, innovation is the most important thing. You must be able to change things that you weren't yourself firmly convinced of a short time ago. I am a freak in this sense, and that's the reason that Wein & Co was always at the top. We have our Web shop – the largest by far in Austria – since 1997, our social media networking is enormous, and we constantly test new ways. When Wein & Co was founded, i.e. in the year 1993, most of our current customers were between zero and 15 years old. In view of this, it's obvious that we have to change!"

With a view to business vision, Kammerer talks about motivation. "I don't believe in these often contrived, engraved principles", he ascertains. If he has a basic principle at all, that would be "We are what we do" – with which he implies authenticity and consistency as values. "Of course we want to be successful, but mainly in the sense that our ideas work with respect to content, and commercially. There is not much more about it. But especially, that which you do must make fun – for each individual employee." Kammerer describes his leadership style as "friendly-authoritarian. In the company, we have very relaxed manners, short decision paths, but also clear goals. There is no doubt that I bear all the risk, so basically, that which I believe is what must happen. However, on the other hand, good, committed employees are the only way to achieve this goal – in other words, a tightrope walk. In any case, more than 15% of our employees are already in the company for 10 years or more; that certainly says something."

For Kammerer, the optimal employee is "in the first place, enthusiastic, and equipped with a good grasp. Everything else, they can learn from us. We are a company managed by the owner, not a group. This automatically provides a different type of atmosphere. Employees who appreciate that they can talk directly with the boss will basically feel good. Of course there are other parameters as well: the interest in wine, success, the position of Wein & Co on the market, a relaxed work atmosphere – sometimes too

HEINZ KAMMERER

relaxed", smiles Kammerer. "Lateral thinkers are important for me. Of course there are career opportunities and training opportunities, as well as – even though it isn't the most important thing – an above-average payment. We have 'produced' all medium-level executives ourselves; only the highest level and a few specialists were hired."

For the future of the wine area, Kammerer expects an upwards tendency with respect to quality: "Everything will go in the direction of quality rather than quantity. People will increasingly realise that wine is a luxury item, and that it should be consumed in reasonable quantities, thoughtfully and consciously. An additional tendency will be the autochthonous one, i.e., the unmistakable characteristics of the different winegrowing areas, which are also travel destinations and cultural spaces." The essential key qualifications for businesspeople in the wine sector, in the future, will be "as it always was, a good mix of risk-taking and sense of reality". Kammerer advises young entrepreneurs "to think carefully about getting started, and only venture to do it, if you have a lot of interest in wine itself. There is no such thing as quick money in this area."

HEINZ KAMMERER

FRANÇOIS PERRIN

Co-owner, Château de Beaucastel
Courthezon, France

François Perrin (born 1954) is co-owner of the winery Château de Beaucastel in Courthezon, which lies in the winegrowing region Châteauneuf-du-Pape along the southern Rhône. He manages the company together with his brother Jean-Pierre and their children Marc, Pierre, Thomas, Cécile, Charles, Matthieu and César; he says that he himself is responsible for preparing the wine. He came into the wine business simply through "succession within the family", says Perrin. The origins of the winery go back to the 16th century. In 1549, Pierre de Beaucastel acquired a barn and a piece of land in Coudoulet near the town of Courthezon. The area is still part of the property of Château de Beaucastel, and the name of the region also appears in the wine descriptions. The descendants of the founder established a manor house and use the land as farmland and pastures; winegrowing is only confirmed since the late 18th century. After phylloxera destroyed the wine farmland in the late 19th century, Pierre Tramier bought the estate in 1909, set up new vineyards, and passed the estate over to his son-in-law, Pierre Perrin. Within the Perrin family, the company is since passed on from one generation to the next.

"THE WINE BUSINESSPERSON MAY NOT FORGET THE HEART OF HIS PROFESSION DURING THE NEED TO CONTINUE DEVELOPING HIS BUSINESS."

Pierre Perrin expanded the vineyard areas further, and his son Jacques changed the name of the winery in 1976, to Château de Beaucastel. He got renowned as a cellar master in the entire region, and when he died in 1978, his two sons Jean-Pierre and François took over the company. François Perrin names, as the most important station in his development, "my first year in our family winery. After my father suddenly died, I had to quickly grasp everything – knowledge of growing vines, making wine, and all the problems that come along with management." Jacques Perrin had set up three principles for the Beaucastel wines: they should contain a high percentage of the vine variety Mourvèdre, be manufactured with natural methods, and not be distorted through technical interventions. "Beaucastel is our family's cradle, and it is our duty to bring forth the absolute best", says François Perrin. "Beaucastel carries with it the culture of Châteauneuf-du-Pape. By producing a hand-made wine and avoiding modernist techniques, we try to reveal the nature of our region and our tradition."

Already since 1950, the winery manages its growing areas in a strictly ecological way, and since 1974 it works in a consistently biological-dynamic way. "As fertiliser, we use half sheep dung, and half grape pulp", explains Perrin. "Beaucastel is mainly a family history – that of our family, whose strength it is to combine, in an admirable way, the talents of different people to make their vineyards come alive under the aegis of common values: absolute respect for the Earth and the region, biodynamics as a philosophy of life, and the search for truth, balance, and elegance." Château de Beaucastel has over 130 hectares of agricultural area, 100 hectares of which are used as vineyards. Three quarters of this are in the Appellation (protected designation of origin) Châteauneuf-du-Pape; the wines from here bear the brand Château de Beaucastel. One quarter corresponds to the Appellation Côtes-du-Rhône, and these wines bear the brand Coudoulet de Beaucastel. Additionally, the Perrin family has vineyards in the Appellations Gigondas and Vinsobres. 30 hectares of land are used just for crop rotation: every year, one to two hectares of vineyards are cleared and a similar area, which hasn't been used for winegrowing for at least 10 years, is planted with new vines. The average age of the Beaucastel vines is 50-60 years.

FRANÇOIS PERRIN

"IMPLEMENTING YOUR OWN IDEAS, SOMETIMES AGAINST THE IDEAS OF OTHER PEOPLE, IS A WAY TO ENSURE YOUR OWN IDENTITY; HOWEVER, IT ALSO MEANS THAT YOU INCUR THE RISK OF BEING MISUNDERSTOOD."

As the only winery in the Châteauneuf-du-Pape area, Château de Beaucastel was immediately allowed to plant all 13 vine varieties recognised there, when the Appellation was recognised in 1935, and it is one of the few companies in the region that continues using all these varieties for its red wines to this day. These are eight red varieties (Mourvèdre, Grenache, Syrah, Cinsault, Vaccarèse, Counoise, Terret Noir and Muscardin) and five white ones (Clairette, Picpoul, Picardan, Bourboulenc and Roussanne); they are grown separately and then blended together. "The art of blending, which is passed within our family from one generation to the next one, gives our wines all of their character", is Perrin's conviction.

"The entrepreneurial spirit in the wine area is very special", he judges. "You have to be close to the soil and to oenology, and at the same time manage business activity. The wine businessperson may not lose the heart of his profession over the need to continue developing his company" – and with this, Perrin means agriculture, the attachment to soil and nature. "The spirit of the farmer must mix with that of the businessman." The fact that his family doesn't shun further development of the company, despite all their conscience for tradition and sustainability, was made clear among other things in 2012: in a joint venture, Château de Beaucastel took over the production of the wines of Château de Miraval in the Provence, which is owned by the prominent American actor couple Brad Pitt and Angelina Jolie.

According to Perrin, his drive to be active in winegrowing is "the recognition of well-done work, of that which is beautiful, good, and serious. Motivation for me is not to get bored, and performance for me is a means to advance." Yet, there is "no personal goal, but many and diverse family goals; to create a healthy family business, which respects its history." Perrin quotes his favourite aphorism by André Malraux: "You don't get similar to those who you admire by copying their works.' We at Château de Beaucastel don't aim to make the world's best wine. Rather, we want to make the best possible Beaucastel! We have never followed any trends. We are happy to see that the decisions of successive generations are now the source of success for our family. To carry through your own ideas, sometimes in opposition to the ideas of other people, is a way to ensure your own identity, but it also implies the risk of being misunderstood. Or people think you are mad! Only the result is what counts, and today, strength of character without concessions is an essential condition to create great wines."

Perrin wants to "transmit, to every person in the company, a spirit that goes in the same direction and aims at satisfaction with oneself", and "offer wines with a great expression, to the best price. The recognised quality of wines which the company produces is an important component of success." Perrin describes his leadership style as "very familiar". The ideal employee, in his eyes, is "one who has the desire to advance". Success factors for employees are "the pleasure and delight in work", and he as a businessman must "provide hope". In dealing with technological progress and digital change, for Perrin the benefits of a family business become clear: "By leaving the new generation with the trouble of caring for that, they learn much better than I, that this evolution is a revolution", he says. "Lateral thinkers are, for me, the possibility to implement new ideas, and contradictions for me are a means to discover new paths."

Perrin explains his understanding of success in more detail, and also talks about value principles: "Decisions are always taken in the family circle, together with my brother, my four nephews, and my three children. After all, now the fifth generation is already on hand. I am proud to belong to one of the generations who built up Beaucastel and made it to what the winery is now. For five generations we are creating 'terroir'. That's a very French concept, and it includes four things: the grapes, the soil, the weather – and the person with his intelligence and will to work. I am proud to be one of these people. To respect the terroir also means to value the soil, the environment, and the history of the place. To strive for authenticity and uniqueness, to uncover all the treasures of Château de Beaucastel. Success, for me, is to fulfil what you have dreamed."

Perrin confronts risks "through a management that is as close to possible to the everyday", as he explains. "Errors are useful for me, but hard to bear", he admits, and adds: "If I were able to go back and change something in my professional life, that would be, not to be dependent on the climate conditions." However, Perrin illustrates the fact that weather is not the only risk factor for the winemaker with an anecdote: at a gala dinner in Toronto, the host opened a jeroboam bottle (one with three litres content) of the top vintage Hommage à Jacques Perrin 1990, worth a small fortune. The cult wine is produced since 1989 only in the best years, in honour of Perrin's father, and is characterised, due to the small yield of the vines, by a special concentration and depth; from the wine critic Robert Parker, Hommage à Jacques Perrin received the rare highest grade of 100 points, five years in a

FRANÇOIS PERRIN

WINE
ENTREPRENEURS

row. However, that night in Canada, the large bottle had a bad cork flaw; the wine was not fit for drinking. The host still had several small bottles of the same vintage in the cellar, which were then used, but Perrin was deeply ashamed, even though he was able to explain that natural cork had its strengths and weaknesses. Once he was back in France, he immediately sent some jeroboams Hommage à Jacques Perrins 1990 to the Canadian wine fan.

"SUCCESS, FOR ME, IS TO CARRY OUT WHAT YOU HAVE DREAMED."

This story also reflects Perrin's personal values, which he lists to be "work, rigour, beauty, honesty, and goodness. Wine, for me, is a possibility to share a feeling. My favourite wine is the one that I will still discover", he defines. He sees the future of the wine sector as "a worldwide development, with the creation of new winegrowing areas". In the future, wine businesspeople would need "knowledge of the bases of winegrowing of the old world, combined with the spiritual openness towards new markets that are developing", according to Perrin. He reduces his recommendation for new starters in the area to a short formula: they should "travel and discover".

FRANÇOIS PERRIN

EDUARDO CHADWICK
President, Viña Errázuriz
Panquehue, Chile

Eduardo Chadwick (born 1960) is the owner and manager of the winery Viña Errázuriz in Panquehue in the Chilean Aconcagua Valley. He manages the company with over 500 hectares of vine areas in the fifth generation. "I actually come from a long family line of entrepreneurs with a passion for wine, so I began my wine career in 1983 at the age of 23", Chadwick tells us. First he studied engineering science, and concedes, in retrospect: "If I could change anything about my career life, it would be perhaps studying theatre rather than engineering skills." At that time, he decided specifically for winegrowing: "Following my graduation from the Universidad Católica de Chile with an MS in Industrial Engineering, I joined my father Alfonso Chadwick-Errázuriz when he had just taken direct control of the historically family-owned Viña Errázuriz, founded by Don Maximiano Errázuriz in 1870 in the Valle de Aconcagua." The Errázuriz came to Chile in the 18th century from the Spanish Basque Country to Chile.

"IMPLEMENTING DECISIONS IN OUR WINE INDUSTRY TAKES A LONG TIME—PLANTING VINEYARDS, BUILDING A WINERY, AND DEVELOPING INTERNATIONAL BRANDS CAN TAKE DECADES."

His father had an important role in his life, as Chadwick admits: "I think having the possibility to join my father in the family estate and learning the skills of viticulture and winemaking from him was an unbeatable kick-start. His life was always devoted to wine and he became recognized as one of Chile's most renowned wine-entrepreneurs. In 1985 he took me on my first trip to Bordeaux and Burgundy to discover the best chateaux in those regions, which was a real eye-opener for what could be done back in Chile. Thus, he was the best mentor I could have at the beginning of my career. My father also instilled in me his passion for the land and the spirit to search for excellence without compromise." Initially, Chadwick dealt with the introduction of new winegrowing techniques which he brought from France, as he recounts: "I set out to learn as much as I could about wine and went to study at the Institute of Oenology in Bordeaux, where I met Émile Peynaud, considered the father of modern oenology. I have since also travelled the world's wine regions with our viticultural and winemaking teams in order to set benchmarks and learn the best winemaking techniques—and then put them to practice at home. These experiences allowed me to perceive Chile's true potential for making fine wines. Later on my family and I lived in Oxford, UK for two years, where I

EDUARDO CHADWICK

took the first levels in the Institute of Masters of Wine. Although I did not pass the final exam, this was a very interesting educational and life experience. Education to me is essential. I really appreciated the opportunity to meet so many members of the industry and make new friends as well as everything I learned in those courses. Living in England and being in one of the world's most important and competitive wine markets was a great experience."

Chadwick's business goal is "to develop Viña Errázuriz in the most sustainable way possible so it will last for future generations, and in doing so, to demonstrate that our Chilean wines are amongst the top world-class wines. When I received my father's invitation to join our family winery back in 1983 I knew very little about the fascinating opportunities and challenges I would have to face to convince the world that we could produce world-class wines in Chile. This life journey has been a real joy, and I feel tremendously privileged to have had the inspiration as well as the help, cooperation, and contribution of so many people without whom we could never have produced the quality of our wines or obtained worldwide recognition for our country."

"ENTREPRENEURIAL SUCCESS MAY BE DEFINED AS BUILDING A SOLID AND SUSTAINABLE BUSINESS IN THE LONG TERM. THE KEY ELEMENTS TO MEASURE THIS ARE THE THREE MAIN PILLARS OF SUSTAINABILITY."

Motivation, for Chadwick, is "the adrenalin that moves everything", as he says. "I lead a family wine business, and my motivation is to develop a very long-term and successful company for every stakeholder of Viña Errázuriz, from the people who work with us in the vineyards and winery, those on the commercial side, and the family-share-holders as well. An additional motivation, which is very relevant to our brand building, is to demonstrate to the world that Chile is capable of producing world-class wines. Towards this goal we have dedicated very significant time and effort all these years to positioning our Errázuriz and in particular, our Icon wines, Viñedo Chadwick, Don Maximiano and Seña, showcasing them amongst the finest wines in the world." Seña is a joint project of Chadwick and the American top winegrower Robert Mondavi, which was created with the vintage 1995, and is currently among the best-known and most-requested red wines from Chile. Both nationally and internationally, Viña Errázuriz received several awards for its wines. Chadwick explains: "I had the chance to decide to join Viña Errázuriz back in 1983, and that was clearly a conscious choice. However I knew very little about the challenges I would face during my 30-year wine career, and I never imagined that we would reach the world positioning that we have obtained for our wines today."

Compared to other areas of the economy, in Chadwick's opinion there are some special features that make the wine sector stand out: "Implementing decisions in our wine industry takes a long time—planting vineyards, building a winery, and developing international brands can take decades. Therefore, one distinguishing characteristic of wine entrepreneurs may be having a very long-term perspective as well as a long-lasting

EDUARDO CHADWICK

determination. You have to be able to withstand challenges and difficulties and have a great passion for the product. Wine to me is a product full of enjoyment. The wine business is also a truly global business. At Viña Errázuriz, we export 95 per cent of our wine production to more than 80 countries. Therefore, the wine business requires clear insight on the developments in the key markets around the world. Furthermore, although it may sound a bit cliché, wine is a people's business, so the relationship with key stakeholders is a very important factor for building premium brands of wines. The premium business is very much related to luxury goods, and understanding the luxury markets is essential. Finally, innovation and deep understanding of consumer trends are also essential parts of building a successful wine business today." According to Chadwick, successful wine businesspeople need "to think globally in order to build a world brand, but they also need to act locally to understand the key local factors in order to be successful in each market around the world."

"INNOVATION AND DEEP UNDERSTANDING OF CONSUMER TRENDS ARE ESSENTIAL PARTS OF BUILDING A SUCCESSFUL WINE BUSINESS TODAY."

Success, in Chadwick's eyes, has to do with long-term thinking, determination, and sustainability: "Success to me is far-reaching. I am successful because I'm never fully satisfied and aim for the next goal", he explains. "Entrepreneurial success may be defined as building a solid and sustainable business in the long term. The key elements to measure this are the three main pillars of sustainability: On one hand, the economic and profitability side of a wine business that should last for a long term, then ensuring that we have sustainable viticulture and winemaking practices in terms of using eco-friendly procedures, and finally and most importantly, in terms of ongoing enhancement of our relationship with our stakeholders and communities, allowing for ongoing improvement in the quality of life of our human resources." Chadwick's recipe for success, as he defines, is "striving for a deep understanding of the key aspects of the business I am engaged in. Then, to select, develop, and motivate a managerial team of excellence. And finally, hopefully, having a generous amount of common sense." Chadwick names, as his fundamental belief, "Nothing is impossible"; and as his philosophy of life: "Life is too short; work must be fun."

He gets to talk about the changes which he encounters as a businessperson: "The world will remain ever changing. And to run a successful business you have to take some risks, ideally, always incorporating the right balances and insurances. First, you want to stay alert to the meaningful changes that will affect your business, ideally trying to lead those that are more important to your endeavour. Regarding the digital revolution and social media, you want to bring young talent into your company that can take on these challenges and incorporate them as part of your company's culture."
Business decisions, Chadwick explains, "should come out of discussion between the top managing team, formed by empowered key players within the company." He outlines some concepts: "Performance to me is benchmarking. Mistakes to me are a learning experience. Contradictions to me are part of life." Chadwick's central value is honesty. "I like leadership by example, and I try and hope that my leadership would fit into this

EDUARDO CHADWICK

WINE
ENTREPRENEURS

description", he says. To be successful, employees "need to be honest, transparent, hard workers and passionate about what they do. Leaders need a broader vision and great managerial and leadership skills in order to deeply motivate their teams." Chadwick's ideal employee is "the one who is most empowered and motivated to comply with his or her challenges, and ideally one who brings additional perspectives, values and ideas to the internal discussion. Lateral thinkers to me are most welcomed into our team." In contrast, the company that wants success for its employees itself needs "deep interest in knowing, understanding and motivating its teams", and "good internal communication"; it must "understand their needs, provide the necessary conditions for work, and make sure that those conditions are actually met", according to Chadwick.

He predicts the future of the wine area as "ever-changing… and full of innovation in all parts of the business, perhaps most particularly in the marketing, communications and commercial areas." To ensure its future success, businesspeople in the wine area have "to be open-minded, to have lots of emotional intelligence, a global perspective, and the ability to react speedily." Chadwick advises young beginners in the area to "take a plane and visit key regions and markets around the world in order to understand the basics of the business."

EDUARDO CHADWICK

FRIEDRICH-WILHELM DAUPHIN

Owner, Allée Bleue Estate
Franschhoek, South Africa

F riedrich-Wilhelm Dauphin is the manager of the Dauphin HumanDesign Group, an international leading manufacturer of office chairs, home and office furniture, near Nuremberg. Together with his wife Elke, he is also the owner of the South African winery Allée Bleue Estate in the Franschhoek Valley. Dauphin, who studied as a merchant, didn't originally plan to enter in the wine area, in addition to the furniture sector, as he reveals: "It was more of a coincidence – as is often the case. When in 1999, in Franschhoek, the farm – which covered about 60 hectares – was offered to us, we seized the chance by reason of the excellent location. Allée Bleue was an investment purchase. And it was a wonderful balance to our previous business activity, between development and sober production. The winery and the farm were, and still are, an antithesis to everyday life: to experience, to see something growing from the soil, in part with our own hands, that's delight, leisure – and also, always, it's in part an adventure. And of course it also has to do with enjoyment. It is quite a different type of enjoyment than the one that we develop with our designer furniture. The enjoyment of wine addresses other senses, opens the door to a different world of pleasure."

"ENTREPRENEURSHIP IN THE WINE AREA – JUST AS IN OTHER BUSINESS AREAS – REQUIRES PASSION, THE COURAGE TO TAKE DECISIONS AND TO BE RESPONSIBLE TO BEAR THE CONSEQUENCES, AS WELL AS THE WILL TO DARE SOMETHING NEW, TO INVEST, EVEN IN PREVIOUSLY UNKNOWN AREAS."

The Allée Bleue estate has its current name due to the driveway, which is lined with old eucalyptus trees with blue shimmering leaves. However, for Elke Dauphin the colour blue also alludes to the blue planet, to sky and water, to force, rest, and peace. The winery is one of the oldest ones on the cape; it was founded in 1690 from Huguenots who were driven from France. Today it includes over 130 hectares of vine area, and apart from wine it also produces fruits, herbs, and olives. In addition, the Dauphin family has also created a bistro, a picnic garden, and a boutique hotel, as well as event premises for conferences and celebrations. The cellar master Van Zyl Du Toit is responsible for the wines.

WINE
ENTREPRENEURS

FRIEDRICH-WILHELM DAUPHIN

"Motivation, for me, is to discover something new", says Friedrich-Wilhelm Dauphin. He sees his most important professional stations not in the wine sector; rather, he situates the first one in the year 1969: "At that time, as a consultant, I presented an English office chair manufacturer with a market analysis, with his opportunities in the German market. He didn't react; as a result, on the spur of the moment, I offered myself as a purchaser of the German office branch and bought the company. Even though I was a newcomer, I soon got a large order from a public office: 25,000 office chairs. Then I followed my own production strategy: demand-oriented, not just functional, but comfortable and with an attractive design. At that time, that was still a real competitive advantage." The second decisive station in his career development was in 1973, continues Dauphin: "We developed a revolving chair which could be packaged in a small space, easily delivered, and easily stacked together conically onsite. That was the breakthrough in exportation – and the launch of one of the leading office furniture manufacturers in Europe."

"BUSINESS SUCCESS IS ALWAYS ALSO CONNECTED TO THE ATTAINABLE SUCCESS OF A GOOD TEAM."

Even so, in the meantime he has got to know, and analysed, the wine business precisely: "Entrepreneurship in the wine area – as in all other areas – requires passion and huge personal commitment including identification, the courage to take decisions and for responsibility to bear the consequences, as well as the will to dare something new, to invest, even in new, previously unknown areas. Wine is always also emotion, not an industrial product; every wine, every vintage is different, each for itself is a new challenge. For that I require good cultivation positions and a talented winemaker. Even if I am currently a wine businessman, I am far from being a good winemaker. Good wine businesspeople stand out by recognising good opportunities and seizing them, counting with risks, calculating them, and at the same time taking measures – just like good businesspeople in all other business areas." Dauphin knows: "Without taking risks, you decrease chances. I have never avoided any risk." He takes his decisions "after an in-depth analysis and with a clear vision", and this corresponds to his guiding principle: "Having clear goals and heading for them with enjoyment and success."

Dauphin continues his consideration of the wine industry: "On our farm we were already growing bio-products, way before the mad cow disease and similar things created a consciousness for that over here. Good wine businesspeople also work in conformity with nature and the natural conditions. Sure, here there are large groups which generate a lot of attention for their brands, with a high advertising budget – for what I consider to be interchangeable wines. And there are talented young winemakers with the correct flair for wine and for the needs of wine drinkers. They convince with enthusiasm and with high-quality wines. The wine business area – even though it isn't entirely independent from the requirements of modern wine drinkers – is, to a great extent, independent, and it allows more individual freedom; you don't need to pick up and implement all the fashions and currents of the so-called zeitgeist. Here, I have other possibilities to test and then implement my ideas."

As a businessperson in the wine area, according to Dauphin you need to "be able to accept the market challenges and be able to learn very quickly. You must make an effort to make the wine distinguishable from others through your own signature, to make its origin, its character, tasteable and visible. We want a wine that reflects the soul of this country. No massive uniform taste. And we want to share the joy that this wine gives us with the consumers. For this, we need a professionally well-trained, highly motivated team – alone, this isn't possible. My way in the wine business has gone along with a constant and fair cooperation with my wife who always developed innovative ideas and identified herself with Allée Bleue. Of course in the wine area you also need a convincing concept, both with respect to marketing and with respect to sales. The world isn't waiting for wine number 'x'. Rather, it is waiting for making the fascination of wine something that can be experienced."

Dauphin is a businessman, as he explains, to "move something myself, shape it, have responsibility. With everything I do, the central issue for me was, and is, to increase the joy of life, that of other people and of course our own. We want to contribute to improve the life and work world of people with high-quality and intelligent solutions. Design for me is aesthetics, which clearly communicates distinctiveness. A good design is oriented towards people, not the other way round. Wine for me is pure indulgence and lust for life. Our wines should give wine drinkers pleasure; they should experience enjoyment with it. And, of course, with our business activity we want to achieve what everyone wants: success."

This is subject to certain conditions, explains Dauphin: "For me, education is the basis for success, and performance, for me, is an essential component of success." Success, he says, is not just the sum of correct decisions; rather it results from the fruitful interaction among people. "Success, for me, is when others benefit from it, too", he defines. "There are different parameters for that: obviously, first of all, the product's acceptance, growth, but also the acceptance by employees, their motivation, stimulating their commitment, as well as their willingness to cooperate. Business success is always also connected to the attainable success of a good team." Since in economically difficult times office equipment is one of the first things in which companies save, Dauphin explains and clarifies: "I am successful because I recognise chances, implement them, and invest." In this sense, he says that his personal recipe for success is "to see chances, perceive them, and to have a perceptible interest in innovations. Dare new things, don't stand still. Today we have over 73 registered designs and patent applications, we have purchased and founded 24 companies, and we employ over 730 employees in 80 countries."

Essential business values, according to Dauphin's opinion, are also important factors of success: "Errors for me are realisations to become even better, lateral thinkers for me are people who extend the horizon, and contradictions for me are an incentive to the solution. We are a performance community on the basis of own initiative and mutual esteem. We deal fairly and respectfully with our customers, partners, and suppliers. In our business philosophy, that's an unalterable foundation of human interaction." These values, he says, are also essential for the success of employees: "Employees can only work in a motivated way if the environment is correct. An employee must get the chance of developing and to assume responsibility in the context of his possibilities." In this respect, as a manager, Dauphin wants to "be a role model and grant free space

FRIEDRICH-WILHELM DAUPHIN

for own ideas", as he points out. In order to have success, employees had to "be able to communicate passion and enthusiasm", and to comply with Dauphin's ideal, they should "be innovative and ready for action above the ordinary. We are a well-functioning team of experienced managers and many outstanding employees, and our daughter Antje will become part of this team", explains Dauphin. Currently, the family business is being converted into a management-led group, in which he, for his part, will become the president of the advisory council.

"THE WORLD ISN'T WAITING FOR WINE NUMBER 'X'. IT IS, HOWEVER, WAITING FOR THE FASCINATION OF WINE TO BE MADE TANGIBLE."

Dauphin has an open attitude towards changes due to technological progress and the digital revolution: "After all, that doesn't affect just the wine area. But for me it's clear that we act according to the needs of the market and of the consumers. If there is a desire for a web shop, we should fulfil it, in the interests of our customers, and in our own interests. Social media, Facebook Twitter, etc. offer opportunities that have been hardly conceivable just a few years ago, to communicate directly with the customers. Surely it may also happen that there is criticism, but we must take it constructively and deal with it – assuming that it is fair, and not discriminatory. Also, a very direct feedback always provides opportunities for further development."

In view of the future of the wine sector, Dauphin first points out to the natural factors of influence and the subject of sustainability: "I assume that the general conditions will change, due to the climate change. That starts with the selection of the vine varieties, and goes all the way to changes in cellar techniques. Winemakers will have to react faster during the harvest; the use of alternative energies will also have an increasing role. Due to an increased demand by consumers, there will be an increase of biologically produced products and raw materials; consumers will also increasingly demand the fulfilment of social standards. In addition, I believe that wine drinkers will prefer more individual wines – small growing areas will be in demand, as will be niche wines." To work successfully in this environment, he says that wine businesspeople need "flexibility, decisiveness, and clear." Yet another essential factor for future success is "individuality – that applies to the cultivation area, the vine variety, and the wine style", according to Dauphin. To a young beginner in this area, to be successful he recommends to have "staying power, talent, and good cultivation positions."

FRIEDRICH-WILHELM DAUPHIN

Owner and managing director, Balthasar Ress winery Hattenheim, Germany

C hristian Ress is owner and managing director of the winery Balthasar Ress in Rheingau. The winery proceeded from an inn which the namesake had founded as an offshoot of a butcher family in 1870. Christian Ress manages the family company in the fifth generation, since he took over the management from his father in 2010. Previously, after several professional stations inside and outside his country, he was already active for 11 years in the winery.

His path to the winegrowing sector "was mapped quite early", says Ress. "I grew up on my parents' winery in the midst of a wine production. For me, it was a fixed component of my environment and my everyday activities from the time I was a child – so that I really grew up into the task, in the best sense. Then after I finished high school, I also lined up all additional training, internships, and jobs to my future task as leader of my parents' company."

"THERE IS NO BUSINESS LIKE WINE BUSINESS!"

Ress studied business management in Wiesbaden, worked in wineries in Germany and France, got to know the wine business in the USA and Great Britain, finished an internship in the marketing section of the champagne cellar Henkell & Söhnlein, and went to the importers of own wines into other countries. "Practically all stations had real value for me and helped me develop myself in specific areas", he summarises. "In retrospect, what turned out to be extremely important especially included meeting specific people whom I could later obtain as important employees or even partners in my companies. I was only able to achieve essential milestones in my professional development together with my most important partners – and so did they. Alones, that wouldn't have been possible."

Entrepreneurship is, in a certain sense, in Ress's blood, as he informs: "I have strived quite early to fashion things and to organise my work time according to priorities which I defined myself. Therefore, even as a child I could see myself being active as a businessperson. It was also important for me, quite early, to be financially independent – even from my parents." Ress names an example: "In the seventh grade, using newspaper ads, I sold the Swatch clocks, which at that time were quite sought-after, and hard to find in Germany, which my father had purchased for me in the duty-free shops in foreign airports during his travels, based on my purchase lists. At that time, that provided me with considerably more money than the pocket money which my parents gave me. I financed my study and internship period myself, by offering services in the area of events, and being active as a DJ."

Thus, Ress's business driving forces are independence, and a quest for quality: "I like to create things and to move them. The path is already part of the goal. For me, it's important to get better and better with what you do. Moreover, even the market demands that from us." Two slogans which Ress names also go in this direction: "Mediocrity sucks!", and "Nothing happens, unless you do it". In this sense, the go-getting entrepreneur not only expanded his winery's vineyard area to currently 46 hectares and initiated a change to biological cultivation, but he also initiated several innovative and media-effective projects – however, these aren't for public relations, as Ress emphasises, but rather have a professional background.

"THERE IS NOTHING THAT REQUIRES MORE STRENGTH, ENDURANCE, TIME, ORGANISATIONAL TALENT, AND CONSEQUENCE THAN CHANGE. ONE WHO MASTERS CHANGE CAN BE SUCCESSFUL AS AN EXECUTIVE."

CHRISTIAN RESS

In 2009, the winemaker from Rheingau started a vineyard on Sylt. On 3000 square metres (0.3 hectares), here there are vines of the early ripening varieties Solaris and Rivaner; Solaris as a fungus-resistance vine variety also reduces the risk of disease. In this project, Ress sees "a challenge, since nature high in the north is problematic". He says that the vineyard in Sylt is protected from wind, and yet well-ventilated, and the North Sea island has more hours of sunlight, during the year, than Rheingau. Therefore Ress is convinced "that the requirements for successful winegrowing are given here, too."

Also in 2009, Ress inaugurated the "wineBANK" in Hattenheim. This is a wine cellar under the winery, "which can also be used as a perfect storage and as a tasting room", explains Ress. Here, wine fans can "store their own wines in manor house's vault cellars, which have a perfect climate, and taste them spontaneously at any day or night hour with their friends or business partners". To do this, they rent one or several compartments in one of the three separate underground chambers, and with a personal chip card, they have around-the-clock access. "Our Rieslings naturally have a high maturity potential. What would be more natural than to give our customers the possibility to let their wines ripen under optimal conditions, and to be able to enjoy them at any moment within a stylish environment", says Ress. A second "wineBANK" in Mainz is currently being planned.

In 2010, the hobby diver Ress sunk some big bottles of his 2009 Riesling RESSpekt in a Hessian stretch. In three especially constructed steel crates, a total of 18 magnum bottles each with 1.5 litres of content, as well as a so-called Balthazar bottle with

12 litres of content were chained at a depth of 22 metres for three years. The objective of the experiment: "We wanted to test what these conditions with constant low temperatures of 6 to 8 degrees Celsius, and a permanent darkness, do to the wine", explains Ress. The maturing process was expected to be slower and gentler in the cool environment, protected from light and oxygen. Most of the bottles were auctioned off immediately after sinking them, and 1/5 of the proceeds went to the benefit of the project "Wein hilft" (wine helps) of the wine author Stuart Pigott. The bottles were recovered in 2013.

"The wine area is certainly a very special area", says Ress. "There is no business like wine business! It is known that many companies in the area are simply nonsense economically, and yet they are managed with passion." He pauses briefly and then comments: "But isn't that even positive in times which are characterised by crises, which in turn are often the result of actions oriented towards short-term successes?" Then he starts again: "The return on capital of the winery which I manage is by no means where it should be. But I work with great commitment on the objective of changing this in a lasting way. Anyway, this doesn't harm the area's progressiveness. In Germany, in the last 15 years, it turned out to be extremely innovative and quality-oriented. The quality of German wines has hardly ever changed in such a clearly positive way, within such a short time."

But the economic dimension isn't everything for Ress: "On the one hand, agriculture also transmits earthiness, naturalness, and closeness to nature. It has an almost magical attraction towards people outside of this area – people who often underestimate the challenges. Many dream of having their own winery someday. After all, there are many examples of wealthy people who can actually fulfil this dream." To be successful in the wine area, according to Ress's conviction "financial and emotional perseverance as well as a high level of goal orientation and concentration" are required: "In this area, you always need an entire year, to be able to bring a new product to the market and to be able to evaluate the effects of a possible change in working methods. Anybody who as a young man or woman enters this area must also know that he or she will generally only have 30 or 40 tries. If you produce lemonade, that's simpler. In that case, you can change something in the recipe every day."

Business success, according to Ress, is "a combination of the image of your own product on the market – basically a result of the product quality -, your own satisfaction, the satisfaction of your employees and partners, and of course also the economic success for all participants – for my partners, employees, and myself. Success for me is the purpose and reward of my work. Whether I'll really be successful with what I am building up will only be seen in the future. Performance for me is the path to the goal, and motivation for me is an indispensable condition for success." On the material level, Ress adds an additional factor: "Design for me is aesthetics, zeitgeist, processing quality, material. All of these are very, very important for any product."

Ress has an essential success principle: "You can't move anything alone. I take the most important people with me on board. For me, lateral thinkers are of immense importance in a team!" In the winery, Dirk Würtz stands by his side; originally he studied business management, political science and philosophy, and then he made a name for

CHRISTIAN RESS

himself as a cellar master and winemaker. Würtz came to the company in 2009 as a consultant, and since 2011 he is responsible for strategy, together with Ress. Together with other partners, Ress purposefully established the winery's market presence in important export markets and founded the import and distribution company B&R Wines in Norway as well as the two trading agencies Veritable Wines & Estates, and Veritable Vins & Domaines, with headquarters in Germany.

With his projects and decisions, Ress also takes risks, but such risks are part of the nature of his activities, as he shows: "I try to manage them as consciously and responsibly as possible – due to the responsibility for my team and the family assets entrusted to me. But of course they are an inherent part of any business. Without risks there are no chances." Rationality and intuition both have an important role for Ress: "Contradictions are a mental challenge for me. With any important decision I try to get a good balance between head and gut feeling", he clarifies. "Errors, for me, are unavoidable. Only people who don't do anything commit no errors. What's important is that you don't commit the same error twice." And in view of technological change, he adds: "Constant changes are indeed an essential challenge in our work." He masters these challenges in the team – with executives who have the corresponding capabilities, as he clarifies.

"WINE, FOR ME, IS THE NATURAL COMPONENT OF A GOOD AND SOCIABLE DINNER."

Ress describes his leadership style as "cooperative". His ideal employee is "reliable, trustworthy, goal-oriented, and motivated". That also corresponds to the values which he himself considers to be most important; he relies on "absolute credibility and reliability", as he explains. "The conditions, of course, are completely different depending on the position and level. But this applies to everybody: Without trustworthiness and reliability, no success is possible – in no position", clarifies Ress. "Especially in the case of executives, they must be capable of implementing lasting changes. To continue getting better all the time, you also need to be able to change things repeatedly. However, there is nothing that requires more strength, endurance, time, organisational talent and consequence than change. A person who manages change can be successful as an executive." To promote the success of its employees, the company in turn must "define goals, give trust, and provide freedom within a clearly defined framework", says Ress.

For the future, the wine businessman predicts "more concentration, increasing company sizes, and as a result, also an increasing professionalization of the area". The sales markets, he says, will continue growing, and the "expectation by the customers with respect to transparency, sustainability and environmental impact of our actions" will increase, as Ress expects. To a young businessperson colleague, who wants to be successful in the wine area, he advises "to intensively be aware that you are entering into a business area in which important elements of the business model aren't influenced by yourself, but by nature. Many people underestimate that. In this sense, agriculture is a very special business."

CHRISTIAN RESS

ROLAND KÖHLER
Publisher
St. Gallen, Switzerland

Roland Köhler (born 1955) is the owner of the publishing group Kömedia AG in St. Gallen, which includes the Intervinum AG and the kbmedien AG. The publishing house publishes books and magazines, including the European wine magazine Vinum. The special-interest magazine was founded in 1980 in Zurich, and starting in 1983 it also appeared in a separate German edition. In 1991 and 1997 the country editions for France and Spain, respectively, followed; the Italian edition, started in 2004, was discontinued after a short time. In 2009, Köhler, with his publishing house, purchased the brand and title rights for Vinum, and after a relaunch, he publishes it in three language versions.

"IF NATURE DIDN'T PROVIDE YOU WITH THE BUSINESSPERSON GENE, YOU SHOULD BETTER STAY AWAY FROM IT."

Köhler started with his publishing career in 1976 with the purchase of a youth magazine, and in 1982 he joined the publishing company KünzlerBachmann Medien in St. Gallen – a "challenge" as he says in retrospect: "I remember my first day in the publishing house very well, the small team, and the manageable number of our products. Since then, every day was exciting, and a lot happened with a fast motion effect. Not just the media world with its innovations and technological quantum leaps, but also the professionalization of our activity, the variety of products, the increased number of customers and partnerships, and of course the constantly growing number of our employees." The company concentrated Köhler on the publication of trade yearbooks.

"2010 was once again an important milestone for me", he continues. "For in that year, I completely took over the KünzlerBachmann Medien AG. That means a lot for me, for together with my committed team I can account for many years of growth and continued development." In 2012, the company was renamed to Kömedia AG. "Kö stands for me as the owner, media for what we do", explains Köhler. "Since the 80s, we obtained over 20 new magazine mandates, and renewed our own products. Today we publish and manage over 40 projects: magazines, journals, yearbooks and Internet portals."

Köhler describes his path to the wine context as "short and intensive", but first he clarifies: "I am not technically a businessman in the wine area, but, with Vinum, a publisher of a wine magazine." In 2009 he obtained the majority of shares in the Intervinum publishing house, "and since then, the whole thing is especially a labour of love. With a total circulation of ca. 85,000 printed copies in several countries, Vinum is Europe's largest wine magazine. It has a high acceptance both among the general audience interested in wine, as among producers, in commerce, and in high-level gastronomy. The Vinum authors in the most important European wine-growing regions – France, Italy, Germany, Switzerland, Spain, and Austria – ensure high informational value and authentic reporting from their corresponding 'Terroir'." Köhler outlines the concept: "Each Vinum country edition has a distinct local editorial colour; the corresponding same international part of the magazine is the connecting element among the different country editions." In this sense, he says, the magazine also takes into account the differences in mentality and brands between Switzerland and Germany.

ROLAND KÖHLER

"MY PREFERENCE IS TO BE AMONG THOSE WHO ARE SUCCESSFUL AND YET HAVE A LOT OF LEISURE TIME."

"Basically, in the publishing business we are in a fairly athletic phase", explains Köhler. "For a successful future, we need a diversified portfolio of print, online, events, contests, corporate publishing, and services." In his property as publisher, Köhler explicitly expresses his belief in the future of print media: "Books and magazines have survived radio, television, and the Internet, because people like to read. Because apart from the moving image, the still image also has its appeal. Some call it haptics, other talk about occidental culture."

Whether a businessperson wants to be active and successful in the wine area or in some other business area is secondary for Köhler: "First of all, the DNA must be correct. If nature didn't provide you with the businessperson gene, you better stay away from it. Lambert Koch, professor at the Wuppertal University, formulated this as follows: 'A person who has no talent to play violin will never truly learn it.' Apart from this basic equipment, the businessperson needs a healthy attitude towards risk and a stable self-confidence, a high degree of intellectual openness, and a lot of curiosity and creativity. He sets goals, takes decisions, can represent even complex processes in a simple way, and does all this with passion." In this context, Köhler also talks about the topic of work-life balance: "The models are those businesspeople who don't talk about work and working hours. Those who despite their success enjoy life, who have the so-called sprezzatura, and thus don't define themselves on the basis of their work-intensive activity. The author Castiglione has defined sprezzatura as the capacity to make even arduous activities look simple and effortless. I prefer to be among those who are successful and who still have a lot of leisure time."

Köhler himself has decided in favour of business activity for a specific reason, as he explains: Subsumed in one word, the goal was freedom. I never wanted to deal with people who promote the culture of hindering. Chains of command, hierarchies, organizational charts, endless meetings, budget restrictions – all those don't leave freedom for creativity, no biotopes for pre-thinkers and lateral thinkers." Even though he emphasises the importance of innovation, Köhler also pleads for a solid base of tried and tested virtues: "Values that I appreciate specially are loyalty, honesty, reliability, and diligence", he says, and authenticity is also important for him: "My favourite quotation is from Alfred Herrhausen. While he was still a bank manager, he once said: 'We must say what we think. We must do what we say. And we must also be what we do.' That is written just like that in our company documentation."

Köhler doesn't have a recipe for business success, and waves dismissively: "Recipes belong to the alchemist's kitchen." His recommendation: "Follow your intuition, decide quickly, be alert, have four fourths of passion in your blood, and never deal with people who don't have qualities." To a young entrepreneur, however, he would recommend "nothing", for "A young entrepreneur doesn't undertake and ask such questions", Köhler is convinced.

The Swiss man considers his leadership style as somewhat tinged with the southern lands; he describes it as "situational, with a lot of Italianità", and explains: "After all, you can't guide the top-creative art director in the same way as the ultraconservative accountant; or guide the sensitive top salesman the same way as the accurate administration leader." The optimal employee in Köhler's company is "diligent, reliable, persistent, resilient, humorous, has initiative, is demanding, can think for himself, is responsible, rooted in the soil, honest, ambitious, loyal, decent, and uncomplicated", the publishing chief defines. He takes his decisions "mainly quickly, without a democratic process forerun", he clarifies. "Enzo Ferrari once formulated this strikingly: 'A formula 1 team must always necessarily be led by an odd number of people. And this number must be less than three.'"

According to Köhler, risk awareness is more pronounced among businesspeople than among hired executives: "To bear personal – monetary – risks is part of entrepreneurship, in contrast to highly endowed managers. As a manager I would be much more willing to take risks, since after all I would speculate with other people's money! Also, the businessman thinks in other time units than the payroll recipient." Köhler is open towards changes, such as those caused by the Internet: "Richard Wagner said aptly: 'Change and transformation are loved by those who live.' There is nothing more to add to that." He names the four topics which in his eyes are the most important in relation to the digital future: "First: social media as the most important factor for the digital transformation, with many possibilities for interaction. Second: Content, since the content that is distributed characterises the brand image. Third: search engine optimisation, which ensures that contents don't get lost in the Internet, but are found as quickly and as frequently as possible. And fourth: mobility, since mobile end-user devices are used more and more frequently for private and business transactions."

ROLAND KÖHLER

Köhler, as a market observer, has precise ideas about the future developments of the wine business: "New big players endanger traditional winegrowing in Europe. The worldwide wine market is in one of the largest restructuring phases of the last decades. The central problem is that in three of the most important wine-producing countries – Italy, France, and Spain – consumption has stagnated or gone back, especially in the case of Spain. Even though the area of vineyards has also gone back, this has not been in the same measure as would correspond to the reduction in consumption. The result is an overproduction, which must be sold as exports. But the classic European consumer markets – Germany, Great Britain, Switzerland, Scandinavia, and the Benelux countries – are also saturated. If cellars, regions, or countries want to establish themselves in these markets, this is only possible in the context of a cost-intensive cutthroat competition."

"THE WORLDWIDE WINE MARKET IS IN ONE OF THE MOST IMPORTANT RESTRUCTURING PHASES OF THE LAST DECADES."

ROLAND KÖHLER

Köhler expands the geographical horizon: "A strong, and still slightly growing, market is the USA, and in part also Brazil. The market area has even higher hopes in the potentially highly lucrative, but unpredictable Chinese market. So, no wonder that the marketing focus changes increasingly to these new core markets. For the French winegrowing, China is currently already the most important export market; the total amount of the yearly sales is well over a billion dollar. The Chinese per capita consumption is still a mere 1.1 litres a year. In comparison, in Switzerland people still drink 36 litres of wine per year and person. If the Chinese consumption changes in the medium term by just one litre per year and person – which is something that experts consider conceivable – the entire European overproduction wouldn't be enough to cover this new demand. However, China itself does a great effort to promote its own winegrowing, both quantitatively and qualitatively. Today, China is already the fourth most important wine-producing country worldwide. China will therefore play an important role in the future, both as a sales country and as a producing country."

Köhler continues with his analysis: "In China, but also in countries such as Australia, Chile, and in part also Spain, a highly rationalised and therefore economical winegrowing is possible. In huge, to some extent automated vine plantations, a single hectare can be managed with only 50 work hours a year. In the legendary steep slopes in Europe – for instance along the Mosel, along the Douro, in Wallis or in Dézaley in Waadtland – up to 2000 work hours per hectare are required. A huge problem in Europe's classic winegrowing countries are also the ownership structures, which are complex, and due to inheritance, often extremely fragmented. While wineries in Australia and China often manage vine areas of 1000 hectares each, for example the ca. 1000 hectares which the Provins Cooperative in Wallis manages are split up among almost 4000 different winemakers. If traditional winegrowing in Europe, which is moreover characterised by some of the most beautiful cultural landscapes, is to be maintained, structural improvements are essential", summarises Köhler. "Only if it becomes possible to market the wines from Europe's traditional winegrowing regions increasingly over a high and independent, i.e., unmistakable quality and its exclusive origin – Swissness and Europeness – will they have a long-term chance against the wines produced in the so-called new wine countries, which are several times cheaper. Controlled biological cultivation as well as sustainable management – i.e., sustainable winegrowing – with reduced carbon dioxide emissions and social responsibility – can also provide the traditional European wines with the emotional added value which makes them attractive in spite of higher prices."

ROLAND KÖHLER

SIR GEORGE FISTONICH

Founder and owner, Villa Maria Estate
Mangere, New Zealand

Sir George Fistonich (born 1939) is the founder and owner of the winery Villa Maria Estate in Mangere in the Auckland Metropolitan Area. His parents came from Croatia to New Zealand in the late 1920s, and Fistonich's father had already produced wine in their new home country, for their own consumption. According to the family tradition, George as the second son should have become a craftsman, and initially he did an apprenticeship as a carpenter. But he didn't remain in the construction work, which he perceived to be too restrictive: "From an early age, I had a strong ambition to become a winemaker", Fistonich makes it clear. "I grew up in an environment with wine and had always enjoyed the taste. Being Croatian meant that making wine was in my blood! However it was only in 1961, when I leased five acres of land from my father in Auckland that Villa Maria was born and my wine career truly began." They only had vines on 0.4 hectares. "My father didn't think that the wine industry had any future. I did a trade but I wanted to get into the wine industry, because I mixed with a lot of the Croatian community, with many of them making wine. For wine, a lot of Croatians had come into the country, and they had wine with their meals. So they tried to make wine in their back yards. I finished my apprenticeship in record quick time and I had six months off; I'd managed to squeeze a five year apprenticeship into three years and ten months. I started making wine at home. I played around with dry red and dry white", describes Fistonich. In 1962 he bottled his first own wine under the name Villa Maria. "I was actually sitting round a coffee bar with two mates when I chose Villa Maria as the name", he continues describing. "Maria was quite an international name, and was also a Croatian name. It sounded quite romantic. Villa is a common expression for a house. Probably today you would come up with a real Kiwi name. A lot of people thought I was married to Maria or my mother was Maria, and all sorts of rumours floated around."

At first, it wasn't clear to Fistonich that his entry into the wine area would also set the foundation of a business activity. "It was entirely by chance", he recounts. "I never went out intending to become an entrepreneur. I had an unyielding desire to make great wine and I've committed to that every day. Being seen as an entrepreneur is merely a by-product of my journey in wine making and Villa Maria." Fistonich especially remembers two essential milestones in his development: "It's difficult to pinpoint the most important stations as the last 50 years have all been important; however there are two points that really stand out for me. The first being in the late 1960's where a beer drinking New Zealand culture slowly started to change. Appreciation for table wines opened up an opportunity for dry red and white wines. I was fortunate enough to win two awards at the 1962 Royal Easter

Show" – the largest Australian consumer fair, which is held every year in Sydney – "for my dry red wines, this opened up an entire nation to the wonders of wine. Secondly would be in 2001 where Villa Maria was the first major wine company, exporting both nationally and internationally, in New Zealand to declare that the winery would become a 'cork-free zone', sealing all wines from the 2002 vintage onwards with a screwcap. It was a bold move, but one that needed to happen to ensure consistent quality."

"ENTREPRENEURSHIP IS REALLY AN OPEN ENDED WORD, CAN MEAN ANYTHING TO ANYONE. FOR ME, IT MEANS BEING INNOVATIVE AND TAKING RISKS."

SIR GEORGE FISTONICH

Currently, Villa Maria cultivates ca. 400 hectares of vineyards in Auckland, Gisborne and Hawkes Bay on the New Zealand's North Island, as well as Marlborough on the South Island. "Wine to me is the greatest man made gift anyone can have or give", says Fistonich. "I drink a new favourite wine every month! We are blessed to produce wine in a country where wine style and quality just keeps getting better." Early on, the ambitious winemaker noted the importance of regional differences with respect to grape quality and wine styles. As the first New Zealand wine producer, he paid his contract growers according to the quality, and not just the amount of grapes they delivered. "It has always been a goal of mine to 1) create great wine and 2) stay a 100 per cent New Zealand and family owned and operated business", Fistonich explains. "Everything I do in this job revolves around maintaining those two aspirations. We've been New Zealand's most awarded winery for 35 years and my ongoing ambition is to put in place the building blocks required to keep this estate as a New Zealand and family owned business, and embed the culture so it moves forward in the same manner that it started." For his merits in the New Zealand wine business, Fistonich was bestowed a knighthood in 2009; thus, since then he may call himself "Sir".

"Entrepreneurship is really an open ended word, can mean anything to anyone", explains Fistonich. "For me however, it means being innovative and taking risks. The wine industry is always evolving. Different ways of making wine are continuously being explored and unless you're at the forefront of this, pioneering and seeking out new and innovative ideas then you risk getting left behind. Entrepreneurship is the same the world over, regardless of sector, business, etc. It requires the courage to do something different, without 100 per cent guarantee of it working." To be successful as a businessperson, according to Fistonich's conviction you need "to be optimistic, a challenge seeker and forward thinking. Always looking around the corner to what the possibilities may be, and acting on them before someone else does." The constant desire for progress also has a role, according to Fistonich: "Motivation to me is having the passion to be better than the person you were yesterday. Performance to me is like a roller-coaster. You'll always encounter good performances and poor performances but what stands out is how you react to them."

Once again, Fistonich emphasises the importance of the willingness to take risk, and vigour: "Changes occur all the time in business and there has and will always be unpredictable situations to tackle. I've always maintained that in times of uncertainty, its best to move forward and not sit still. Embrace the change and hire experts in specific fields who can best handle the evolving nature of the wine industry. There is always a need to take risks, especially if you wish to innovate. So I see them as a necessity and an integral part of moving forward."

Fistonich's recipe for success is simple: "Being brave, bold and authentic", he defines. "Success to me is enjoying your life. I am successful because I surrounded myself with great people, both personally and professionally." However, he once again talks about the risks as well: "Success has always been a slight enigma as it's very personal and means different things to different people. For me, entrepreneurial success would consist of seeing an opportunity, taking a risk and exploiting that opportunity, and in the end making sure it pays off. This may not happen every time, but as long as it happens most of the time, I consider that successful!" Fistonich takes his business decisions, as he says, "quickly", and he formulates, as his life slogan: "Stay healthy, enjoy your friends, family and work and always drink great wine."

"MISTAKES TO ME ARE STEPPING STONES. A NEW AND IMPROVED PATH WILL OFTEN BE CREATED BECAUSE OF MISTAKES BUT ONLY IF YOU ACKNOWLEDGE AND LEARN FROM THEM."

The businessman is conscious that Villa Maria didn't become what is today one of the largest and most successful wineries in New Zealand only due to his own efforts, as he explains: "Values which are important to me are my family and looking after the team that work for me. Villa Maria wouldn't be what it is today without the incredible support of my family. Equally, it's the great team of individuals who come to work every day, enthused about their jobs and this company who are the success story here. Looking after them, making sure they are happy at work is paramount." In this respect, Fistonich encourages his employees to follow their own strengths, while highlighting the value of team work and cooperation. His employees' personal development is important for him, and apart from his own passion for top-level results, he also considers his capacity to transmit this passion to those who are connected with his winery to be an essential factor of his success.

Fistonich describes his leadership style as "collaborative, decentralised and leading by example." For him, there is no one optimal employee: "A variety of different employees are essential. If everyone thought the same, then we wouldn't debate ideas and discuss different solutions. Lateral thinkers to me are very creative and idea generators. Contradictions to me are a part of business and life. If treated properly, they can lead to healthy debate and great outcomes. As long as the employee is enthusiastic, passionate and committed, then they have all the tools to be a great asset to any company."

SIR GEORGE FISTONICH

WINE
ENTREPRENEURS

In this sense, Fistonich also considers an open company culture to be relevant for success: "I've always believed in an open door policy. If my door is open then come in and chat. I think being approachable at all levels is essential. Often the smallest voice in the room can have the best ideas so we nurture an environment where everyone feels encouraged to speak up and share ideas." For decisions – whether in staff issues or other issues – you may not underestimate your own gut feeling, he warns: "The biggest cost in any business is employing the wrong people and not following your heart. The worst decisions I've made include employing people I wasn't satisfied with. On paper they were perfect, but sometimes instinct tells you different and I didn't follow my intuition." Despite these experiences, Fistonich wouldn't change anything in his life, as he explains: "Hindsight is a wonderful thing but without previous mistakes and risks, I wouldn't know and enjoy what I do now. Mistakes to me are stepping stones. A new and improved path will often be created because of mistakes but only if you acknowledge and learn from them." And he summarises: "Employees need to be excited and enjoy their job and what they work for. They should be passionate and committed. This goes the same for leaders and management. Ideally, everyone should have these qualities, irrespective of your position or authority."

"FOR ME, ENTREPRENEURIAL SUCCESS WOULD CONSIST OF SEEING AN OPPORTUNITY, TAKING A RISK AND EXPLOITING THAT OPPORTUNITY, AND IN THE END MAKING SURE IT PAYS OFF."

In the future, too, Fistonich expects a dynamic environment in the wine sector: "Predicting the future is complicated as change is so rapid however I do think that over the next decade, we will become more so than ever, a global society with the necessity to cater to every nation being a must. I also think we will see more brands, more companies and more products. Only strong brands will have longevity in this ever changing environment." The inner attitude will be critical for success: "Qualifications only stand for so much. Attitude, passion and enthusiasm will stand for a lot more." According to Fistonich, one who wants to enter the wine area and be successful there must "work hard, learn from experts, be true to himself and never cut corners."

SIR GEORGE FISTONICH

DOUG SHAFER
President, Shafer Vineyards
Napa (CA), USA

Doug Shafer (born 1955) is the owner and manager of the winery Shafer Vineyards in Napa (California). His father John bought the company in the Stags Leap District in Napa Valley, 1972, after working for over 20 years in the publishing business. "Our family moved to Napa Valley from Chicago in January of 1973", reports Doug Shafer. "My dad had been interested for several years in buying vineyard property in California and starting a second career, at almost age 50, in the wine business. On one of his trips looking for a property that featured a hillside vineyard (or hillside potential) he found the site we own today." Ca. 85 hectares of vineyard area – part of it on steep cliffs – waited to be revived; in 1978, the first own vintage was bottled.

"AN ENTREPRENEUR IN THE WINE BUSINESS MUST HAVE A COMPREHENSIVE UNDERSTANDING OF VINEYARDS, WINE PRODUCTION, HUMAN RESOURCES, AND PR, MARKETING AND SALES."

"When we moved here I was 17 years old and more interested in girls and basketball than anything else", Shafer remembers. "Over time though, as those big life decisions come at a kid in preparation for college, I started to pay attention to what my dad was doing and it looked pretty good. He wore jeans, drove a pick-up, operated a tractor, and hung out with buddies in the grape business. It seemed a lot more attractive than working in an office and wearing a tie." Already during his high-school time, Shafer helped his father replant vineyards and clear land to plant new vines. "Some of my first work experiences in the wine business were summer jobs during college", he tells us. Among other things, he worked for Robert Mondavi, but "one that particularly shaped my outlook was working for Hanns Kornell at Kornell Cellars. That's where my work ethic first began to develop. When you worked for Hanns if you had a spare moment, you better grab a broom and start sweeping. He wouldn't stand for a single moment of idleness."

Shafer then went to the University of California in Davis, and immediately knew what he wanted to study: "When I went to U.C. Davis, I majored in viticulture, with an eye toward a career related to vineyards and winemaking." However, after that he didn't immediately entered his father's company. "After getting my degree at U.C. Davis, my first real job was working for Randy Mason, as his assistant winemaker, at Lakespring

Winery", he describes. "That's where I learned all the 'grunt' jobs in the cellar and the importance of being detail oriented. You check it, you check it again, and you check it a third time. Randy was a great mentor and remains a friend today. In 1982, my dad asked if I would come be the winemaker at Shafer Vineyards and I turned him down. In fact I turned him down several times, knowing that I didn't have the experience. In the end he prevailed (he was my dad after all) and I became winemaker at Shafer in January of 1983." In this function, the junior refined cultivation and extension, to provide the wines with more character of origin, set up new vineyards, and continually expand the portfolio. "Wine to me is art you can drink", he says.

"EVERYTHING WE'VE ACCOMPLISHED HERE HAS HAPPENED BECAUSE OF HARD WORK, SWEATING THE SMALL STUFF, TRIAL AND ERROR, PICKING OURSELVES UP AFTER FAILING, TENACITY, CONSTANT EXPERIMENTATION, AND ALWAYS ASKING IF THERE'S A BETTER WAY TO DO IT."

DOUG SHAFER

In 1994, Shafer got in charge of managing the company, and since then, together with the cellar master Elias Fernandez – who came to the company in 1984 as an assistant and 10 years later took over Shafer's position – and his father, he works to ensure the wine quality and the future of the family winery. In the long term, he wants to keep Shafer Vineyards as a small family business, dedicated to the production of world-class wines from their own vineyards, as he says. An important focus for him is sustainable agriculture: The winery works ecologically since the 90s, and since 2004, it gets all of its electrical energy from its own photovoltaic systems; the water on the winery is also recycled.

Shafer is responsible for the operational processes both in the vineyard and in the cellar. His motivation to become a businessperson arose from his father's example, as he explains: "When I was in high school, I saw my dad move from the corporate world in Chicago to becoming his own boss in a vineyard in Napa. I saw how much he loved his work here. It was infectious and I saw that as a great fit for me. In that sense it was a conscious choice. At the time I didn't think much beyond vineyard management or perhaps winemaking. I didn't see myself as running a winery then." Shafer highlights some peculiarities of the wine sector: "The biggest difference I see between the wine business and other types of business is that wine is vertically integrated, in other words we produce the necessary components for the products we make. We grow the grapes and then turn around and make and sell the wine. This is unlike most other business models. If, for example, you're manufacturing cars, you don't mine and smelt the metal used in your product's body. You don't source and make the glass for your windows. You purchase all of that from vendors." Due to the verticality of the business, a wine businessperson must cover the entire value chain with his abilities, according to Shafer: "An entrepreneur in the wine business must have a comprehensive understanding of vineyards, wine production, human resources, and PR, marketing and sales. It pays to be someone who is naturally curious and had wide interests because you need to have much more than just superficial knowledge in each of these areas."

Shafer's business objective is "to provide an unforgettable experience. That can be any number of things including an experience with the wine, with a winery visit, with a visit to our website, or even in our interactions over the phone. In the late 1990s Dad, I, and the team here spent some time defining our core values. It was a valuable exercise as it continues to give guidance as we move forward. They are: respect and care for each other, our customers, our suppliers, and our environment; integrity and authenticity in all aspects of our work and interactions; service to our community; excellence in everything we do." Shafer makes it clear that communication via new media and social networks is also based on a long-term orientation in customer care: "For Shafer, tools like Twitter, Facebook, Instagram and Pinterest fit into our long-term approach. They aren't about selling cases of wine in the next 24 hours, or even the next month. They're about creating and maintaining long-term relationships with customers."

Shafer explains his personal motto: "'There is no silver bullet'... in other words, there's never a magic solution. Everything we've accomplished here has happened because of hard work, sweating the small stuff, trial and error, picking ourselves up after failing, tenacity, constant experimentation, and always asking if there's a better way to do it. I ask myself, 'Is the wine better? Are my employees happy? Are my customers happy? Did we make a profit?' If all of those answers are yes, then we've been successful. Can it be measured? Yes. I'm measuring it all the time, although sometimes it's more of a gut feel than a row of numbers on a spread sheet."

For his business decisions, Shafer has a precise pattern, as he explains: "Decisions at Shafer revolve around three key questions. The first question is always, 'What's best for the wine?' The second question is, 'What's best for the business?' And the third is, 'Is this a good fit with our core values?'" However, Shafer also appreciates impulses from his surroundings: "When making larger-scale decisions I like to hear from a pretty wide circle of people on our team. I find it especially useful to listen to opposing viewpoints. I value civilized disagreement. The least useful thing I can think of would be a management team that's my 'rubber stamp committee'. From there I will sometimes go back and forth on things. Ultimately I like to 'sleep on it'."

Shafer handles business risks level-headedly, and tries to keep them as small as possible: "Both my dad and I have avoided key risks by doing two things", he explains. "First: Taking a long-term approach. Since we aren't beholden to any investors and do not need to show growth on a quarterly basis, we have taken cautious steps in terms of our spending. As a result we own our land, own key pieces of equipment and technology such as our own bottling line, and we carry no debt. This has allowed our business to weather the inevitable ups and downs of the economy. Second: We have focused on what we're good at. We believe we're good at producing and selling about 30,000 cases of wine a year with a small, hard-working team of employees. We have not expanded in ways that would require us to tackle a lot of unknowns, create new layers of management, or take on debt."

DOUG SHAFER

Shafer attributes his recipe for success to simple formulae: "Work hard. Learn from your mistakes. Mistakes to me are a step toward learning. Never rest on your laurels. Hire people who enjoy working hard and have the innate desire to learn from their mistakes and constantly look for new ways to improve. It's a cliché to say this but I've found truth in the idea that you hire good people and you train and empower them to make the smart decisions on the fly. You must also give them the right tools to do their jobs whether that's the right computer equipment in the office or new technology in the cellar." The ideal employee, for Shafer, is therefore "someone who enjoys working hard, loves Shafer Vineyards, and has an innate and ongoing desire to do the job better. You can teach a person specific tasks but you can't teach them to want to perform at a high level. That's either in them or it isn't."

"I'VE FOUND TRUTH IN THE IDEA THAT YOU HIRE GOOD PEOPLE AND YOU TRAIN AND EMPOWER THEM TO MAKE THE SMART DECISIONS ON THE FLY. YOU MUST ALSO GIVE THEM THE RIGHT TOOLS TO DO THEIR JOBS."

DOUG SHAFER

Shafer sees the future of wine business as being multidimensional: "Some things will stay as they always have. People will still gravitate toward wines that taste good, they will want to be welcomed warmly at your winery, they will wish to enjoy relationships. They will still want that sense of discovery – finding a wine or a winery that they love. Other things will change over time. Some red and white varietals may swing in or out of general favour. The economy will move up and down, determining which price points will be more or less successful. New technology may change the way we do things in the cellar and vineyard. And as the world becomes more digital and more global, I believe there will be a desire for things that are anchored in authenticity and speak of a singular place. Wines that offer that will enjoy a lot of success."

According to Shafer, the requirements for someone who wants to be successful in the wine sector in the future are "taking a long-term approach and learning to use new technology for the aims of improving wine and fostering relationships with customers." In his opinion, young wine businesspeople must "start where the rubber meets the road. Learn how to prune. Learn how to shovel a tank. Know the science of fermentation. Get your hands dirty. Learn the business from the dirt up."

CHRISTOPH MACK

Chairman of the board, Mack & Schühle
Owen, Germany

Christoph Mack (born 1962) is the chairman of the board and majority shareholder of Mack & Schühle AG in Owen (Esslingen County). Founded in 1939 as a wine shop in Hechingen, today the company is one of the largest wine importers and distributors in the Central European area, and supplies especially the food retail, specialised shops, online business and gastronomy. Mack is active in the family business for ca. 30 years, and conducts it in the third generation. Apart from that he is also the president of the Bundesverband Wein und Spirituosen International (Federal Association for Wine and Liquor International – BWSI) in Wiesbaden.

"I was born into the wine area; my family is rooted for generations in wine commerce, production, and oenology", says Mack. "One of my earliest child memories is the clinking when empty wine bottles bump into one another on the conveyor belts of the bottling facilities. Even though as a youth I had several professional interests and would have liked to be a physician, it was still always somehow clear that I would continue the family history."

> "FOR ME, TO LIVE AS A BUSINESSPERSON MEANS THE WILLINGNESS AND THE READINESS TO ASSUME RESPONSIBILITY AND TO THINK AND ACT IN AN INTEGRAL WAY."

Mack gathered experience for this purpose both inside and outside his country: "A very internationally oriented career shaped me. I learned the practical bases of wine making at home and in German and Austrian cooperative cellars, and that's something I wouldn't want to miss", tells Mack. After that he studied oenology at the Centre for Winegrowing and Wine of the Zurich University for Applied Sciences in Wädenswil, where he wrote his thesis on biological acid reduction in wine. Internships then took him to additional countries in Europe and overseas. "The study of oenology in Switzerland, my activities in France, Italy, South Africa and California, both in oenology and in marketing, are still of great value for me", says Mack. They also ensured that he knows three foreign languages.

CHRISTOPH MACK

Mack sees himself as a wine producer and wine marketer in one person, but he distinguishes between these two roles when he considers the development of his company: "From the point of view of the producer, one of the most important steps was the founding of the Italian group mondodelvino, which is quite important today, with my partners Alfeo Martini and Roger Gabb." The company group MGM Mondo del Vino, whose acronym is made up of the initials of the founders' last names, was created in 1991, and is currently one of Italy's most important wine producers. "From the point of views of the marketer, the cooperation with the Gallo family in California was a decisive development", continues Mack. "I personally, as well as our company group, have enormously benefited, and still do, from the marketing performance of the world's most successful wine marketer. In addition, the early entrance into our family business and the successful development together with a highly motivated and continuously growing team are influential for an entire lifetime."

In 1992, Mack became managing partner of the company, and since 2001 he is part of the board of directors. "For me, living as a businessperson means the will and the readiness to assume responsibility, and to think and act in an integral way", he defines. "That was never a conscious decision, but rather an intuitive one. Leadership and responsibility are decisive criteria, not only for the businessperson himself, but for any organisational culture and community. Performance is natural for me, and part of the tasks of life. For me, there is motivation if something is fun for you. It is a lot of fun for me to have the possibility to accompany and participate in the fashioning of the positive development of a business society."

In his business activities, Mack is guides by certain values and principles: "Sustainability, and an integral and humanistic approach, are very important for me. Values such as tolerance, respect, thoughtfulness, gratitude, and humility are as important as discipline, will, and the readiness to always give your best." Here, for him the important thing is not primarily a specific basic principle: "I don't really have a life slogan", he explains. "But I like to hold on the statement 'The way is the goal', and to try to concentrate on the attitude: 'The past can't be brought back, the future is an illusion, therefore try to do your best at any moment, to shape a good future for your surroundings and for yourself.'"

Mack's basic convictions are also reflected in the Mack & Schühle company model, which the chief executive officer quotes: "Our central task is to ensure that our customers are completely satisfied with our services, and to make them more successful. Sustainability, transparency, and quality assurance are part of the success concept."

Mack perceives the wine sector as being ambivalent: "The wine area, from my point of view, is unique and can't be compared with any other business area. On the one hand, it is completely hybrid – or diffuse – characterised by the smallest winery and self-marketer structures, to family-managed middle-sized companies, to large cooperatives and multinational organisations. On the other hand, it continues being a very comprehensible branch, of a practically familiar extent." In respects, too, Mark determines contrasts: "On the one hand, the area is characterised by the production of rather large amounts of standardised wines, driven by the price – comparable with many other agricultural products. On the other hand, all over the world there are a growing number of individual and in part intellectual small and large wineries and producers who go their own path. Thus, the really wonderful luxury item wine, which in general receives a positive and public attention, is difficult to understand, and impossible to generalise", summarises the businessman.

"IN THE LONG HISTORY OF WINEGROWING, PROGRESSIVENESS AND INNOVATIVE POWER ARE ACTUALLY BASICALLY NEWCOMERS."

In summary, he says, the wine economy is very traditional: "Compared to the long history of winegrowing, progressiveness and innovative power are basically newcomers. A tendency which we might say passed over from the New World countries to Europe, and is very positive for the product and the market. But still, compared to other luxury items, luxury products, or fast-moving consumer goods (FMCGs), the wine world is still a rather thoughtful and conservative little group", judges Mack.

Despite its special features, according to Mack the wine sector is governed by principles similar to those of other areas of the economy. "The ways and keys to success, from my point of view, are really no different in the wine area than in other business areas", he says. "You must have your sight firmly on the benefit for the consumer and his wishes.

That means a commitment to quality, price-performance, innovation, and communication, and for me it also includes especially authenticity and sustainability." But he notes: "In comparison to many other consumer products, wine is rather a low-margin product. Someone who isn't willing to think in the long term but rather thinks about a fast profit, or isn't willing to invest and act sustainably, should better only participate in this area as a consumer."

Mack understands success in the most comprehensive possible way: "Vision, courage, motivation, and passion are keys to success. Here I always try to live with an integral approach: earnings are important, but they aren't an isolated goal. If a company that consists of a motivated, positively loaded, and happy team develops dynamically in all areas, is critical with itself, is communicative and lives innovatively towards the inside and outside, recognises the market needs and in part anticipates them, gets an acceptable profit, appropriate for the area, is financially independent and willing to invest, and acts sustainably, then I consider it to be integrally successful." And in view of his international career, he comments: "We Germans link happiness with money. I am surprised, again and again, how happy people in other countries are, people who have so much less. We must really learn that too."

Mack formulates his personal recipe for success as "giving your best at any moment and don't consider yourself to be important", and adds: "You have to reinvent yourself over and over again, without forgetting where you come from. Success for me is a great delight. I am successful because I can be content." For his business decisions, Mack uses "my own magical triangle: team, head, and gut feeling". This can sometimes result in misperceptions: "Errors are completely normal for me. Only a person who doesn't

CHRISTOPH MACK

do anything commits no errors, and one who commits no errors takes no decisions at all. Lateral thinkers are heartily welcome for me, and contradictions are a welcome stimulation for me. Only someone who follows the path he recognised as correct in a sustained way can be successful." For Mack, risks are part of a company's everyday life: "In general, I think: The moment the ovum and the sperm cell merge, the risks of life start. Each company must be able and willing to take risks. However, they must be of such a type that they can occur at any moment."

Mack is also open towards new technological developments: "Digital revolution and social media aren't unforeseen challenges; rather, they have been part of the real life of society and economy for quite a while. The wine area is no exception. I am willing to adapt to changes, as long as I have the force to do so. However, for me the Paracelsus law applies here too, or I live according to the rule: 'How much salt and pepper does a good soup need?' From the business point of view, I am completely open towards all communication media, as long as they are lawful and don't harm anybody. Personally I don't need Facebook or anything like it."

In view of the business culture and its underlying human understanding, Mack quotes once more from the company model: "To achieve our integral services, we value dynamic teamwork a lot. We promote each individual and demand from them, and we know that the best results are achieved as a group. Each employee has the trust of the company." Mack describes his leadership style as "open, team-oriented, let do, and if required, clearly intervene." His point of view of the ideal employee corresponds to this; such an employee "thinks and entrepreneurially, is team-oriented, strong-willed, communicates competently, and is a specialist in his area, but with a holistic approach".

However, the businessperson is also responsible for the success of his employees, explains Mack: "A business must provide some space for the development of the employee's personality. It is important to promote and to demand, and to delegate responsibility and decision-making powers. There must be a positive symbiosis between the company and the employees. It is important to have a common approach and success. Tolerance, team spirit, free space, and a pleasant environment are just as important as a performance-oriented payment. Of course a company must give its employees the correct tools, to let them act successfully and to be able to develop itself. The focus is always the win-win situation."

Mack basically considers the future of the wine area to be optimistic: "As long as people get enjoyment from getting together for good food in good company and from communicating with one another, wine will also have a pleasant role in the future. After all, wine is a wonderful product – pure pleasure, in an incomparable variety. To cook, eat, enjoy wine, talk, be with friends – that's the joy of life for every day and for many people who are living their life."

Mack is sure that "The wine business will continue developing positively, with all of its changes, as long as it acts sustainably and strives for additional qualitative development. I believe that wine consumption in Germany is very stable in the long term and that it has a good growth potential. In our assortment, German wine becomes

CHRISTOPH MACK

increasingly important. We cooperate more and more with German producers, wineries, and cellars, who would like to penetrate more into the markets and use our strength in sales and communications. If in the southern European winegrowing countries consumption decreases, I believe that this is the result of a change in the dealing with wine. People enjoy in a more conscious and selective manner."

"A PERSON WHO ISN'T WILLING TO THINK IN THE LONG TERM, BUT WHO THINKS ONLY ABOUT A FAST PROFIT, OR WHO ISN'T WILLING TO INVEST AND TO ACT SUSTAINABLY, WOULD BE BETTER OFF BY ONLY ACTING IN THIS AREA AS A CONSUMER."

But Mack also sees dangers: "Something that might become a problem in the future is a tendency of politics to get involved in all sorts of consumption and to insidiously work on paternalism or even disempowerment of the consumer. That also applies to alcoholic beverages. Wine enjoyment has nothing to do with drinking bouts", he clarifies.

To be successful in the future, businesspeople in the wine business, according to Mack, must display "sustainability, creativity, diligence, honesty, and a lot of competence in communication and distribution technology – in principle, all the qualifications that are also needed for any non-wine businessperson", he considers. Mack recommends young beginners in the area to cultivate these properties and, as he emphasises, to remain authentic.

CHRISTOPH MACK

WINE
ENTREPRENEURS

FRÉDÉRIC DROUHIN

President, Maison Joseph Drouhin
Beaune, France

Frédéric Drouhin (born 1968) is the chairman of the board of the winery Maison Joseph Drouhin in Beaune in Burgundy. He manages the business together with his three siblings Véronique, Philippe and Laurent; their father Robert is chairman of the supervisory board. With 73 hectares of vines, the Joseph Drouhin domain is one of the largest wineries in Burgundy. The vineyards consist, to over two-thirds, of grand-cru and premier-cru positions, and extend over the Chablis (38 hectares), the Côte de Nuits and the Côte de Beaune (32 hectares), and the Côte Chalonnaise (3 hectares). They are managed biodynamically, and for some community and regional descriptions of origin, the Joseph Drouhin house cooperates in the context of partnership that last several years. Additionally, the company manages a winery in the USA, the Drouhin Oregon Domain in the Willamette Valley. Both companies grow exclusively the two vine varieties Chardonnay and Pinot Noir.

> "A COMPANY IS BASED ON THE QUALITY OF THE PEOPLE THAT MAKE IT UP. YOU CAN'T LEAD EVERYTHING ALONE; YOU HAVE TO BE CAPABLE OF GETTING ALONG WITH THE BEST."

Frédéric Drouhin is responsible for the strategic development of the Joseph Drouhin Domain. He got an MBA degree in Marketing from the University of Hartfort in the U.S. state of Connecticut, and expanded his business experience in several companies before entering his family business in 1993. He reports about his development: "The Maison Joseph Drouhin was founded in 1880 by my great-grandfather, and is managed today in the fourth generation. The transfer of know-how – the passion for wine – is perceived and trained quite early, starting with playful experiences such as the time of the grape harvest, preparing the wine, children playing in the wine cellars, then participation in meals with customers, where wine of course plays a special role. Thus, I grew up in this environment, and I am proud about what was achieved by previous generations, and together with my two brothers and my sister, I would like to hand on this tradition and set it up for the fifth generation. At first that meant to pursue an education which corresponded to my passion and my intellectual interest. Since our company is very open to the world – we export over 80%, into 90 countries – I wanted to pursue an education at an American university, to fundamentally get to know the culture of this country, our most important market. Our profession is very varied; it includes agriculture, oenology, economy, marketing, finances, and business relations. Thus, I got to know all these areas of our company in a quite natural way, and expanded my knowledge, to finally take over the general management in 2003." Drouhin refers to meetings that have characterised his professional development: "Two people were very important in my development: our former oenologist Laurence Jobard, but also my father with all his collection of experience, for he has experienced the development, even the revolution of wines from Burgundy, as well as the strengthening of winegrowing countries of the world." Additional contacts continue enriching his activity, as Drouhin explains: "It's also very important to exchange experiences with the sons and daughters of other winemaker families from France and other countries, who share the same values and the same challenges of a family business. That happens in the association of the Primum Familiae Vini, in which eleven winemaker families are united: Champagne Pol Roger, Baron Philippe de Rothschild, the winery Egon Müller Scharzhof, Hugel et Fils, Marchesi Antinori, Perrin et Fils, The Symington Family Estates, Vega-Sicilia, Bodegas Miguel Torres, Sassicaia Tenuta de San Guido and Maison Joseph Drouhin. Thus, this exchange was possible not just with my own generation, but also with the previous one."

"THE DIGITAL WORLD CHANGES ALL THE TIME, AND YOU HAVE TO ALWAYS BE ACTIVE AND REMAIN UP-TO-DATE, TO KNOW HOW YOUNG PEOPLE COMMUNICATE, FOR THEY ARE THE FUTURE BUYERS OF OUR WINES."

Drouhin perceives the wine business area as divided into two parts: "Today there are two types of businesses in winegrowing: the family businesses and the large industrial groups", he explains. "These two can very well be compatible, and don't aim at the same customer group. In a family business there are certain values of continuity: transmitting, to the next generation, respect, ethics, visions, passion, and a goal, namely to produce quality wines which are representative and indicative of the winegrowing area." His own values are correspondingly "the values of family, ethics, and morals", says Drouhin. "High demands, thirst for knowledge, and a sense for values, passion, and boldness have been transmitted together with the knowledge and the sense for quality", he emphasises, and adds: "For me, education means to acquire knowledge, in order to give something back." His goal is "discovery, training, and preparing the members of the fifth generation, who feel the passion and the desire to continue the company development."

To be successful as a wine businessperson, numerous conditions are required, Drouhin explains: "The professional qualifications must be spread widely: an agricultural and oenological training, as well as training in economy, marketing, and finances. You must not forget that winegrowing is based mainly on the vine, and if you plant a vine, that's for at least the next 30 years. Thus, everything requires its time. The idea of management is therefore not that of a publicly listed company which must provide better results every quarter. There is no orientation on short-term profits, but rather on long-term profits which must be reinvested. As I mentioned before, you must also set the

FRÉDÉRIC DROUHIN

WINE
ENTREPRENEURS

goal of being a model of quality, with the demand of making every year a good one, regardless of the climate conditions. The vine gets its basis from the soil, which you must maintain, and using pesticides or fertiliser can change this soil, and therefore the nature of the wine, in the long term. As a result, you must apply more oenological tricks, resulting in a standardization of wine. The methods of biological and biodynamical cultivation help maintain this heritage of wine culture, and – I am convinced of this – produce wines which have more 'soul'. It is one thing to make good wines, and quite another to know how it is done. Finally you also need the competence to communicate and market the wines." However, the basic condition for success, according to Drouhin, is something that he recommends anybody who enters this area to have: "Passion!"

Even if he is busy primarily in management and not so much in the vineyard and cellar, Drouhin is very close to his company's nature and product: "If I were able to change something in my professional life, I would care more about the operation and less about management", he confesses. "Day after day, I am interested in knowing how my vineyards are doing, how I can prevent diseases, and then, when a new vintage is growing, to follow the transformation from a simple fruit, the grape, into a special wine; also, to ask myself whom I'll meet today, with whom I will talk about my passion as a winemaker."

Success, according to Drouhin, also results from the product: "For me, wine means to participate jointly in something – enjoyment, feeling. I am successful because my friends recommend my wine to their friends." And yet he is quite modest: "Success, for me, means not to flaunt it too much." But for him, initiative and willpower are also important, as he defines: "Performance is inseparable from ambition. Motivation, for me, means to start now and not tomorrow." The concept of success has many different facets in Drouhin's eyes: "To be able to objectively measure a company's success in the world of wine, there are several indicators: first constancy and the increase of reports in the trade press which evaluate the wines every year. From the commercial point of view, performance can be measured by the market share, both in volume and in money. A successful company can provide its production with a better image than the competition, and can thus penetrate more strongly into the sales segment. From the financial point of view, you can measure profitability in relation to the amount of capital invested. Finally, if you know the company from the inside, you can measure the employee fluctuations: Do they remain loyal to the company? Are there promotions within the company?"

Drouhin describes his leadership style as "determined, direct, and dignified"; as a businessperson he must "have an open ear. You need a clear goal and the resources available for that, you must keep your promises, and show your appreciation when the goals are met. That applies to all employees up to the management level." The ideal employee for him is "one who proposes solutions for problems, instead of expecting them from others. A lateral thinker for me is somebody who draws attention to himself. The employees must make the business culture their own, must have a partnership attitude, professional ethics, and efficiency, and must be proud of their task." At the same time, Drouhin emphasises: "A company is based on the quality of the people that make it up. You can't manage everything alone; you must be able to get along with the best." His favourite quotation is from the American president John F. Kennedy, who said: "Don't ask what your country can do for you; ask what you can do for your country."

FRÉDÉRIC DROUHIN

Once again, Drouhin speaks of the importance of a strategic orientation and the long-term orientation: "Mainly, you need to have a clear goal: In what direction do we want to go, how, and with what resources? In Burgundy, production is very diverse, and goes from the regional designations, which are in competition with the vine variety wines from all over the world, to the big wines, which are among the top class, or top wines, with which you can't compromise. You must therefore take your decisions according to the product made and the sales markets." The company chief isn't afraid of risks: "For me, it's better to commit errors than not to take any decision at all. In our profession there are several recurring risks such as agricultural damage (frost, heat, hail), problems in making the wine, getting grapes, the business performance, or commercial or financial failures of the distributors. You have to be able to accept natural catastrophes in agriculture, and at the same time know that you can protect yourself, in part, from certain risks. However, since our winery extends over several dozen kilometres, the risk is spread out."

"FOR ME, IT'S BETTER TO COMMIT ERRORS THAN NOT TO DO ANY DECISION AT ALL."

Drouhin goes into more detail: With respect to getting wines, there is a lot of competition in Burgundy, since the wine growing area only increases slightly, and many wine-growers bottle their production themselves, and don't sell any grapes to buyers such as us. Therefore, you have to both expand your own wine growing area, and regulate the purchasing relations with producers officially, with contracts. With respect to making wine, there is a daily control, to be able to intervene in case there are deviations from the planned winemaking process. In the business area, capital participation at a distributor allows a better control over the fate of your own wines on the market, and participating in the business strategy, since you also know the financial aspects."

For sales, technological progress is also an important success factor, as Drouhin explains: "Internet and the social networks are an excellent connection to consumers all over the world, and they allow us to get an audience for our point of view, in addition to the wine trade press. Nowadays it's therefore possible to maintain a much more direct contact with consumers, to see what they say about our own wines. It's therefore important to make access to such information easier, either through an official website or by participating in blogs. Since 1994, we have an official website, which has later also been adapted for smartphones and tablets, and we have printed a QR code on all our labels to allow customers to immediately and very easily access the datasheets for our wines and information about our winery. The digital world changes continuously, and you have to be always active and keep up-to-date to know how young people communicate, for they are the future buyers of our wines. The Internet has also contributed to price transparency and less control in the movement of merchandise. Somebody in Japan can do his purchases at sellers other than the ones in Japan, while getting a better price – even though that isn't always the case."

FRÉDÉRIC DROUHIN

With respect to the future of the wine sector, Drouhin has specific ideas: "I believe that in the next 10 years and beyond there will be more wine drinkers, and that the average wine consumption per capita in other countries – except for France – will increase. The drinking habits for wine will change fundamentally, that is, it will be less connected to classic eating. The demand for quality wines will increase, not only for wines with a protected designation of origin, but also for wines from other large winegrowing areas – and none will be able to satisfy the demand. In countryside wines and vine variety wines, France will increasingly get competition from the rest of the world. I also believe that Malbec from Argentina will be very much in vogue. In the future, Oregon and New Zealand will become the two best winegrowing regions for Pinot Noir. Global warming, which results in a change of the historically planted vine varieties, will become an important topic. There will be more drastic and more frequent extreme climate events. Brands will get a greater weight. In sales, there will be a concentration, but more and more small, local dealers will appear on the scene as well. The price of land will be covered less and less by the bottle price, especially in the case of AOC wines. Investments in wine gardens and production systems will increasingly activate investors who are outside of the area of sales and owners."

FRÉDÉRIC DROUHIN

GARY VAYNERCHUK

Owner of Wine Library and VaynerMedia, wine dealer, communicator, and social media consultant
Springfield (NJ), USA

Gary Vaynerchuk (born 1975) is the owner and manager of the wine business Wine Library in Springfield (New Jersey) and of the VaynerMedia agency, which is specialised on social media and brand consultancy and maintains branch offices in New York (New York), San Francisco and Los Angeles (both in California). Vaynerchuk got known as a video blogger; he is also active as a public speaker, a book author and investor, and has founded a variety of companies, alone or with partners. After Robert Parker, he is considered to be one of the most influential wine critics in the USA.

"I ALWAYS THOUGHT OF ENTREPRENEURSHIP AS WAR. I ALWAYS WANTED EVERYBODY I COMPETED WITH TO SUCCEED... AS LONG AS I SUCCEEDED A LITTLE BIT MORE THAN THEY DID."

Vaynerchuk's family came to the United States from what is today Belarus, when he was three years old, and settled in Queens (New York), while there his father was able to take a job at liquor store in Edison (New Jersey) owned by a family member. His father would go on to take ownership of the store, and Vaynerchuk already worked in the shop while he was in high school: "From the ages of 16 to 18, I was a cashier at Shopper's Discount Liquors (what would eventually become Wine Library). That gave me the opportunity to observe how customers behaved in the isles, and really started building up my awareness of consumer behaviour", he recounts. When he got bored at the cash register, he read wine magazines such as Wine Spectator and Wine Advocate. Since as a youth he wasn't allowed to taste wine for legal reasons, he sampled the aromas found in the wine in the original – apart from all sorts of fruit and vegetable types, also grass, earth, stones, wood, and tobacco. "I probably consumed more New Jersey grass in my teens than any lawn mower", he says with a wink.

After he finished college, Vaynerchuk – who in the meantime was a passionate wine collector – took over his father's business in 1997, and converted it into the wine business Wine Library. As the company's only wine purchaser, he tasted every wine personally, before including it in the company's assortment. He used the nascent Internet technology quite early, as he tells us: "In 1997 I was selling wine with an email list while most stores were still faxing their customers. Building on that, I quickly came to recognize the importance of e-commerce, and launched WineLibrary.com, one of the very first wine sales sites. As soon as Google AdWords came out, I was the first (and for a long time the only) person to advertise against people searching for "wine." All of this helped me to grow the store from a $3 million business to a $60 million business, and it was just the beginning." Today, Vaynerchuk's Internet wine shop is considered to be the largest online discounter for wines in North America.

The next step was his video blog, which he called "Wine Library TV": "Within a year of YouTube popping up, I knew it would be an incredibly powerful platform. Armed with a Flipcam and a NY Jets bucket, I started Wine Library TV in 2006 to share my knowledge and passion for wine with a community that desperately needed a fresh voice. It wasn't long before 100,000 people were watching my videos every day", Vaynerchuk describes. He says that he had been bothered by the rigidity of conceited sommeliers and arrogant wine dealers, which, in his opinion, were either not able or not willing to teach their customers anything. He also disliked the apparently mysterious conventions of the area, which made wine look intimidating for outsiders, as he tells us.

In "Wine Library TV", he instead spoke in an unconventional, often even disrespectful way about wine (and in between also about the New York Jets, his beloved American football team), and encouraged his viewers – which as "Vayniacs became his followers and exchanged opinions both on the Internet and in real meetings – about honest, uncomplicated tasting. He cleared away wine myths, explained the influence of natural conditions of origin such as soil and climate on the wine aromas, carried out comparison tastings on camera, and gave tips for purchasing wine. Vaynerchuk defines his basic intention as follows: "First, I want people to try different wines. How can you have a favourite if you only know a few? Second, I tell people to trust their palates. If a wine appeals to your palate, then it's a good choice. Don't feel pressured to like popular brands or what experts recommend. Buy what 'brings the thunder' for you." The wine communicator repeatedly invited visitors, including several celebrities, to his show. For five years, the video blog was running every day on the Internet, until 2011.

Since then, Vaynerchuk concentrates more on his consulting company, which he has also founded in the meantime: "In the spring of 2009, my brother AJ and I launched VaynerMedia, a strategic creative agency focusing on social and digital", he explains. With VaynerMedia he helped some of the American companies with the highest turnover from the "Fortune 500" list of the magazine with the same name, "execute against their KPI's, and build their digital brands through micro content and other storytelling techniques. The idea took hold, and what started as a 6-person project 5 years ago has swelled to a 400-strong team spread across the country." As a private investor (known as a business angel), Vaynerchuk participates in over 50 companies – mainly in the technology area. His most recent activity in this area is to create, together with Matt Higgins, co-founder of RSE Venture, the 25-million investment fund "VaynerRSE, a $25 million seed fund that will help invest in and launch the next generation of world-changing technology companies", according to Vaynerchuk. "The biggest thing that's happened to me is following trends. I like fast following. We have a desire to support entrepreneurs and go into spaces that others haven't gotten into or take on complexity that scares others off." As a marketing consultant, Vaynerchuk can point out, not least, that he has established himself as a brand – by carrying out an intensive dialogue, via social media and networks such as Twitter, Facebook, YouTube, and Instagram, with his fans and followers.

His business attitude appeared quite early: "I have been a businessman for as long as anyone close to me can remember. You can be fancy and call it being an 'entrepreneur', but at the end of the day, I do business. While most eight year olds were learning how to properly squeeze a lemon, I was managing seven lemonade stands across my neighbourhood in Edison, NJ. When I turned twelve, I set my sights on my local mall, where I became something of a legend selling baseball cards on weekends", Vaynerchuk remembers. However, he didn't purposefully develop into a businessperson: "I don't think it's a conscious choice at all. I didn't even know what those words meant until I was 30, and 'entrepreneur' suddenly stopped being used as a dirty word."

"I'M NOT ENTITLED TO ANYTHING, AND IF I LOSE, IT'S BECAUSE I DESERVE TO LOSE."

Vaynerchuk's motivation is of a non-material type: "I don't like stuff. Matter of fact, I hate stuff. I don't want planes. I don't want cars. I don't want watches. I don't do it for any of that stuff", he clarifies. The goal of his business activity can be described as multiplication or – using a biological analogy – as reproduction: "To the outside world, it's always been to buy the New York Jets. To myself, it's following my beliefs to create a handful of extremely successful companies that then go on to create new generations of entrepreneurs. Think of it like a coaching tree in the National Football League where a coach leads a team to victory, and then the members of that team all go on to become great coaches."

According to Vaynerchuk, a successful businessperson needs "passion for the product. A lack of romanticism around the product (that is to say remembering it's a business). The ability to push back against trends. One of the biggest problems in the wine world right now is that everybody will ride the same wave. All of a sudden Barolo, or Gruner, or Pinot gets hot, and everybody follows like sheep. Before too long the new thing becomes the establishment and gets boring, so you need to be able to trust your palate. I think that's something that is lacking at the highest levels." Vaynerchuk warns, "that people can become 'fake entrepreneurs' because it's the trendy thing to do. A Hollywood movie comes out, and all of a sudden script-kiddies think they can put a hoodie on and become the best thing ever (that plus there are certain practicalities to becoming an entrepreneur in the first few years out of school). With all of this talking comes a lot of preconceived notions about what an entrepreneur 'should' or 'shouldn't' be, what 'real' entrepreneurs say, or what 'real' entrepreneurs should do."

Vaynerchuk doesn't want to give universal recommendations for business success; rather, he wants to explain "what works for me. Entrepreneurship runs in my blood, and I feel like I've always had a pretty good eye for what works and what doesn't." He lists some of his fundamental principles: "I have never been on the defense. I have always been on the offense. I love to hustle! As an entrepreneur, I'm just a counter-puncher. All of my moves are predicated on the moves of my opponent. I make my decisions because of movements I see in the market. It's all reactionary. Speed has always been more

GARY VAYNERCHUK

valuable to me than profit. It was always about growing the base, growing the company, and moving quickly. I have never worried about the bottom line. I have always focused on the top-line revenue." Vaynerchuk describes his leadership style as "motivational. Outwardly frantic, but shockingly calm."

Independence, a fighting spirit, and long-term thinking propel him, as he reveals: "I never cared what my parents or teachers thought. I always paid my dues. I never worried about the short-term effects on my life because I just knew there was no other choice. With me there was only one gear. I just had to do it because my business is my life. It's my blood. It's my oxygen. I just wasn't worried about work/life balance when I was 24. I never cared what my friends thought. I never once envied anybody. I couldn't have cared less about any 27-year-old contemporary who worked on Wall Street and make 200,000 dollars and drove some fucking fancy car. I really didn't give a fuck. Want to know something kind of sick? I actually preferred for them to think that they were beating me, because I knew how it was going to net out. I always wanted to beat everybody. (Even dear friends.) I always thought of entrepreneurship as war. I always wanted everybody I competed with to succeed... as long as I succeeded a little bit more than they did. I always wanted legacy. I was always concerned with how I'd be looked at in the long term. I wanted entrepreneurs to read about me in schools one day. I was just always more concerned with the legacy of it, than the currency of it. When I'm not spending time with my family, who mean everything in the world to me, I speak and share my experiences in business with people around the world. I have also found a passion for storytelling." Thus, Vaynerchuk's books "Crush It!", "The Thank You Economy" and "Jab, Jab, Jab, Right Hook" became bestsellers in a very short time.

"MOST NON-ENTREPRENEURS CAN MEASURE SUCCESS EASILY SINCE IT REALLY COMES DOWN TO DOLLARS AND CENTS, BUT FOR US, IT'S MORE ABOUT BEING ABLE TO PLAY THE GAME RATHER THAN BEING ABLE TO MAKE THE MONEY."

Vaynerchuk has worked out everything for himself, as he emphasises: "I had a lot of patience. (Still do.) I felt zero entitlement. I'm not entitled to anything, and if I lose, it's because I deserve to lose. I think one of the things that most attracted me to entrepreneurship was that nobody was entitled to anything. Even with all of the success I'd had, I loved the idea of starting an agency four years ago with nobody in the agency world knowing who I am, nobody respecting me, and nobody thinking I'd be able to do it. I prefer to be underestimated. I love it. I prefer the climb. Starting over is attractive, not a negative." Success, for Vaynerchuk, is not primarily of a monetary character: "I would personally define entrepreneurial success as being able to sustain the lifestyle of being an entrepreneur. Most non-entrepreneurs can measure success easily since it really comes down to dollars and cents, but for us, it's more about being able to play the game rather than being able to make the money. Some of the most entrepreneurially successful things I've seen are events like getting your company acqui-hired simply so that it wouldn't go under."

GARY VAYNERCHUK

Vaynerchuk places the company above the people connected to it. With respect to perspective, it is necessary to have "a respect for the history of the business coupled with a disrespect for the people who made that history. I'm constantly shocked and humbled by the people who say that I've influenced their career, but I'm confident that the ones who will win are the ones who say 'fuck GaryVee, I'll do it my own way.'" Even though he carefully observes the market and is very trend-oriented, Vaynerchuk doesn't like to give future forecasts for wine: "I'm not a big fan of making predictions, but I can make some guesses. I think you'll begin to see some major challenges to long-held beliefs. I can see artificially flavoured wines becoming a bigger thing. Wines on the rocks. Smart technology integrated into bottles that monitor things like temperature, humidity, age, even things like trichloroanisol which is responsible for a possible cork taste."

According to Vaynerchuk, the awareness of the present is essential: "My core thesis has always revolved around one question: Are you marketing like the year you actually live in? That's it. It's not about where things are going to be in five years, and it's definitely not about how we've always done it. Do what works. Right now."

GARY VAYNERCHUK

MAG. WILHELM KLINGER
Manager, Österreich Wein Marketing
Vienna, Austria

Wilhelm Klinger (born 1956) is manager of the Österreich Wein Marketing Gesellschaft (ÖWM – Austrian Wine Marketing Board) in Vienna. When he started to work full time with wine, he was in the beginning of his 30s; his parents' home was already gastronomically characterised: "I come from Wels in upper Austria, where there is hardly any winegrowing. But my family has a nice country inn in the Hausruck district, where there has always been a somewhat better wine than in the surrounding areas. And since I wasn't interested in anything other than good eating and drinking, after a study of Romance Studies and Drama study I ended up in the wine area", Klinger summarises.

At first he studied French and Italian at the Salzburg University in the teaching profession, and he is master in Philosophy. After that he completed a Drama study at the Vienna Franz-Schubert Conservatory and completed the state stage matriculation exam. For three years, Klinger had individual contracts at the State Theatre Salzburg, where he worked as an actor and carried out tasks in cultural management. In the context of an author cabaret, apart from Salzburg he also acted in Vienna, Graz, and Munich. In the summer 1986, Klinger directed the PR work of the Bregenz Festival.

> "TO BE ABLE TO DECIDE YOURSELF, BEAR
> RESPONSIBILITY, AND ALSO TO HARVEST
> THE FRUIT OF YOUR WORK, REALLY GIVES
> A SENSE OF PURPOSE."

Apart from his culinary passion, it was also Klinger's communicational capabilities that then took him to the wine sector: "The first position in the wine area was immediately the most important one", he reports. "From 1987 to 1993, I learned the fine wine trade from the start, with the renowned wine importer Alois Stangl in Salzburg, as 'number two' after the chief. Our assortment of top wines from Austria, Italy, France, and Spain was state of the art at that time. The key to success was my enthusiasm for wine and culinary arts, but especially my language knowledge, for I speak English, French, and Italian fluently." At Stangl, Klinger learned all areas of the wholesale and retail trade with wine and coffee. He was entrusted with purchasing, importation logistics, processing orders, and invoicing, as well as advertising and staff recruitment, and finally rose to the position of marketing leader. During his six years in the company, the turnover increased by a factor of five.

MAG. WILHELM KLINGER

WINE
ENTREPRENEURS

This established Klinger's career as a manager in the wine business. He took over the operational management of the wine specialty shop chain Wein & Co, and in this function, he established a retail business with nine branch offices. "As the right hand of the visionary owner Heinz Kammerer, I was able to delve deeply into the retail world", says Klinger. From 1993 to 1995, he was responsible for purchases, assortment, marketing and staff recruiting, and represented the company to the outside as the representative of the managing sole shareholder. Now there are 14 Wein & Co branch offices in Vienna, Linz, Graz, Salzburg, and Bregenz.

Thus, Klinger had ca. 8 years of management experience in wine trading, when in 1996 he "took care of the management at the winegrower's cooperative Domäne Wachau in Dürnstein, together with Fritz Miesbauer. With 660 hectares, we had enough wine to also play a role in the food retail business. That was a special fire baptism, for some annual meetings required good nerves and stamina." For four years, Klinger was responsible for marketing and distribution and for the strategic repositioning of the Free Wineries Wachau (Freie Weingärtner Wachau), as the Domäne Wachau was called until 2008. Here, among other things he reordered the assortment, built up exportation, and internationalised PR work.

> "WHAT YOU DO, YOU SHOULD DO WITH PASSION
> AND CONVICTION, AND RADIATE ENTHUSIASM
> ALL AROUND YOU. WITHOUT OPTIMISM,
> NOTHING IS POSSIBLE."

"At the beginning of the 2000s, I was hired by Angelo Gaja, who had just finished setting up the winery Ca`Marcanda in the Maremma", Klinger continues narrating. At Gaja, until 2006 he participated as an independent consultant, and worked for the optimisation of wine export and sales, market watching, global media relations, worldwide product presentation, and sales training, as well as import consultancy in the area product selection. "With the exclusive image of the Gaja brand in my luggage, I went all around the world, and in six years, I was able to make a good name for myself on the international arena as well", Klinger summarises. In a way as Angelo Gaja's right hand, the Austrian with language and stage experience was responsible for over 50 export markets.

Then he started his current position: "When in 2007 I got in charge of the management of Österreich Wein Marketing GmbH, I was able to look back on an extensive experience in this business area, which covered almost all areas of the diverse and exciting wine business", explains Klinger. "For eight years now, I can make this experience available to my country, at the top of ÖWM. That's not always simple, since suddenly you can't sell something tangible." ÖWM was founded in 1986 and understands itself as a service company for the Austrian wine business. Its tasks are image and PR work, promoting sales, advertising, as well as increasing the export and value creation for Austrian wine.

MAG. WILHELM KLINGER

In this respect, for Klinger it was quite a change after being almost 20 years in the wine business, as he intimates. "However, roof marketing does have special facets, and with the necessary political support, it is possible after all to get things done in the long term", he says. "It is just that the market reacts to our activities with the inertia of an ocean liner. However, I still think that we have finally taken it into the correct direction; in part, this is due to the fact that in the last three decades our wine economy has had a very positive and dynamic development; and the ÖWM permanently contributes to this."

In this respect, Klinger has internalised his mission: "The vision of a sustainably successful wine country Austria shapes my daily activities. All objectives have the orientation of creating a high esteem and a corresponding qualified demand for Austrian wine at the national and international level and to thus make the Austrian wine business more and more profitable, economically successful, but also more sustainable ecologically." The ÖWM manager doesn't lack determination, self-confidence, and ambition: "I am firmly convinced that I can formulate these goals in a credible way and also successively achieve them, and that at the end of my career, my personal reputation will be strengthened through this vision and its realisation. I want to become one of the best and most convincing messengers worldwide of a responsible wine and eating culture, and give people a lot of enjoyment for life by enticing them to moderate enjoyment." This also corresponds to Klinger's life slogan: "Life is beautiful!"

Even if he might technically not be a businessperson, Klinger understands and feels himself as an entrepreneur: "Lateral thinkers, for me, are sisters and brothers in spirit." He clarifies his motivation by mentioning, once again, his professional start: "I studied Romance studies and did the state exam for the teaching profession. In the trial year, it quickly became clear to me that working as a teacher, with all respect, is nothing for me. Good teachers, bad teachers – they all earn the same, society thinks less and less of their pedagogues, and you need a thick hide and a lot of fantasy to imagine that you can achieve a change under such conditions. Being a businessperson in the area fine wines is the most beautiful thing that I can imagine as a profession. For me, wine is life. To be able to decide yourself, to bear responsibility, and also to earn the fruits of your labour, really give a sense of purpose. I come from a family of businesspeople, and I consider an independent existence to be completely natural, even though today I am active not on my own but as a manager of a public organisation."

To be successful as a businessperson in the wine business, according to Klinger you need a certain product orientation: "The sober matrix is: You need to produce enough liquid, and sell them to the best possible price. Therefore I always say: fine wine marketing works opposite to the way that textbooks preach. The consumer is important, but he comes last. First are the vineyard and the grape variety. All strategic decisions are made there. The wine must be good and communicate his origin clearly; that's the only way to make things work. And now we can go on our way, with our stories, our passion, and our daily commitment, to find the customers for this great product, of which we are totally convinced that it is good. One who eyes the customer while making the wine will play in the B-league, in the best of cases."

MAG. WILHELM KLINGER

WINE
ENTREPRENEURS

Klinger goes into more details: "The most important thing with wine is the cultural component. This must be emphasized more strongly, due to two reasons: first, only a culturally secured higher positioning can achieve long-term profitability, and second, the wine economy will only have a successful future by communicating a cultivated dealing with the alcoholic beverage wine." Klinger has especially one group of producers in mind: "I strongly believe in the dynamic artisanal small businesses – the 'artigiani', as Angelo Gaja always says. And these 'artisans' of wine are the world's last universalists. They need to be able to do everything: be good farmers, fermentation technicians, plant managers, as well as communicators. The motto is, from the tractor to the airplane towards New York. And that's very exciting."

For him, success is "to be happy in the knowledge that I did it well", defines Klinger. "I am successful because I like people and I also like myself. For me, performance can be retrieved every day, because my work is fun for me. Motivation is automatically there, every morning. You need to do whatever you do with passion and conviction, and radiate enthusiasm all around you. Without optimism, nothing is possible."

To evaluate his – Klinger's – business success, however, you have to consider the concept in a differentiated way, according to the ÖWM chief: "Normally, business success is defines according to profit, preferably sustainable, i.e., the businessperson must manage to create a profitable business, sustainably, with his employees. In my function as the manager of a non-profit organization, I must needs define success in a different way, for my business existence is hard to measure. I do have market information that shows that we do our contribution to take the Austrian wine business on a good path in general terms. Market shares, price development, export data, and the international reputation of Austrian wines speak clearly in this case."

With this background, Klinger considers economic aspects as important success criteria. "But for me as a businessperson, it's also important to create a good work environment for our employees, and here, the ÖWM is surely exemplary", he clarifies. "Our team has 80% women, and in the governing body, including the general manager, there are two men and five women. We manage public money carefully, and even so, we are a highly motivated troop, who enjoy work. We are especially proud of the fact that we managed to compensate the reduction of public money through an increase in branch contributions, which the boards of the branch representatives decided through unanimous decisions."

According to Klinger, business decisions are thus also community work: "We prepare decisions well in the team, act on the basis of careful planning, often jointly with the affected areas and their committees. I am especially proud of the trusting and constructive cooperation with our board of directors and the representatives of the owners."

Klinger confronts risks or wrong decisions openly. With a wink, he remembers his time in Dürstein: "If I would be able to go back and change something in my professional life, that would be not to bottle the fertile Riesling vintage of 1996 in the Domäne Wachau, but to sell it in the barrel, for when I later got it served in Chicago, I myself dreaded it." But then he becomes serious: "I learned to live with the risk; otherwise I wouldn't be able to be a manager. The only thing I consider quite frustrating is the financing risk, since we depend a lot on public money. Also, the extravagant bureaucracy becomes worse and worse; it has itself already become a great risk, threatening the creativity and effectivity of companies."

Klinger describes his leadership style as "collegial, competence-based, and sometimes a bit volatile, since I, as a creative person, always have a lot of things going around in my head. I repeatedly have to refrain myself." Ideally, he wishes his employees to be "friendly, loyal, dedicated, with a positive charisma, resilient, and able to learn. And he or she must have fun in what he or she does." These characteristics, he says, are also conditions for success: "Without intelligence, nothing works. But it's also important to have passion, the ability to learn, and self-organization. You must also be able to get other people enthusiastic for something, and apart from passion that also requires teamwork."

To favour the success of his employees as a businessperson, or to enable it in the first place, Klinger knows that a lot of experience is required: "You have to deal with the topic of human resources much more than you think. I myself first needed to internalise the meaning of the topic personal development. I believe that without moderation through outside consultation it will hardly work."

"WITHOUT AN HONEST ASSESSMENT OF YOUR OWN PERSONALITY, THERE WILL BE NO SUSTAINABLE SUCCESS."

In his business activities, Klinger lets himself be guided by essential values: "Honesty and loyalty are the basic requirements. That starts with yourself. Without an honest assessment of your own personality there will be no sustainable success. For me, errors are there so that you can learn from them and not commit them a second time. Contradictions, too, are daily bread for me, a part of life. And there are many other things, for instance consistency and sustained efforts. And then, joy and passion are contagious. And I am always a person who believes that more can be expected from the consumer than everybody believes. I don't like to give things away too cheaply. The important thing is to change the consumer, from one who consumes to a co-producer, as the slow-food founder Carlo Petrini always says. Only if the customers understand our products will they stop demanding cheaper and cheaper prices."

Fundamental values should also apply to the entire economic area, demands Klinger: "The greatest challenge is a prohibitionist tendency in parts of society and their political representatives. In France, the so-called hygienism already threatens the economic outlooks of its famous wine economy. Therefore this business area is itself required to support measures against alcohol abuse and to promote a responsible use of the cultural product wine. Therefore the program 'Wine in Moderation' is actively supported by us. We consider the changes in communication, for instance in the area of social media, as a chance, for we don't want to react to these developments; rather, we want to be actively involved at the top."

MAG. WILHELM KLINGER

WINE
ENTREPRENEURS

Klinger's observations and the demands derived from them also refer to the future of the international wine sector: "The competition among an ever-larger number of high-value wineries will become harder and harder", he estimates. "Prohibitionist tendencies increase and they must be handled proactively by the business area. The responsibility for the customers' health increases. The wine economy must learn to advocate a wine consumption that makes life more beautiful, healthier, and more worthy to live. Total abstinence can also result in an inhuman perfectionism, which can take away, from the people, the desire to live." In this context, Klinger is convinced that "the communicative capacities become more and more important, for the narrative element in wine marketing, the credible and inspiring telling of stories, is truly the best wine marketing."

For young businesspeople, Klinger has concrete advice: "Someone who wants to be successful in the wine area needs a good philosophical background, in other words a good general knowledge with a high humanistic level, should be multilingual, and be able to get people enthusiastic. Today, wine competence is more important than ever, as is good networking. And well, you need to take care, do sports, fast sometimes so that after a violent phase, which the job can cause, there is an opportunity to regenerate body and spirit."

MAG. WILHELM KLINGER

Utz Graafmann
Founder and manager, Wein-Plus
Erlangen, Germany

Utz Graafmann (born 1961) is the founder and manager of the European wine network Wein-Plus in Erlangen. The Internet platform offers an editorial area with a wine guide, wine glossary, and online magazine, as well as a service area with a Web catalogue, a wine search engine, and services for members. Over 200,000 users have registered into the open information and communications network. For a fee, Wein-Plus members get access to all content (wine evaluations, glossary entries, magazine articles, etc.), and can make use of marketing and purchase benefits. Apart from membership fees, the company gets financed by sales of advertising, marketing and Web services throughout the platform. Also, through a sister company, Wein-Plus is active in events and publishing.

"IN OUR AREA, CLASSICAL CRITERIA SUCH AS INCOME, TURNOVER, AND GROWTH ARE OFTEN ONLY SECONDARY MOTIVATING FORCES."

Graafmann studied computer science in Dortmund, and in 1983, the same year he graduated, he founded a software company for established physicians (the name APRIS is made up of the initials of the business object – Arztpraxis-Informationssystem, i.e., Information System for the physician's office). Graafmann found his way to wine when starting a second APRIS office in a wine area, as he recounts: "I was born in the Ruhr area, and there, I traditionally had more contact with beer than with wine. When it was wine, it would usually be very simple, not to say bad, wines. That changed in 1986, after I opened a branch in Franken for the company I had at that time. There, for the first time I had contact with good wine, and this quickly and strongly triggered my passion for wine." In 1987, Graafmann moved both the company headquarters and his home to Erlangen.

"In 1998, the Internet become more and more available", the online pioneer reports. "Here I recognised a chance to exchange information with other wine fans, and to find out more about my passion. What was available at that time in printed wine magazines didn't satisfy this desire, in any case. That was the starting signal for Wein-Plus, which I started at that time, in parallel with APRIS, and with the assistance of a half-time employee. After that, the development of Wein-Plus went on very quickly, and it has now long been both my passion and my profession. My computer science study gave me the required basic knowledge, to understand, even today, the technical part of Wein-Plus, and to know what is feasible and what isn't. However, computer science as the science of managing information is also ideal to be able to manage the complexity of a company with all of its aspects."

At that time, Graafmann already had 15 years of business experience, when he started Wein-Plus: "Founding and managing my first company, APRIS, gave me a lot of valuable experience as a businessperson. Here I learned how marketing, sales, organisation, and managing employees work. In 1998 I was then able to combine this knowledge with my passion for wine, and to use this in Wein-Plus." After that, as Graafmann recounts, the platform grew quickly: "In 1999, Wein-Plus, together with Norbert Tischelmayer, started the glossary, which is currently the world's most comprehensive online wine encyclopaedia, with almost 20,000 keywords. In 2000, with Marcus Hofschuster there followed the first tastings for the wine guide, which in the meantime has made a name for itself due to its strict and objective opinions, and ca. 100,000 professional wine descriptions and evaluations. In 2009, we introduced membership at Wein-Plus. In 2013 there was the first Wein-Plus convention in Frankfurt, and shortly after that, a second one in Munich. With our wine and consumption fair, we have successfully transferred the core ideas of Wein-Plus from the Internet into the real world." After he had already gradually retired, over the years, from his daily business at APRIS, in favour of Wein-Plus, Graafmann sold his first company in 2007, to concentrate exclusively on the wine network.

"TO PREPARE DECISIONS AND TO TAKE THEM IS PROBABLY THE MOST IMPORTANT ACTIVITY OF A BUSINESSPERSON. SOMEBODY WHO CAN'T MAKE UP HIS MIND WILL PROBABLY HARDLY BE ABLE TO SUBSIST IN THE ROLE OF A BUSINESSPERSON."

The computer scientist can't imagine anything else than an independent professional existence: "Since I finished my studies at the age of 21 years, I am a businessperson, and I have never worked as a dependent. For me it is important to be able to orient my actions every day according to my own values, and not have to subordinate myself to the values of other companies or businesspeople. Only as a businessperson can I really follow my own visions", explains Graafmann. "Also, I am fascinated by the idea of creating something new, something that doesn't exist yet. Lateral thinkers for me are the impellers of progress. And yet, size and growth aren't goals for me. Specifically in the case of Wein-Plus, I find it fascinating to be able to think and act entirely in the interest of our members. To create as many benefits as possible for our members, through synergies, networking and the penetration of a very small and pointed market segment. To help them enjoy wine better and – if they are themselves active as businesspeople in the wine area – to become more successful in our area."

Here Graafmann himself immediately differentiates: "I believe there is no such thing as 'the wine business area'. It is subdivided between the part of the discount and food retailing wines, with a considerable volume and turnover, on the one hand, and the fine wine area on the other hand. I can only speak for the fine wine area, which is what we address exclusively. Here we talk about the freaks, people who are mad about wine. This includes the producers, as well as in commerce and among the consumers. These people know how to enjoy and to live. Income, turnover and growth are often only secondary motivating forces in our area. That's what makes our business area so special. We all have the same 'virus' and we can probably only be successful if we have this virus – for me, apart from the 'usual' criteria for good businesspeople, this is probably the most important prerequisite in this area. Personally, I love to be right in the midst of things as a businessperson, and to help others to exercise their passion even more."

Graafmann explains: "Successful wine businesspeople love the product wine. Somebody is successful if he also loves his clients and manages to transmit his passion for wine to them as well. At the same time, it is essential for survival that, apart from the necessary infatuation with the product, you also have the capacity not to neglect the commercial and organisational aspects of a business. As in probably any business area, successful businesspeople know where they want to go. They dare to think far into the future, and they remain faithful to their visions. Even if there are a few stumbling blocks along the way. And they learned this difference, to be independent or a businessperson – in other words, to work on the business rather than in the business."

Graafmann measures the business success "not with the classic parameters such as turnover, number of employees, or profit. For me, success is when, thanks to Wein-Plus, people have more enjoyment of the topic wine. Whether it is professionally or privately. Of course this is not a Samaritan activity; of course I expect a return in form of the yearly membership payment. The number of our members is thus an indication of how successful we can be helping others. But I also measure success with egotistic goals such as my own satisfaction with my life and with getting into the office every day. This is just as valid as the satisfaction of our customers, employees, and other partners. Success, for me, is achieving my goals, and I am successful, because I always knew where I want to go. If I were able to go back and change something in my professional life, in hindsight I would surely change many small decisions, but I am sure that I would change none of the large steps."

His recipe for success is based on long-term thinking and endurance, as Graafmann explains: "Even my first company, APRIS, was based on long-term customer relations and proceeds from its customers. I always considered short-term one-off proceeds to be rather boring. I managed things the same way with Wein-Plus. For instance, I prefer to invest my energy into obtaining long-term members than in one-off advertising income. In the same way, in general I rather tend to work for after-tomorrow than for today or tomorrow – even if I encounter a lack of understanding for this among employees, but also, quite often, from the bank or the tax consultant", reveals Graafmann. "The long-term orientation makes it necessary to always act openly and honestly", he emphasises. "Journalistic independence, and a clear separation of advertising and publishing, is a special value in this case. It would be simple to quickly earn a lot of money by overstepping this limit. But I would just as quickly gamble away my credibility, and thus the basis for my own future."

Accordingly, Graafmann takes business decisions with as much farsightedness as possible: "Here, the long-term point of view is very important", he says. "Only he who knows the target can hit it. Only he who knows where he wants to get to has a guideline for his business decisions. Preparing decisions and taking them is probably the businessperson's most important activity. Somebody who can't make up his mind will probably not be able to subsist in the role of a businessperson. The worst decision is usually not to decide. Personally I don't have much trouble here. When I do my job correctly, I usually have the required bases for decisions available. The bases for decisions may be numbers, data, facts; but more important, usually, is the knowledge about how partners and employees think, and of course my own intuition. Contradictions are, for me, reasons to think about it once more. Gather lots of information, get sufficient input from other people, analyse very carefully; but in the end, I also trust my own intuition."

Graafmann accepts the risks of his business activity almost serenely: "After over 30 years of experience as a successful businessperson, I handle risks in a rather relaxed manner. Risk is really another word for an unexpected event. However, as long as I always keep enough options of action open, precisely with a small business I can always react soon enough. We have it enshrined in our business vision that Wein-Plus is specifically willing to take risks in form of new projects. For me, errors are always an opportunity. We know that not all new projects will be successful, and we consciously accept risks here. But in the end, we know that in the final result, the failed projects are more than compensated by the successful ones."

To describe the goal of his business engagement, Graafmann quotes from the company model: "'Wein-Plus is the leading wine network on the Internet. Our mission is information and networking. We help people in the wine area get informed, enjoy wine better, bundle interests, communicate and cooperate with one another. We connect supply and demand, help people buy the right wine, and help producers and merchants find the right customer for their wine.' This model is not just some marketing text stamped on by some marketing guy; rather, it expresses very precisely what I and my team live and stand for." Once again, Graafmann emphasises the importance of independence: "Obviously we don't do commerce with wine, and we aren't directly or indirectly involved financially with wine dealers. Our tastings for the wine guide are strict and differentiated like nowhere else. Marcus Hofschuster as the editorial director is known for his integrity and absolute incorruptibility, and all wines are exclusively tasted blindly in our neutral tasting room in Erlangen."

Graafmann formulates, as his personal motto: "'Create, and maximise the benefit for your customer. Your benefit will then come almost automatically.' That is to say: I am convinced that the long-term benefit for the customer should always be in the foreground. The 'business model' or the profit can then be obtained almost by itself. The same happens with employees: It is not of much use to push them and to force them to performance. Nor is it possible to motivate employees through some sort of direct influence; not through commissions and gifts. It's much more important to give the activity and thus also the business a sense, in the eyes of the employees, and to create a working environment in which the team can freely develop within a fixed framework."

His leadership style, too, is goal-oriented, explains Graafmann: "I guide on the basis of trust, and I train my employees for autonomous action. In this case, goals and the 'what' are in the foreground. As for the 'how', every employee must find it himself for his own area of responsibility. At Wein-Plus, we have combined the management level and the clerk level. Thanks to this flat hierarchy, at Wein-Plus every clerk is his own manager. I myself concentrate on the role of the businessperson, that is, working on the business rather than in the business." The optimal employee, in Graafmann's eyes, "loves wine and people related to wine. He acts autonomously and with a customer orientation."

Room for manoeuvring, according to Graafmann, is also an essential requirement for the success of the employees, as long as they know the general direction and their framework for action: "Performance for me is not the result of energy, but rather the result of effectivity (doing the correct things) and efficiently (do things correctly). Employees must know their goals, and must be able to act freely within a clear framework. The activity must be joyful for them, and they must be paid fairly. For me, motivation is the result of the correct framework conditions."

"I CONCENTRATE ON THE ROLE OF THE BUSINESSPERSON, IN OTHER WORDS, WORKING ON THE COMPANY RATHER THAN WORKING IN IT."

Graafmann can be considered one of the pioneers who brought the wine subject to the Internet and has thus advanced the digitalisation of the wine area. But for him, there is more about it: "With Wein-Plus, I have surely contributed my part early for this change. Consider that Wein-Plus was founded before Google was. But we must not forget that, even though the information and communication paths have change drastically, the product wine itself, the real purchasing motivation, the effort to maximise enjoyment, and the people, are all still the same they were 20 years ago. Therefore we don't define ourselves as an Internet company, but as a network that connects wine and people. The Internet and social media are only a tool for this purpose. This is the case with our mission statement as well: Our home is the Internet – but where it makes sense, we will also use media outside the Internet to support our core goals."

Graafmann considers the future development of the wine sector as basically positive, but he does recognise changes: "The wine volume and the wine quality on European markets will continue increasing. In the product and in the equipment, as well as in communication and distribution channels, we will see many new ideas and concepts come, as well as go. The willingness to innovate, which until now has been relatively restrained in the wine sector, will continue to increase at all levels. Not all companies will want to continue in the area, and they will say goodbye to the market – whether by their own will, or because they are forced to. I currently see a lot of changes coming for the wine retail market in Germany. The discounter and the food retail will step up the pace with respect to wine competence and wine quality, and in the low-threshold area they will gain an additional participation in turnover. The dedicated wine fan will choose the Internet, more and more, as his order method. It will be decisive for success how well the providers will grasp and put into practice multichannel sales. Logistic will play a growing row. Same day delivery, click & collect, as well as other service offers will be considered to be self-evident by tomorrow's customer. All of these are huge logistic and organisational demands for tomorrow's wine business."

To act successfully in the wine business of the future, "flexibility, love for the customer and for the product, as well as the knowledge about the difference between businespeople and independent people" are required, according to Graafmann. "That is not much different from businesspeople in other areas. However, in our area, the love for the product has a special role. A positive one, for without such a love it would be diffi-cult to talk face-to-face with the customer and to understand him. But also a negative one: Quite often, businesspeople in our area fail, because apart from their love for wine, and the desire to work in this area, they don't fulfil many other requirements."

Graafmann therefore recommends young beginners in the area: "Understand your cu-stomer, and only start a company if you can really solve one of your customers' pro-blems. That, however, is something that you can only judge and understand if you are yourself in the midst, and are infected by the wine virus. But you must also be sure that you are born as a businessperson, and that you have the required personal equipment to do it."

LEO HILLINGER

Owner and managing director,
Leo Hillinger winery
Jois, Austria

L eo Hillinger (born 1967) is the owner of the winery Leo Hillinger in Jois, in the Burgenland. As a descendant of a wine dealer family, he went to several viticulture schools and passed several internships, among others in the Palatinate. At the age of 19 he went to California, where he dealt for the first time with natural winegrowing, and in 1990 – at the age of 23 – he took over his parents' company.

Even as a child, Hillinger was interested in the processes in his grandparents' vineyard, as he tells us. The Austrian says that his internship in the neighbouring country was especially influential for his professional development: "The most important thing was my stay in Germany. My father was a wine merchant, and we had practically no vineyards – less than a hectare. My father only made three wines: red wine, white wine, and medium dry in two-litre bottles. Thus, there was no love for the product. I, too, really had no idea before I went to Germany. It was only in Germany that I got to know the great love for wine. It was in Germany where I saw that even young people deal with the product. Only in Germany I learned that I have a talent for tasting. And then I really started to love this product."

"THE BASIS IS ALWAYS THE QUALITY. BAD QUALITY, GOOD MARKETING, FAST DEATH – THAT'S A TRUE SAYING, FROM ME."

Another important station was then in the USA, Hillinger continues: "I became a fan in California. That was impressive for me, from the marketing point of view. Biological acid reduction, that wasn't a topic previously – I learned that in California. Making wine, large, nice, fat red wines, as well as marketing –I learned that in California." Additional trips took Hillinger to South Africa, Australia, and New Zealand. "Foreign countries have really characterised me extremely, to be open towards all sorts of wines, and of course also from the marketing point of view", he summarises.

After taking over the small family winery, Hillinger successively expanded the vineyard area to currently 50 hectares, which lie in Rust (30 hectares) and in Jois (20 hectares). In 2004, in the midst of the vineyards he set up a new, technically ultramodern, and architectonically distinctive production site, which includes a tasting lounge and a seminar room. The largest part of the building is buried in the hillside, as Hillinger explains, to benefit from the earth climate. In 2005, in Pandorf in the Burgenland he opened his first flagship store, which sells exclusively his own wines. From 2009 and 2014, a total of five additional stores, bars and lounges were opened in Austria and Germany. More than half of the produced wines are now exported to 18 countries. Since 2010, the Leo Hillinger winery consistently practises biologic-organic winegrowing. The company is currently part of a foundation that belongs to the family.

Hillinger talks about his localisation in the wine business: "I was always a very glitzy person. In 1990, I had a debt of 400,000 euros, at an interest rate of 17%, and of course I had no money for marketing. So, I had to do that with my person – my person was the marketing. I had to get on the stage." He "did that relatively aggressively, not according to norm. As a result, of course others smiled about me and said, this guy is crazy. Finally they ran out of arguments. They said: 'Well, the marketing is not bad, but the quality is.' In practice, groundless things." Hillinger must still fight again and again, as he explains: "I am now not talking about the customers, but there is a huge amount of envy, unnecessary envy. That's a pity." Hillinger thinks that wine producers should concentrate on their wines and on their brands – and, if necessary, get help from experts to do that. "I, for example, am a terrible accountant", he reveals. "So I need people who do that. If I can't do marketing, I get professional help. If I can't do design, I get professional help – and not many people do that. Design, for me, is the basis for communication."

"ANYTHING THAT I DON'T EXPERIENCE MYSELF, I CAN'T SELL."

For Hillinger, devotion to the product is an essential motivation for his business activity: "Motivation, for me, is when people love my wines – my products, my wines. My drive is, first of all, that I am able to work with the coolest product on Earth. Wine for me is a blessing, an elixir of life; simply everything. I live out my dream. Making wine for me is the greatest bliss. I can't imagine anything more beautiful. 25 years ago I wouldn't have dared to dream this dream. I can live out my hobby as a profession and vocation, and work in it. I stand up early in the morning and thing: 'Once again, I fell into the honey pot!' I could cry from joy every day, since things work out so good for me. I have the world's best employees; that motivates me a lot. Somewhere there are things I need to think about. But the family is doing well; I am free from debts for the last three or four years. You can't imagine what effects that has. And what motivates me most is when people are happy with the product. When I am able to make people happy, when people call me and say, for instance, that they are currently on the AIDA and have just drunk one of my Sauvignons – 'such a good stuff'. Or when the only wine on the wine card, in a bar in New York or Mauritius, is a Hillinger wine, that's motivating. Then I always think: 'I really didn't do a lot of things wrong in my life.'"

Hillinger thinks that the wine area is a special one, compared to other business areas: "Of course there are business parallels, as well as paths and structures that you can compare. But the wine area is certainly individual. Very sensitive; thanks God it is sensitive. One winery can't be compared with another one, because there are different positions, different vine varieties, and different end consumers. And especially: In a worldwide view, the wine area is a niche area. The way we Austrians make wine and take it to the world – with one percent of the world market – we are a niche product." To be successful, the wine businessperson needs a high-quality product, Hillinger explains: "I don't want to create international vogue wines that can be confused, but rather very typical Austrian top-quality. The basis is always quality. Bad quality, good marketing, fast death – that's a very true saying, from me. It's very important that the quality is top-quality, unqualified. We constantly organise blind tastings. We do these with end consumers, with merchants, and especially, also, with journalists. They are surprised, because we really come out quite at the front – certainly in the price-performance ratio, but also qualitatively, since journalists taste for quite a bit more. And only then I can stand out, I can come and tell the people outside that we are the very best. We are among the best. I only want the very best, I want to say that we are among the best, and in that case we can be noisy, and we can be impudent. You can only do that if you have really big eggs."

"I AM SUCCESSFUL BECAUSE I FOLLOW MY GOAL VERY CONSISTENTLY."

An important success factor for a businessperson, in Hillinger's opinion "in any area, is cooperation with, and leading, employees. The employees – we currently have 75 – are really the company's base." Thus, "the employee structure, motivation, and especially loyalty for the company" are a type of key qualification. "My employees, my executives, they all have their area." Only in the vineyard and in the wine cellar he participates himself, Hillinger says, "since some people have other ideas, with respect to senses, about wine". Thus, the winery's oenologist, for instance, is "a freak", and the wines which he produces according to his own ideas "can't be sold", Hillinger formulates drastically. "If the grape material is top-quality, not much needs to be done in the cellar. After many years of experience and many experiments, I know: the fruit must be perfect, and it must go into the bottle unchanged." Therefore, he says, it's important to participate in the decisions in wine manufacture as well as in the vineyards, where he has hired biologists for several years.

However, "otherwise, the executives always have their own area; they are controlled by me, but in a very sensitive way", Hillinger clarifies. "They are responsible; they are more or less independent in a protected workshop. I am always there if they need help, and I motivate them. I pay them well and treat them well. That's damn important. I give each of them the possibility to develop fully. I also let them unleash their creativity. That's also damn important. You can't restrict people. And if it sometimes doesn't work, with me there's no beating people up; I always have a protective shield. That is to say, my authorized representative is a man who confronts the employees directly." Depending on the communication occasion, there is a role distribution at the leadership level, explains Hillinger: "We have bad boys and good boys; that's important." The authorized representative takes care of that "if something doesn't work well. He does that differently. I am emotionally charged, and he is quite relaxed. I sleep it over for two nights, and then we go through it once more. That has turned out to work quite well in this direction, and my strong point is simply that the employees work for a long time in the

LEO HILLINGER

company. It almost never happens that we have to separate from an employee, or that an employee wants to separate from us."

In 2012, Hillinger was named the "Entrepreneur of the Year" in the category Commerce and Consumption Goods. This renowned company prize is issued every year by the auditing and business consulting company EY (formerly Ernst & Young). "For me, performance and training are the basis of success", defines Hillinger. But in his eyes, business success is, first of all, an issue of stringency and perseverance: "Once, I was asked in an interview what are the three most important things for me as a businessperson. I told them: 'There are three things: consistency, consistency, and consistency again.' There are a huge amount of creative people who don't push through. And in life you have to push through. I am successful because I pursue my goal consistently. If I give birth to an idea, I follow through on it. I now open the seventh shop – wine bar and shop combined. In the entire world, there is no winegrower who has his own shops and wine bars. If we invest somewhere between 300,000 and 500,000 euros for such a shop on 90 or 100 square metres, we must have really big things, to get through with it."

Hillinger is currently not only active in the wine business, but also in the real estate and investment area. "But in the wine area, we finance ourselves from the cash flow", he emphasises. "We don't really work with banks, since we have no debts." For his winery he has additional plans: "I simply want to make this strong brand even stronger, that's my goal. I want to position myself internationally in such a way that Austrian wine is always associated with Hillinger. That's my deep desire." He looks back: "If you have started very low, from negative, if, like me, you had nothing and the only thing that belonged to you was the dirt on your fingernails, then you somewhere live out your small profile neurosis, and you want to be a big name someday. There are so many countries in which we definitely still have potential for catching up. We want to be in the best sales and in the best restaurants; that's important. We want the brand to become definitely unbeatable."

But Hillinger not only has business goals: "Success, for me, is secondary", he admits. Personally, privately, I want to spend more time with my family and my children. I want to be not just a good businessman, but at the same time also a good father as well as a good husband. That's important for me, very important." Despite his success story, Hillinger wants to always "stay at the bottom. I always say: 'If you fly 20 cm above the ground, at most you can break a wing if you fall; but at 400 or 500 metres, you can also break your neck.' So, always stay at the bottom. Arrogance is foolishness. Remain a realist." According to Hillinger, this once again requires an orientation towards both quality and marketing: "That's a very, very important point for me. To always thank the employees and have them participate in success, including financially. Praising is very important – praise the people, also externally, and be financially grateful. If the company registers a profit, the employees should participate in it, that's damn important. And not just those who are in sales, but also the people in the office who work in the background."

For Hillinger, innovation and changes are an integral part of the business existence: "Lateral thinkers, for me, are models. Contradictions are of an essential importance for me, to be open for new ways. Errors, for me, are important for learning", he clarifies. This openness, he says, also applies to technological novelties: "We make complete use of social media. We were among the first to even have a homepage. We make use of everything, from Facebook to all the different other social networks. We simply manage this offensively, and in part also aggressively. That is to say, everybody who buys a wine from us should also access the Internet, to get all the information. We organize a huge amount of events – for instance, 'Bike and Wine' – for which we can of course draw on our customer base; and quickly. We can get across information extremely quickly through social networks. In the future, we must just think things through, so that we don't transmit too much information, but concentrate that. In the future we'll handle this quite differently. We need professionals who advise us well in this aspect, to avoid us from getting too boring or intrusive; that we rather handle social networks a lot."

In this sense, Hillinger clearly sees more chances than risks in the digital change, as he illustrates: "Of course there is a risk, no doubt about that; but in the future, the generation is a different one. For instance, I say: I have looked at a photo album with a child that was four or five years old. And the child takes the photo album, moves the fingers over the pictures, and tries to enlarge them. The new generation won't order much without using the Internet. We had our new homepage ready in two months, but it cost us 17,000 euros. That's hard to imagine; it's just the tip of the iceberg. There are still a huge number of possibilities. If you are innovative and open, that's a really large opportunity."

An important qualification for wine businesspeople who want to continue being successful in the future "is foresight", in Hillinger's opinion. "You have to think globally, you can't go through the world with blinders, saying, I do it that way, I don't care." The producers should consider "individually the country, the varieties", but they should also position themselves in a targeted and conscious way on the market: "People should of course concentrate on varieties, but they should also look at the international scene, to make sure that you don't stand just anywhere." Hillinger expects competition to intensify: "It will definitely get harder. People always want a good price-performance ratio. That's a very important topic in my success, the fact that I had known about trends even before they started." Flexibility is just as important: "In the wine area, you always hear about tradition, but still there are certain trends that simply exist, and that are then quickly implemented."

However, Hillinger says that "You don't need to participate in experiencing all trends. Let me give a very clear example: orange wine. I can't participate in a trend that I don't experience myself. I can't really identify myself with all this. It isn't my wine, I don't like it, I don't drink it, and so I don't participate in this wine extension. Anything that I don't experience myself, I can't sell either. I can't make it, and I can't sell it. My cellar master would do it immediately, and he already did it. Once we were with him, tasted a wine, and he asked us our opinion. And I said: 'I don't want to be rude, but if I had to sell this, I would have to lie. That won't work.' It is important to concentrate on what you can do best."

LEO HILLINGER

Hillinger expects that in the future "surely the large and strong brands will get even larger and stronger. Then there will be this middle layer, but in the lower layers, people will leave sooner. That is to say, the discounter will also have good qualities, a good price-performance ratio, because people get to trust this discounter. And as a result of the trust, once you participate with the discounter the quality for the price may not be too bad."

When asked for advice for a young beginner in the wine sector, Hillinger once again talks about his credo: "First of all, the quality must be right. He must make wines that are understandable even for simple people, and about which a sommelier is also enthusiastic. It must be an 'everybody's darling'. And especially: He must get in the role. He must surprise with quality, but also as a person. That's difficult for an introverted person. In that case, he'll need help. People want to experience people. They don't want to come and see someone who is behind a table, from his head and shoulders downward. They also want to experience personalities." Another point also reflects Hillinger's development: "I would always advise a young person to go to other countries. He should take a look at several countries, learn several languages, learn to accept religions, simply go into the open throughout the world and spend some years in other countries, before he gets home. While the parents are still relatively young, go out, out, out! And don't make excuses – you have to be consistent about this!"

LEO HILLINGER

ANGELO GAJA
Owner, Az. Agr. Gaja
Barbaresco, Italy

Angelo Gaja (born 1940) is one of the grand masters of Italian wine-growing, and to describe him as a legend among winegrowers is no exaggeration. He represents the family's fourth generation; his great-grandfather Giovanni founded the family winery in 1859, in Barbaresco in the Piemont. The name Gaja has a Spanish origin and – as Angelo Gaja tells us – it came into the Piemont, when in the 18th century a Spaniard married a woman from Barbaresco. Since the company's foundation, the first-born Gaja sons are always called Giovanni and Angelo, alternately; so, Angelo Gaja's son is called Giovanni once again, just like his father and great-grand-father.

Gaja studied winery in Alba and Montpellier, and in 1959 he received his oenology diploma. After that, he completed a study in Economics in Turin. In 1961, he started working in the family's winery, and for seven years, he managed the company's own vineyards. At the same time, he participated in tasting courses, completed the oenology internships outside his country, and visited wineries in Italy, France, and the United States. In magazine articles with a technical and economic emphasis, he continuously furthered his education, and looking back, he reveals a clear set of priorities: "To find the time to do this, I refrained from television," he smiles. He also considers these first years as the most important work stages in his training: "Learning how to manage vineyards, refining the tasting knowledge, and constantly learning of the markets for premium wines."

In 1970, Gaja hired the oenologist Guido Rivella, who is still responsible for the wines from House Gaja. Angelo Gaja is considered a forerunner of radical yield reduction, of introducing malolactic fermentation, of using barrique barrels and of planting French grape varieties in the Piemont. He pursues a consistent quality strategy, and developed the winery considerably over the years: Currently, he manages the family company, which at the beginning of the 60s had 21 hectares of vineyard hills, ca. 100 hectares of vine surface in the Piemont, and over 130 hectares in the Toscana. With Barolo, Barbaresco and Super-Tuscans, Gaja became world-renowned, and received numerous prizes and honours. In 2007, he transferred the day-to-day business to his oldest daughter Gaia.

He says that, from the beginning, his objective has been "to tame" the wine variety Nebbiolo, typical for the region, "to unfold all of its facets," describes Gaja. For this purpose, he established the relationship between vine variety and soil: "The basis was having top locations, which especially my father had purchased. He had a great eye for that, for his profession was surveyor and landscape architect, and incidentally, he was mayor of Barbaresco for almost two decades." His son, Angelo, started, at the end of the '70s, to separately vinify the Barbaresco top locations Sori San Lorenzo, Costa Russi, and Sori Tildin. Giovanni Gaja (1908-2002) has influenced his son's development, as the son states. He says that his father was convinced that "without commitment, suffering, and the willingness to sacrifice" there can be no quality. "Out of every ten vintage years, three or four have a low quality. In such years, my father preferred to sell the wines openly rather than bottling them, to preserve the dignity of their origin. A wine may only bear the name of origin if it is worth its quality," explains Gaja. It was also his father who said: "He who knows how to drink, knows how to live." With this motto, his father introduced him quite early to wine – against the desire of the grandmother. He said that the family must teach the offspring, how to savour wine responsibly. Grandmother Clotilde Rey (1880-1961) already prepared House Gaja's path towards a quality without compromises. She introduced the late harvest as well as low-yield clones, and at the end of the 30s, she created a new, self-confident label, on which, for the first time, the name Gaja appeared in large letters. In 1948, she ended sharecropping and hired all employees full-time so that from then on she could give them precise and binding quality specifications.

"MY FAVOURITE WINE IS THE ONE THAT I'LL PRODUCE NEXT YEAR."

"People need respect for the developments and the past. You have to understand history in order to be successful," says Angelo Gaja. He says that it is a matter of ensuring life experience for the next generation, and to transmit it. "The past has its value but it doesn't explain everything in the future. The modern age of wine started 40 or 50 years ago," according to Gaja. He says that this modernity is characterized by clarity: by clean and precise wines, and not least by improved cellar hygiene. On the one hand, he says, technical progress produces pleasing wines which come from large wineries and are immediately accessible for the consumer. On the other hand, regional wines appear, in which geographical conditions are transferred to the wine. "Regional wines are not oriented towards the taste of consumers, but towards their origin and the mentality of the producers," defines Gaja. He says they are produced by artisanal wineries, the artigiani. "All wine producers are important – the wine-growers, the cooperatives, the large wineries – but the artigiani are something special!" These artisanal wine-growers, according to Gaja, "are madmen who believe in a dream." They advance the quality of wine; it is only due to them that there is progress, according to him.

Gaja refers to the situation in the communist countries after World War II: "In what is nowadays more or less Georgia or Moldavia, wine was produced according to the specifications of the planned economy in collective farms, and sold in supermarkets in Moscow. Both the wine production and the sales of wine were political processes," he emphasizes. For artisanal wine-growers, who have their own vision, such a thing would be impossible. "In communism, there was no freedom and, therefore, there was no good wine quality either."

ANGELO GAJA

Gaja thinks of himself as an artigiano: "I want to be an artisan," he admits. It was his grandmother Clotilde Rey who caused him to have this understanding of himself: even before he was 10 years old, she asked him what he wanted to do with his life. He didn't yet know a reply for that, and she told him: "You must become an artigiano!" Four stages are required to achieve that, explains Gaja: "First: work, make, do something. Whoever wants to achieve something in life must be active. Second: knowledge. You must always acquire knowledge about your work, develop abilities and know-how; you must constantly learn until you master the activity. This is only possible if you do something into which you put all your passion. Third: transfer knowledge. You have to transfer skills, i.e. teach the work to other people, the family, the children, the employees. And fourth: communicate knowledge. You have to transfer your own knowledge about the work, take your abilities outwards – in summary: tell." Only a person who goes through and masters these four steps will become a true artigiano, he says.

"You have to narrate stories about wine, and you should also teach about it," continues Gaja. "Wine-growers must learn to tell about their wines – not just to repeat technical facts, but also include the region's and the family's history as well as their own dreams. This is about emotional messages. The narrator must arouse curiosity about the wine. The artisanal wine-growers are the best narrators!"

Apart from his grandmother and his father, Gaja names other inspiring people who have been examples for him – also as examples of those "mad" artisanal wine-growers who have persistently made their own dreams come true: Edoardo Valentini (1934-2006), the "father" of the Trebbiano d'Abruzzo; Mario Incisa della Rocchetta (1899-1983), the creator of the Sassicaia; Ferruccio Biondi Santi (1849-1917), the "inventor" of the Brunello di Montalcino; and Aldo Conterno (1931-2012), who was famous for his Barolo and – according to Gaja – said in view of the sales slump after the worldwide financial crisis in 2008: "Now, even those who don't pay anyway no longer buy."

During the crisis, the economy (including the wine economy) bet on innovation, research, and technology. "These elements are important for progress, but you mustn't forget manual work. In wine production and tourism, human labour is the most important factor for quality, therefore, we must give more emphasis to the value of artisanal work," demands Gaja. "Agriculture is an important and huge reserve of qualified workforce, and the wineries can be perfectly integrated into the system. They have the objective of selling their wine in bottles, but if that isn't possible, they sell it in barrels to the merchants."

Gaja considers the entrepreneurship in the wine business, too, "as artisans." According to his father's motto, for him it is important "to set limits (for growth) and to sacrifice (by abstaining from bottling vintages that have a bad quality)": I always wanted to produce local wines, wines that highlight the specific features of the grapes' growing area, and not pleasing wines that pamper to the taste and demand of consumers. I never made an effort to produce wines whose taste everybody likes," he clarifies. According to Gaja, a successful entrepreneur in the wine business distinguishes himself "by being active in a branch of agriculture in which the time factor has an essential role. By the ability to understand and implement the potential of a wine region, and to carry out marketing,

ANGELO GAJA

appropriate for the wines produced in that region." The key qualifications to do this, he says, "are the same that apply in all other areas – just as they do in the wine business: to know what must be produced, how to approach this, and where to sell the product. It often happens that entrepreneurs devote themselves strongly to wine production but then neglect sales, or vice versa." In Gaja's opinion, to be successful in the wine business, "first, you must carry out a strict analysis, and then, by individualizing the requirements of the market segment in which you want to appear, carry out the activity without hesitation, and make an effort, to meet the requirements. To be successful in the short term, you also need a good deal of luck."

"YOU HAVE TO TELL STORIES ABOUT WINE AND ALSO TEACH ABOUT IT."

Gaja says that his own success is a consequence of his family history: "I had success because it was placed in my cradle by my father. I benefit from the reputation of our house, which was founded long before my time, by my father and by my grandfather. And I trust that my work will also benefit my children. In agriculture, there is a strong awareness that your own work also benefits future generations." In this sense, Gaja – farsighted and modest – considers his recipe for success in "having ancestors, who were already active, with great prowess, in the same agricultural sector in which I work, and thus have made it easier for me to achieve success myself."

With respect to success, Gaja insists on distinguishing several concepts: "Success is what entrepreneurs achieve when people notice them, for example when other entrepreneurs consider their work methods to be an example to be emulated, one which can be used for experience, and which can be put into practice, with the objective or the hope to even exceed them. The highest degree of success – which cannot be measured by the sales volume or the number of bottles produced – is achieved by entrepreneurs who give a good example. In a market, such as the wine market, in which there are hosts of producers –in Italy alone there are over 35,000 cellars that bottle wine – the wineries which give a good example are at the forefront, those whose wines are faithful to their origin and have a high quality, and which are recognized on international markets by professional tasters and experienced consumers due to these properties; which appear on the wine lists of selected restaurants and which have a high demand in the most qualified wine cellars and specialty stores. Success is not just the result of intuition and passionate work, but also of fortunate circumstances. To be successful in the world of wine usually requires the work of several generations." Gaja distinguishes success from satisfaction and gratification: "Satisfaction is achieved by the wineries which expertly confront the market requirements and which increase the production volume – mainly in the low and medium-level price classes – as well as their sales volume, and thus get earnings which they can then reinvest in the company. Gratification is what wineries of any size get, which work mainly or exclusively in the domestic market and do an honest job, to allow their employees and owners a dignified life; that means that they pay taxes, fulfil their social obligations, have no debts, but don't make large investments either."

ANGELO GAJA

For Gaja, the motivation to be active as an entrepreneur is "the passion and delight of work," as well as "the knowledge of being favoured by fate, for my activity allows me to stand with one foot in nature and with the other in the world of business." He "absolutely didn't" make a conscious decision for entrepreneurship. "My father determined my future, by telling me that I would have to continue the family business, that I was to produce grapes, to make wine out of them. I didn't perceive this as arrogance, but as a gift that was bestowed upon me," explains Gaja, and adds: "For me, success is a light drug, which should be shared among my employees, who help me have this success. My employees are great experts in their corresponding areas of specialty, and know more about it than I do. And yet, I know about the different areas, and when I talk about a certain topic with my employees, I know exactly what I am talking about." That, he says, is the basis of entrepreneurial decisions: "The first step is to listen. And then, I advise them in my capacity as an artisan, who has a good overview of everything, what the most important strategic decisions are which must be taken." Gaja confronts entrepreneurial risks "without hesitation, as soon as I have thought about them – sometimes for a long time. Often, instinct and intuition play a role as well."

Gaja describes his leadership style as "plain" and specified: "I don't like yes-men. I value people who devote themselves to their work with dedication and enthusiasm." Employees who want to be successful have to "work for the cause itself, put aside their vanity, and be committed to the company's well-being." According to Gaja's conviction, leading employees must "correctly interpret the company's history, be able to make strategic decisions, and not get involved in simple solutions." To promote his employees' success, he says, the entrepreneur must, for his part, "transmit trust, clear up errors without flaring up, and help them grow while maintaining the company's philosophy."

Gaja's slogan is to "Live and let live." He says that his personal entrepreneurial goal is "to produce wines that are faithful to their origin, that inspire me. "For me, wine is the means that has allowed me to confirm myself." Here, he says, the fundamental value, and the principle that determines his actions, is "the conscience of working together with other producers, to increase the demand for quality wines – Barbaresco, Barolo, Brunello di Montalcino, Bolgheri – in my own interest, and in the interest of the other wineries who use this designation of origin. To show esteem for my colleagues, especially for those who use different strategies and conduct other projects than I do." In this sense, for Gaja a lateral thinker is "somebody with whom you should compare yourself; and for me, contradictions are also signs of an active spirit, which wants to be adapted to the times." He wants to achieve "that my children become integrated in the company's leadership, and operate it with mutual respect in a friendly atmosphere." Here he gives me two additional definitions: "For me, motivation is the cause and effect of the passion for one's own work," and "Errors, for me, are something that help you grow."

Gaja considers that he has two duties towards his children: "On the one hand, I want to be a good example. I want to give the following generations many good examples but without the compulsion that they have to do it exactly the same way that I do. The children should be able to do what they want." On the other hand, it is important to transmit the passion: "My children should dedicate themselves to their work with passion – as I do – they should want to achieve something. Passion for work is like a windscreen wiper: it doesn't prevent rain, but it lets you drive even during bad weather." Gaja himself transfers this image from a metaphor to reality: "My activity is related to agriculture. The amount and the quality of agricultural production are subject to large climate risks. Tourism, too, may be influenced by climate conditions."

Another factor that influences the market and the activity in the wine economy is the media change; Gaja has found his own way to handle it: "We are original. We have intentionally not created a home page; we don't sell to private consumers, nor do we sell our risks over the Internet. Private consumers or tourists, who want to visit our cellar, have to give a modest contribution for charity directly, and show us the payment slip; they don't pay anything to us. I frequently write articles about wine and related topics, which are then published on diverse blogs. The great wine connoisseurs, wine guides, and magazines about wine-growing will always exist, but social networks have opened the dialogue for a large number of passionate wine fans, who may sometimes be quite competent, but previously didn't have a way to talk. It makes sense to listen to them and to learn from them.

Gaja considers the future of the wine market basically as "good"; but here, too, he has a different point of view: "The threat lies in campaigns in favour of non-alcoholic beverages, and that also affects wine. In the future, it will be necessary to separate the image of wine – which has a long history and gives evidence of an ancient culture – from the image of beverages with a high alcohol percentage, and of other soft drinks which have a dash of alcohol. Wine is something different!" When asked about future key qualifications for entrepreneurial success in the wine business, several of them occur to Gaja: "Knowledge about the production area, a sense of belonging, the capacity to influence company decisions, and speaking skills. It is especially important to transmit the cultural aspects of wine and to have regard for the maintenance of the vineyards and the environment, without boasting about it." A young entrepreneur who wants to be successful today in the wine business must "have courage, be a good observer, a good listener, acquire technical knowledge and marketing knowledge, and plunge unhesitatingly into the wine sector. Satisfaction and gratification won't stay behind for long. And if you are also assisted by luck..."

> "TODAY, THE WINE-GROWING SECTOR IS THE SECTOR IN THE AGRICULTURAL AREA THAT OFFERS THE BEST OPTIONS TO ACHIEVE ECONOMIC RESULTS, WHICH ALSO PROVIDE SATISFACTION, GRATIFICATION, AND SUCCESS."

He says that Italy has a great wealth of regional grape varieties, and it is important to cultivate this "localized identity." Gaja is convinced that "not every wine must always be perfect. Nature knows no perfection. If somebody serves you a perfect wine, I would be quite sceptical! There may be small deficiencies; these are characteristics of wine, and artisan wine-growers appreciate them." Gaja evidently encourages independent wine-growers as well as merchants and clients who care about quality: "It is not about

ANGELO GAJA

perfect wines, but about original wines, which reflect the identity of the producers. The markets are not just for large-scale industrial wineries – there are opportunities for individuality!"

ANGELO GAJA

STUART PIGOTT
Wine journalist and author
Berlin, Germany / New York, USA

S tuart Pigott (born 1960) writes about wine as a freelancing journalist and author. He grew up in London and initially started a study in arts and painting, before he finally got a master title in cultural science. His first encounter with wine – specifically with German wine – however, already started in his school days. "The back story", he narrates, "was my visit as an exchange student in the Palatinate. That was in the spring 1976. I didn't get along at all with my exchange student, but with his family, I did. At that time they managed a small restaurant in a suburb where they had a bungalow. And in the refrigerator of this bungalow there was a lot of beer and wine, and when I arrived a magical word was uttered to me; it immediately entered my sparse vocabulary: 'Selbstbedienung' (self-service)". During this stay in Germany, he drank his first Riesling, says Pigott. "Yes, that was the first time that I consumed alcoholic beverages with pleasure and enjoyment. And in this case it was mainly wine; now and then a beer. Then it got started. When I drove home, the family gave me a suitcase, and the suitcase was full of wine bottles. That was, as it were, the beginning of my wine cellar."

During his studies, Pigott then worked "as a barman in a restaurant which had a very good wine card. That was the restaurant of the Tate Gallery in London. And it is true that my professional confrontation with wine goes back to spring 1981, when I got this job." And yet, he says that he was merely a "wine connoisseur with zero knowledge", when "wine discovered me. At the same time I started to write about wine – its present and its history. It is exactly 30 years ago that my first article was published. In the April 1984 edition of 'Decanter', a professional magazine which still exists. Through this job in the Tate Gallery, I got to meet several people in the London wine scenery, in other words in the professional world, and those introduced me to other people. In retrospective, I must stay that getting into the London wine scenery was surprisingly easy for me. Among other things, I met the acting editor in chief of the 'Decanter', Alice King. She asked me whether I wanted to write something, which I did. It remained in the editing office for a long time, but then, in April 1984, it was published, and suddenly I was a wine journalist – at first, part-time. And then, at the end of my studies – that was in the summer 1986 – I suddenly realized: I really don't know any other job; this is the only thing that I can do. And then I was forced to continue with it. German wines quickly became my main topic, in part because there wasn't much competition. In retrospective, my study was very important for my current activity; my professor, Christopher Frayling, taught me critical thinking."

STUART PIGOTT

WINE
ENTREPRENEURS

After completing his studies, at first Pigott tried to "keep afloat as a freelancing culture historian and writer. A tough struggle, which unfortunately didn't challenge my creativity", he reports. Then, however, he dared to try a new start: "In January 1989, I rented an apartment in Bernkastel an der Mosel, to intensify my contact with German wine and with Germany – present time and history. Gradually I spiritually drifted away from England." Pigott remembers an influential talk he had with a British colleague at the beginning of the '90s: "We were in a press trip on Madeira Island. She uttered magic words, saying: 'Gonzo wine journalism'", which basically means to devote oneself and dedicate oneself completely to a topic. That colleague had "given me this procedure in journalism as a conceivable method in journalism for the wine topic. Up until now, I hadn't thought a second about that; that was a decisive moment." Another milestone in his development had been moving to the German capital, according to Pigott: "My career developed slowly, until at the end of 1993 I moved to Berlin." After his first book in the German language was published in autumn 1994, that was followed by "a large amount of stories in German and foreign media about me, the British writer living in Berlin. With my preference for clothing from Vivienne Westwood and a language that is unconventional but German, I am considered to be 'multicoloured'", says Pigott.

"ANYBODY WHO, AS AN ENTREPRENEUR, THINKS THAT THERE IS NO RISK OR THAT YOU CAN ADVANCE A LOT WITH MINIMAL RISKS IS A COMPLETE IDIOT."

Now it is clear to him what he wants and how he wants to achieve his goal: "Inspired by the American journalists Hunter S. Thompson and Tom Wolfe, I developed a revolutionary kind of cultural history of wine. I simply call it 'Gonzo', and with that I mean unconditional research, which gets one deeply involved in the topic. For ten years I have worked with this method, and created a trilogy about wine and globalization. The research costs during all this time brought me close to bankruptcy several times, but the thing was never discouraging", clarifies Pigott. His book, "Wein spricht Deutsch" (Wine speaks German), which was created in 2007 in cooperation with the photographer Andreas Durst and the co-authors Ursula Heinzelmann, Chandra Kurt, Manfred Lüer and Stephan Reinhardt, is now considered a standard reference work. "However, it became clear to me that my knowledge about wine was between patchy and deficient. Therefore, starting in October 2008 I studied for two semesters in the famous professional school for wine growing in Geisenheim in the Rheingau", continues Pigott. "During the studies I had to commute between Berling and the Rheingau. And this time I was consistent and brave: I attached a practical exercise in wine growing." A winery in Franconia left him "ten rows of Müller-Thurgau vines in a super-sloped position for a year", to farm them. "On 15 September 2010 I presented my first wine in Berlin. Today I prefer to write about the exciting history of wine", decides Pigott.

For almost 19 years, Berlin was Pigott's "headquarters"; since the end of 2012 he also lives in New York. "That started a new phase", he says. "Coming to New York is surely the next decisive step – a return to the English language, my mother tongue. Thinking that this might open quite different possibilities; I mean, first of all when writing, and secondly, to bring these texts to market. So, an entrepreneurial aspect."

STUART PIGOTT

His motivation for entrepreneurial activity is, first of all, one of content, as Pigott explains: "I am fascinated by my subject. I mean, wine as a theme. But I am not less fascinated by journalism, and especially journalism in this extremely exciting world of media that we have now. In which things are transferred at an incredible speed from one medium to another. I feel very well in this world of modern media. Even though I absolutely don't participate in Facebook." Freedom and independence are important for him: "Well, if I were to manage an editorial office, I would need to have a similar freedom to act as I currently have. Otherwise it wouldn't be attractive for me." However, Pigott also wants us to consider: "Nobody is really 100% independent. I am dependent on my economic situation, I am dependent on the legislation and even more on how these laws are interpreted and how they specifically influence the environment of a person such as me. My type of entrepreneurship is of course quite uncommon. Because for a long time it didn't look like entrepreneurship at all. I spend a long time for specific investigations, follow specific topics. That's what is called 'Publizistik' in German. I don't like this word. For me, that is journalism. Recherche, this word gets a lot to the point: re-cherche, search again; re-search, search again. It doesn't matter in which language, it means the same. And the entrepreneurial aspect appears in short but very intensive phases, when a new orientation is taken. Of course it must have an economic side, it needs to work. Beyond that, I would say that it must also be promising in the economic area. Otherwise this problem becomes conscious. A limited profitability may be accepted strategically. That's also an entrepreneurial decision, where you say: on the one hand, I earn a lot of money; on the other hand, I can allow myself to get started with this without a sure income – let's say, to assume a full risk."

Ultimately, Pigott takes entrepreneurial decisions "from a gut feeling. But before it comes to that, I obviously ask around and look around. I have to say that in the last years I took one seriously faulty decision from the economic point of view. An Internet enterprise which I cofounded foundered. Here you can see that, no matter what decision you take, you really have to be prepared for such a failure. And if a person is prepared, nothing really bad will happen; for if you are prepared for that, you won't invest your entire capital in it. Only a naïve person would do that, and go into financial ruin." This takes Pigott once more to the topic of risk: "Anybody who, as an entrepreneur, thinks that there is no risk, or that you can get far with only minimal risks, is a complete idiot. Of course you must try to weigh such risks, and especially not to get started with things where there is hardly a chance. But if you want to have a great success – and I don't want to claim that I have had a great success – at some moment you certainly have to tackle things where others shake their heads, saying: 'That can't work!' The entire history of entrepreneurship is full of such stories."

Pigott defines success as "to be read", and he goes into more detail: "Performance, for me, is to write stuff that is read, and motivation is that which forces me to do that." He considers himself a lateral thinker, considers contradictions to be "an essential part of life" and mistakes his "daily bread". However, "I have to repeat that so far I didn't have any major success", he emphasizes. "I had medium-sized successes, but I had many of them, and that adds up. And especially in my line of business, this adding up of diverse successes certainly works. I haven't sold a hundred-thousand issues of any single book, but these things stack up, and such a stack is certainly something."

STUART PIGOTT

Also relevant for success are the general conditions in the wine area of business, as Pigott explains: "The first point is that wine is a long-term product. A vineyard lives at least 30 years. Even if nowadays in some climate areas you can quickly change over, you should keep this thought in mind if you are a winegrower – but also as a journalist, I think. This long-term aspect, this product inertia, results in the conservative character of the wine area. Of course there is also a reaction against it, the attempt to act against this inertia, this conservative element, as many young wineries do in Germany. But that's the basic situation. And any entrepreneur in the wine area, no matter what part of this area he chose, should be well aware of this."

According to Pigott, to be successful as an entrepreneur in the wine area, certain key qualifications are required: "Somebody who isn't media-capable, i.e. can't handle media well, certainly at least needs a right hand who can do that. But that is something extra that has been added. I think that the basis is professional knowledge, which hasn't changed. A lack of professional knowledge will be punished. Even the most innovative person can fall on his face. Here is a good example: There is a winery in Oregon – Brooks. The founder, Jimmy Brooks, died some years ago, and his sister, who didn't know anything about wine, took over. She managed the company exemplarily. But she soon realized that she needed a certain minimum of professional knowledge. And she got that from the Internet, from a really good source. That was enough. That's a good example. Even somebody who is very capable as an entrepreneur requires this minimum, this basis of professional knowledge."

Pigott talks about media once more: "I believe that you can't consider social media in isolation. That certainly has to do with certain technology – especially the smartphone which has evolved from the mobile phone and basically goes back to the '80s. The PC came at the same time, and all this has basically come together. I see this with mixed feelings; on the one hand, I have a much more open media landscape than what I saw before. On the other hand, for a journalist – somebody like me – it has become much more difficult to earn his income with this type of work. That might not affect me that much, for as I said, I have this stack of medium-sized successes in my past, and I have made a name for myself. But how is a young journalist supposed to get along with this situation? Very, very difficult." Pigott sees precisely the economic side as a great challenge: "Where is the money supposed to come from? It was difficult enough for me in the last 10 years as a freelancing journalist. I think that today you would first have to earn your money with some other activity for 5-10 years. And the third aspect of this new media landscape, of course, is that all these communication resources can be hacked. That can happen to anybody; and it may be a criminal or your own government who is behind that. That isn't funny!"

An entrepreneur also needs leadership qualities, says Pigott – even when his own situation is a special one: "My employees change. There were short phases with no employees at all, then I had quite a few, who took over different tasks and participated in certain projects. I must admit that I am not good in leading teams. It is fortunate that I don't have to do that on a large scale. In that case I would have to study this in more depth – that would be exhausting, and not simple at my age. I think that's a realistic assessment. It might even happen that somebody says to me: 'You are our chief editor for the next two years." And it is conceivable that I would accept such an activity; but then, I would have precisely this problem from the very first day." In that case, Pigott speculates, he would "discover or start to discover the first day" what the optimal employee would be for him. He mentions an event that already confronted him once with these reflections: "A few years ago, before I worked so much with others, a young guy presented himself, and said: 'I would like to be a trainee with you for a year.' And I thought, 'Shit, what does that mean?' Then I started to give it some thoughts, and considered: The first task for such a person would be to clean the toilet. For if he doesn't do it, I would have to do it. I think a good entrepreneur is always ready and capable of suddenly taking over any task. I think it is important that employees understand that. And I also considered: The last task for such a trainee at the end of his year would be to write a Stuart Pigott report – a long Stuart Pigott report. That would be published in my name, and only after it is published would I announce that my employee has written the report. Thus, he would completely take over my role. But finally this person found something different, and the situation hasn't really repeated."

As a journalist, truth is of fundamental importance for Pigott; honesty, clearness and truth are central values for him, he says, and clarifies: "What parts are published and in what context they are placed is something that you can discuss for a long time. But to pretend that invented things are facts, rewrite quotations according to your mood, as many of my colleagues do – I don't consider that acceptable! That has to do a lot with my situation as a journalist. After all, I live from the trust my readers place in my stories, and that is the foundation of everything, including the financial aspect."

"A GOOD ENTREPRENEUR IS ALWAYS READY AND CAPABLE OF SUDDENLY TAKING OVER ANY TASK HIMSELF."

Pigott considers the future development of the wine market to be rather turbulent: "I observe everything since the beginning of the '80s. In general there was a quite positive development, but there were also highs and lows. The last low of course was 2009 due to the financial crisis. I assume that I'll have to go through something like that at least 2-3 times more in my lifetime. It wouldn't surprise me if it gets worse next time. The irresponsibility of the financial industry is breath-taking; that isn't anything good for our world." In addition, says Pigott, wine isn't a vital base product. "Who needs wine? OK, in some countries it is deeply embedded culturally and is considered a food product, at least in its simplest variety. There, of course, it has a much higher economic stability than in our modern western society, where it is now basically just a luxury product." Pigott gives an example: "Before the financial crisis, on the shelves there was no Sauvignon Blanc from New Zealand for under 4.99 euros. That was the cheapest ware, and as a category, it was virtually the most expensive common wine category worldwide. You could even get the normal red Bordeaux for less than half that price. And then suddenly the financial crisis appeared. New Zealand had the bad luck of having two vintages with a large volume production in a row. So suddenly there was a high excess production, in other words a large offer and an extremely limited demand. And the price for barrel ware went down to 50 cents, delivered in Germany to the large wineries. From

STUART PIGOTT

that, you can extrapolate that the shelf price went down to ca. 1.99 euros." However, Pigott certainly expects, for Germany, "a certain revival of the mid-level price segment. There are many good reasons for that; not least the new and young wine drinkers that are growing up. Part of them will stay with their wines for 4.99 euros. But others will want to have something better, or will at least want to cover part of their requirements with better wines. And they earn more money, have better jobs, and are able to spend more money. That's a very simple development; all in all, a good thing. I hope that we don't economically move away from that."

"THE LENGTHY ASPECT, THE PRODUCT'S INERTIA, RESULTS IN THE CONSERVATIVE NATURE OF THE WINE BUSINESS."

Pigott emphasizes the economic dimension in view of the new generation of entrepreneurs and journalists: "It is nice, and also good, to become known quickly. Nowadays this is much easier than 15 or more years ago. But I would recommend anybody to build up his company on the most solid foundation possible, economically. I consider things such as sudden price rises risky, even if they go through. There are options to become well-known more quickly in the area, and it is super if that works; but I would be careful with fast and drastic price increases. There are lots of examples of companies and even entire areas which fell on their face doing this."

Pigott's own goals are both economic and charitable, as he explains: "Of course it would help to have more money on the account; no question about that. I think that I could and would expand my charitable activities quite a bit, if I had a larger amount of money on my account." The issue for him is "a positive change in our world. And that has not only economic consequences; the other consequences are much more important still", he is convinced. With his project "Wine helps – wine fans against AIDS" he supports the German AIDS foundation: "The proceeds go to HIV and AIDS projects in southern Africa, where about 67% of all infected people worldwide live", explains Pigott. Those are not only children – after all, an old man is also a human." Should he get the corresponding income, he would expand his social commitment "to other areas as well. Where the limit is, how much you can do, etc., those are open questions. But that would certainly be a goal. But that goes hand in hand with being more independent as a journalist and more ambitious as an entrepreneur. All of these things fit together for me, and by even more entrepreneurial ambition I mean: I have in mind to convert my blog into a real Internet platform with many invited authors, a much larger variety of topics. That would be something exciting. Wine for me is a wonderful topic, one that is inexhaustible." Accordingly, his favourite wine is always "the next discovery", he formulates. And he establishes the connection between wine, language, and the mission he set for himself: "If everything would be so simple that you could reduce it to a saying, I would have written no books and wouldn't be able to give lectures. We live in a very complex world. The more I deepen into the history – that, which I also call the backstory – the more I get aware of that. I studied cultural science – in English that's called cultural history. That is only possible if you narrow down your field of vision a lot and insist on getting simple rules out of this complex world."

STUART PIGOTT

GERHARD EICHELMANN
Wine critic, author, and publisher
Heidelberg, Germany

Gerhard Eichelmann (born 1962) is the founder and manager of the Mondo publishing house in Heidelberg. In his property as wine critic and author, he published the wine magazine Mondo, and in 2001, the Weinführer Deutschland (Wine Guide Germany). In addition, picture books (in the series "Mondo Wine Library") and wine pocket books (in the series "Mondo Compact") are part of the publishing house's portfolio. Eichelmann studied economic sciences and political sciences in Göttingen, Paris, and Würzburg, is a graduated economist and management expert, and was active for 12 years as a business consultant, before he changed, in 1997, to the publishing and wine area.

> "FOR ME, PERSONAL INDEPENDENCE WAS THE MOTIVATION TO BECOME INDEPENDENT AND TO ESTABLISH A PUBLISHING HOUSE, BUT I ALSO SEE IT AS SUCCESS OF A BUSINESSPERSON THAT HE ACTS INDEPENDENTLY, AND IS RESPONSIBLE FOR HIS OWN ACTIONS."

His change "had two backgrounds", he explains. "One was a familiar background." He became father, but as a manager in a large, international business consulting, he was hardly at home: "I was really constantly somewhere else, came home Friday evening, and had to get away again on Sunday." So he decided to look for "a professional change". The second reason was the fact "that with what I do in strategy consulting, I couldn't get independent, because I exclusively dealt with large projects with volumes of several millions, and exclusively with large customers. I was never interested in small middle class consulting or something like that, and I never did it; I was specialised in cross-border expansion projects, especially in the financial services area."

Eichelmann already met the wine topic in his family history. "I come from a winery area, from a village where there is wine, and in which everybody grew wine – my ancestors, my grandfather, and my father, too, have always conducted winegrowing; as a sideline, not as their main profession", he describes. "Sometimes they sold a bit, but that wasn't important. That was mainly for relatives and for own consumption, and for

GERHARD EICHELMANN

a while, a small amount was delivered to the cooperative. However, that never had any importance, except that I was present on the vineyard from an early age." The parents' vineyard had half a hectare, says Eichelmann. However, he had "not been very enthusiastic", since he "saw the work, when, as a high school student, he was sent somewhere to the vineyard, to make holes, to be able to plant new vines. For in the case of such small companies, only a few are mechanised, and a lot is done manually."

He then initially got winegrowing "completely out of sight, since I had nothing to do with it", relates Eichelmann. "The interest arose once again due to drinking wine, due to the joy of wine. I was in London for a long time, and there I got together with others, who regularly tasted, where people were simply open for everything, independently of the grape variety, independently of the country, from which the wine comes. Simply a great situation, somewhere at the end of the eighties or beginning of the nineties. There I got into closer contact with wine once again." Finally he got infected with the "wine virus": "When you are interested in wine and then go into a bit more depth, it's so exciting! It was especially the variety that interested me at that time. Then when I was back in Germany, I was frankly disappointed by what could be read in the German language about wine. I found that in other languages – English, also French – there was a qualitatively higher-value wine literature." That, for him, was the occasion to think whether "these ideas of a high-quality wine journalism could also be implemented in Germany", explains Eichelmann. On the basis of these considerations, he founded the Mondo publishing house, and the magazine of the same name, "and then, of course, later came the first book. That really started the success story. That was somewhat surprising for me, that someone like me, as a career changer, without being known, not known at all", could have success. "Previously, I had written virtually nothing about wine. I had worked as a journalist during my studies, but I never had anything to do with wine journalism. But I did notice that I wasn't the only one who had the impression that something was missing in Germany; rather, many wine fans had the same impression; therefore success came relatively quickly."

Eichelmann sees himself and his activity situated more in the publishing business than in the wine business: "I have to admit that I have somewhat of a problem in considering myself part of the wine area. I think that the wine area, in the narrow sense, is production and commerce. I see myself as a publisher, who happens to publish about the wine topic; in part I write them myself, but in part they are from other authors. I consider myself to be more part of the publishing area than the wine area; as an example, you can notice that, as a publishing house, we have never exhibited on a wine fair. We aren't interested in ProWein; the only fair on which we appear is the Frankfurt Book Fair, and the only association of which we are members, is the Bookseller's associations of the German book commerce. Our area is publishing, not wine, though of course we are strongly tied in with the topic of wine, since as a publishing house we concentrate on the topic of wine and related topics."

Nevertheless, Eichelmann recognises connections: "Of course there are general parallels, which affect all areas – for example, with respect to new media, etc. These challenges, which you have to confront. Nowadays it isn't enough to produce good contents or make a good wine; rather, it's important to also make the good wine known, and to sell it. The wine area has changed quite a lot, with respect to the producer side. As a result, today the winemaker has much more requirements in field service, in wine marketing, distribution, sales. That's the fundamental change which I see in the wine area, which of course goes along with a change in the change in the order of magnitude. For small winemakers it gets increasingly difficult to subsist. There is a concentration process; you can see that in Germany, too. Even if the area has always had only a small part of the market. That is no different in the book trade, in the publishing business. There you see the same concentration process, which is boosted by the fact that small publishing houses can't afford to invest a lot in new media. Thus, there are numerous parallels."

Eichelmann would consider the digital change with Internet technology and social media "neither as a chance nor as a risk. It isn't a risk. Sometimes I think it's irritating", he laughs, and explains: "After waiting a few years, we now decided to publish the Germany Guide as an app for different platforms. I don't think that we'll earn money with that, but it's required, people now expect that. And I believe that every change also provides an opportunity." In this respect, both the book and the Internet presence are being reviewed. "Today, the requirement is that the contents that you create are no longer shown on a single platform, but on several. I said – and that was really solely my own decision: I don't think that what appeared so far in the book should be transferred one-to-one to an app or to the Internet; rather, we need to have three different products, three different platforms, on which we show our work; this includes having a different structure, according to the way the corresponding platform is usually used, and which can decidedly have different contents; they don't have to be identical."

Eichelmann comes back to the wine business in general: "Wine, for me, is – well, it's an elixir of life. Since I am personally not just a publisher, but also an author, I of course know what goes on in the wine area, and I am close to the ball. But we live from the sales of our books." He "doesn't want to depend on the drip of the wine area", Eichelmann clarifies with a wink, "but from drip of the consumer, the reader, who buys the books, or doesn't buy them." He delves more into this: "I believe that in the wine area you have to clearly differentiate between production and sales and commerce. The requirements asked for are quite different. In commerce, of course, you also see a process of concentration. You can see a coming and going of small wine dealers. But you can also see that many manage to define themselves, and have the chance of being successful through niches or a good local positioning. On the production side, at the winemaker, the concentration process will also continue strongly. A lot is happening in German vineyards and wine cellars; someone who stands still will be overtaken. There will have to be branding. Branding, not just in the supermarket area of large cellars, but also at wineries who will position themselves as a brand and who will also have a corresponding force of market behind them. A small winemaker, who produces 20,000 bottles a year, can of course not afford this. But you can also see how many top winemakers in Germany have doubled their area and their production in the last ten years. I believe that will continue increasing. And you shouldn't turn up your nose saying, larger automatically means that the quality decreases as a result. On the contrary: I believe that there are benefits of size, that winemakers who increase their area increase their potential and can thus be more powerful on the market."

GERHARD EICHELMANN

GERHARD EICHELMANN

Within wine journalism, Eichelmann wants to occupy a top position: "Performance, for me, is an absolute basic principle. Motivation, for me, is my independence and the endeavour of being good, of being better than others", he explains, and he deepens the thought: "My independence is important for me. I want to be the best with what I do, consistently. That also means that when I evaluate wines or wineries, in the end I don't care at all whether I appreciate a winemaker a lot or perhaps even am his friend, or whether I can't stand a winemaker. I simply must evaluate his performance, and do that in a neutral way. That's important for me, for that's the crucial thing: I want to be good, I want to be better than all others." Being independent was the main motivation for him to work on his own, Eichelmann clarifies: "Of course I have to say that even as a business consultant in the management I was really already a businessperson, that didn't appear overnight; and that in consultancy I really had to deal with quite different orders of magnitude, as I mentioned before. There, it was about large projects with an order volume of several millions. That changed, everything got smaller. But I already had responsibility previously, and I couldn't have imagined accepting a management job somewhere. I even got offers, but it's always that way as a consultant: When you are active with the customer and he is satisfied, you get offers, but that was never a topic for me. For me, independence was simply the most important thing – and of course the family environment."

"I BELIEVE THAT THERE ARE SIZE ADVANTAGES, THAT WINEMAKERS INCREASE THEIR AREAS, INCREASE THEIR POTENTIAL, AND CAN THUS GET EVEN STRONGER ON THE MARKET."

Eichelmann also defines business success in this sense: "Success, for me, is independence. Take your own decisions, be responsible for them yourself. This personal independence was, for me, the motivation to become independent and establish a publishing house, and I also consider it to be a success for a businessperson if he acts independently, is responsible for his own actions, and can assume responsibility himself when things go wrong." He says that he himself has achieved this goal: "I am successful, because I am the best in what I do. You simply have to go about with a certain stubbornness, carrying through what you consider to be correct. The success, I think, came in part through the contents, which of course, once again, are strongly related to wine, or depend on the wine area. If we hadn't managed to achieve credibility on the market via the German Wine Guide – that is, among both producers and consumers – the product would have failed early." The fact that the Eichelmann wine guide is currently one of the two most significant ones in Germany "is surely a sign that it has been accepted by customers, but also by winemakers. I simply believe that the contents were in demand, because people might have said, here is a publisher, an author, who sees to things that really matter, including the simple wines. At that time, that may have been the decisive difference to others, that we said, we always consider a winemaker's entire collection and judge a winery accordingly; we aren't interested in individual highlights, individual raisins, especially when they are not produced in quantity. And I think that that has simply aroused and met the interest of consumers, and they recognised themselves in it. For if somebody says, I have no use for the book, I can't comprehend what was written and evaluated there, he won't buy it a second time, and the topic is quickly done with."

For his decisions, according to Eichelmann, there are "no models. You take business decisions – especially in small, comprehensible structures – yourself, by having some idea, how something develops, and that you have to change something. I consult that with my wife, I talk it over with individual friends, depending on what the topic is. But there are no models. For me, it's simply important that the quality isn't compromised, otherwise you will lose." At the same time, Eichelmann is aware that risks and "contradictions exist, and you sometimes have to accept them. That's a normal part of life. You take decisions, and they can be wrong or right. Errors, for me, are forgivable – the first time. We have already published books which made us lose money. That happens, you can't change that. And yet, I don't regret it. For instance, we have published two books about biological wines, with which we earned no money. But it was also important to do something in this area, and that will continue this way. We will surely continue publishing titles, where it is obvious from the start that it won't be a great model of success. But there are also titles which you have to do at some moment, if you think that it's important – perhaps, for instance, a collection about German vineyards, even if you say, that won't become a hit. That's the freedom which you have as a businessperson: to say, I don't need people to calculate for me that every title will have such-and-such a return on sales; rather, I can simply say, that's a title that I consider important, and I want to, and will, do that."

"EACH CHANGE ALSO BRINGS AN OPPORTUNITY."

Eichelmann talks once again about the independence which is not only the motivation but also the goal of his business activity: "I have my independence. It also allows me to realise book projects, perhaps next year, which I like. Independently of whether they work financially or provide a profit. That's also an independence which simply consists in that I say, I must not needs maximise profits. If I had wanted that, I would never have changed my area of business." Eichelmann smiles and outlines the situation in the publishing business: "The development in the last 20 years was that practically all publishing houses who published wine books drastically reduced their programme. There is virtually nobody left who gets wine books on the market. Nowadays, no publishing house is willing to publish a book any longer, if the author doesn't bring the money. That's a devastating development. It's also a development in which we consciously don't participate. If an author says, I have something interesting here, I either say, it's interesting, and in that case it is our risk as a publishing house, and the author only has the risk that we pay him according to sales; but I don't say, first give me 50,000 euros so I can publish your book. That has been a devastating development in the last few years, which of course is increased by the fact that today you can now no longer carry out the large print runs which you may have had in the nineties. That still works for wine guides which are established, which are sold year after year, but with other titles you have to be glad if you are in the upper four-digit range. However, it may also be the case that you are in the lower four-digit range or in the upper three-digit range, and that's something that sometimes happens to us. In that case, it's obvious that you can't earn money from that." Eichelmann is outraged that publishing houses for cookbooks also demand purchase commitments from top cooks for new publications, and he repeats: "I find this development to be devastating. Nobody is willing, any longer, to undertake a business risk. I believe that is so because, ultimately, there is no interest in it; because

GERHARD EICHELMANN

there is no belief in a book, rather, it's simply commerce that's in the foreground. As I said before: I take the liberty to say, I simply make a title, even if I believe that I won't earn money with it." But he relativises: "Of course it shouldn't annihilate too much money, that's obvious – we won't deal with a title that has no prospect of success."

As a businessman, Eichelmann is also an executive, but he admits: "Actually I don't want to lead alone. I give specifications, I say what expectations I have for an employee, and then at first I give him free rein. Then, if I don't like something, I simply say that, or I correct that and say, this must be so-and-so." The optimal employee, for Eichelmann, is thus one "who acts independently, takes decisions, and still has an overview over everything. Lateral thinkers were always important for me. That has surely characterised me quite early, and today, it's still very, very important for me that there are lateral thinkers. I believe that there must be a passion for wine, and of course also the will to do something well, to be good. The businessperson must provide the employees with trust, show them trust, give them clear guidelines, but then also foster them, to ensure that they are positively tuned. I don't need employees who just serve their time. Most of our employees are freelancers who also have other activities, but I think that of course the same passion for the topic is there, with respect to the editors of the Germany Guide. You can notice if somebody no longer feels like it; in that case, it becomes necessary to separate, or to sit down with them and say, that can't continue this way. Of course it might happen that one is overwhelmed by this situation, because he is currently overloaded in his other job, or in something else that he does, and that he gets a bit careless. But I tell them all: 'Let us know on time. We always have spare capacity, we can always restructure something. I can stand in.'"

Eichelmann talks, once more, about the developments in the wine area: "I believe that on the commerce side there will be a concentration process, and the same process will also occur on the producer side. There will continue to be a quality offensive. If we reduce everything to German wine, German wine will continue putting on weight at the top. In the medium term, the weights will move around a bit, with respect to regions, with respect to winemakers. But in general I have a positive outlook, and I believe that it should be possible to get consumers to pay a bit more attention to quality. That, however, is a general problem in society, which affects not only wine but foods in general: to pay more attention to what you really consume, where it comes from, how it tastes. Simply to pay attention to quality; that starts with potatoes and ends with wine."

For wine businesspeople, the product quality will be the success factor, is Eichelmann's conviction: "Since I evaluate wines and pay attention to quality, design, in wine, isn't important; otherwise it is. I would wish that it were really the quality", which is the key qualification for the future. "In our publications, of course we also want to help the winemakers who aren't able to sell well, but who may make great wines. Hence, I think that we try to evaluate the quality of German wineries and their wines as neutrally as possible, that we help, in part, to counteract this tendency, where everything is only market, only selling, only talking a lot to people, always bring something new and modern – that really can't be it. But of course that becomes more and more important. It becomes increasingly important for the larger wineries, which then have millions in turnover. In that case it can't be avoided. As soon as you produce a few hundred thous-

GERHARD EICHELMANN

and bottles a year, that's simply critical. In that case you need good sales, and you need faces that represent it."

With respect to young beginners in the area, Eichelmann also considers quality to be the most important condition for success: "I am interested only in the quality of the wine; I am not interested in packaging, or anything else." To a new businessperson, he would therefore advise: 'Play on quality; you must first of all do an outlay, perhaps at first produce better wines than what you get paid for.' But in the medium term, that will pay off, since I think that the consumer gets increasingly independent and critical, and that there are more and more consumers who look not just at the name, but who actually say, I'll try this out myself, I'll decide myself, independently of what the wine guide says, or what medals the wine has won. The development is very good, and the press is very open towards young winemakers. Sometimes you can almost think that they are hyped in excess... But it's a good thing that there is this kind of openness by the press, which may not have existed 20 years ago, but at that time there weren't so many young talents either, young winemakers who said, I have to bet on quality, in order to advance." In this respect, Eichelmann welcomes the fact "that there are journalists who simply look for something new – something new, something new, something new, and a young face. And a young female winemaker who is also pretty, has already half won", he laughs.

GERHARD EICHELMANN

ROMAN NIEWODNICZANSKI

Owner and managing director,
Van Volxem winery
Wiltingen, Germany

Roman Niewodniczanski is the owner and manager of the winery Van Volxem in Wiltingen on the Saar. Niewodniczanski, who studied economic geography, comes from a family of businesspeople from the Eifel region, with ancestors who were already active in the beverage area; his grandfather Theobald Simon founded the Bitburger Brewery. His family "was very, very busy socially, and in business, in a variety of areas", Niewodniczanski recounts. "This entrepreneurship was practically laid into my cradle." He had always wanted to fulfil himself: "I founded the first companies when I was a child. And accordingly, it now fascinates me to stand on my own feet."

"THE WINE AREA IS A FANTASTIC, VERY EXCITING BUSINESS AREA, SUBJECT TO A PERMANENT CHANGE."

He spent his study time in Trier, where he "studied different things, among other things business administration and strategic management", he tells us. After "a short excursion into business consultancy, which gave me no joy", as he confesses, he "took the decision, actually quite quickly, to buy a winery. At first I didn't know that that would be along the Mosel. At first I thought it would be in South Africa, Australia, or New Zealand." After "an intensive research, for several years", at the beginning of the year 2000 he decided in favour of a tributary valley of the Mosel, the Saar Valley, "because at that time, winegrowing there was in a severe crisis. That was a time during which I travelled a lot worldwide, and saw that wine was about to have a great revival", says Niewodniczanski. His love for wine, as he says, is due to his grandfather Theobald Simon, who – even though he was the owner of a brewery – was "a friend of the Saar region, the Mosel region, a friend of Bordeaux and Burgundy"; what was decisive was a bottle of 1971 Riesling Selection Goldkapsel from Egon Müller.

"Thus, I then founded my company and took over a traditional company, renovated it, built it up. And I see the chance of setting up a significant name at the international level", says Niewodniczanski. This is not about coincidences, but about "a very purposeful history, quite systematic with pros and cons, very strategic, rationalised." He decided in favour of a winery along the Saar for three reasons, he says: "We have a very, very rich history. I can prove with original documents that Van Volxem was already a supplier of European royal houses and luxury hotels. We know that on the basis of manuscripts, proofs of purchase, and price lists – St. James Hotel in London, Grandhotel Königsberg or Hotel Adlon in Berlin, Kaiserkeller in Berlin, Hotel Vier Jahreszeiten in Hamburg. I can prove that. It's a very, very important point, if you want to work today in the premium business, to be able to trace that back. Reliability and trust are based very strongly on the long term, and that was an important point for me."

The second reason had been "the financial crisis, the economic crisis of winegrowing, which gave me the opportunity to buy a lot of land in a very short time", says Niewodniczanski. "I purchased land from 580 owners. As a result of the Napoleonic Code from 1803, the vineyards were strongly fragmented. There had never been a structure like my company, not in such a size. Due to the crisis, I had the historically unique opportunity to set up an extraordinary winery, in a very short time, with a reasonable amount of capital – a winery that has a value in top-quality positions which will only show its effects gradually over the decades. This is a very long-term thing." The Van Volxem winery building is a former Jesuit monastery, which Luxembourger monks set up in the place of an ancient Roman farmstead. Today, the area of the vine surface is 53 hectares, which grow 97% Riesling and 3% White Burgundy. The vines have an average age of 40 years; the plants in the Wiltinger Gottesfuß location are even up to 120 years old.

The third reason to acquire a winery in the Mosel winegrowing area – which according to Niewodniczanski is one of the world's most beautiful and stylish, but from the point of view of the winegrower also one of the most brutal and difficult wine regions – was the climate change: "So far we have been the coolest region in Germany, and we benefit from the climate getting hotter, perhaps like no other region." Niewodniczanski mentions the vintage 2014: while in other German growing areas there had been a lot of rain even during the harvest, the harvest at the Mosel was clearly better that year: "We have juicy, healthy, golden-yellow grapes. That's great. We benefit enormously. And the main reason for me was: I wanted to do something that others don't have. I wanted to create a wine style which was clearly different from others, without using the attributes good or bad. It doesn't make sense to make wine or your own products stand out by denigrating the competitors. That's nonsense. The point is rather to offer the customers something which they perceive as attractive, and to establish a market that way." Van Volxem, he says, stands for wines with a dry taste, which are meant to be drunk with the food: with every mouthful, "the customer should see an inner movie, which shows an insanely great autumn in all colours", says Niewodniczanski. Every wine tells his story, about laborious work under dramatic difficulties."

The wine area, according to Niewodniczanski's judgment, is "ultimately a very middle-class area; diverse". There are "large players, those are highly professional, but ultimately, the wine area is a wild area." Apart from large, international, marketing-oriented groups in commerce, "which also maintain a wine factory, we deal with a very middle-class and very complex area, in which you'll see a lot of lateral entrants, which is what makes the area so interesting. And for me, the premium area is exciting, for the higher you get, the more interesting are the people which you meet." The wine area, according to Niewodniczanski, is "a fantastic, very exciting area, subject to permanent change. That's what most people aren't aware of. In this area, you must practically continuously reinvent yourself. We must continuously review and adjust, fine-tune, the path we took."

ROMAN NIEWODNICZANSKI

A successful wine businessperson "may not think about money", clarifies Niewodniczanski. Such a person needs "passion, dedication. He must be deeply and strongly convinced, with every fibre of his body, of his success, and then simply create the conditions, the strategy, in his life and work, to make this possible." For himself, success is "the basic condition for happiness, the air for breathing", he defines. "I am successful because I have a lot of happiness in my profession – an infinite amount of happiness. Wine, for me, is the world's most beautiful triviality. If I hadn't become a winegrower, today I would be unhappy. For being a winegrower is for me the most marvellous profession, and my fulfilment. With it, I have fulfilled the dream of my life." Niewodniczanski sees performance as the "basic prerequisite for success", and he explains his goals and his motivation in more detail: with his business activity, he wants to achieve personal happiness for himself, "quite simply satisfaction, fulfilment, also recognition. With that I don't mean recognition by society, that my name appears in a book. Recognition, that I stand in front of the mirror in the morning, and that I can look into the mirror and be satisfied with myself. That's the most important thing. If I am not satisfied with myself, I won't be able to create everything else, either."

"THAT'S BUSINESS THINKING: LONG-TERM, SPANNING YEARS, AND HOPEFULLY EVEN GENERATIONS."

Niewodniczanski considers success in the long term: "Wine stands for trust. Business success is success, if you create values. That's the most important thing. To create lasting values, which the next generation – which doesn't necessarily have to be your own family – can then continue developing. That's business success. That you change things with your ideas – landscapes, business areas, processes. You have an idea; at night you wake up, and you have an idea. And 20 years later, somewhere it says 'Red Bull' on an airplane. That's business success. To change an entire genre, to help influence a business area, and to be able to continue developing it. That's ultimately also a cultural achievement. Success is surely something that is able to cause additional success, because it motivates. Failure for me would be sinking; I couldn't stand that."

Additional reasons to be active as a businessman, for Niewodniczanski, are "a certain form of vanity, also a certain form of playful disposition; enthusiasm for the product and enthusiasm for the business area, total enthusiasm. Many businesspeople think too much with a financial orientation. If you look at the most successful companies today, you'll notice that many of them weren't even guided by financial aspects. I am completely product-oriented. My entire conviction, my passion, are based on my belief to be able to create an extraordinary wine with my team. That's the only thing that interests me. Unfortunately, I do have to occupy myself with the topic of sales, and numbers, and profitability – marginally, since I very much dislike doing this. But if I offer somebody my wines, that's as if I give him my children to guard them. Initially, that has no financial relevance. Unfortunately we are under economic pressures and must deal with these subjects, but that's really an extreme situation. I noticed this repeatedly with top businesspeople and top managers – that they are best when they simply want to create value for their customers, and are convinced of the idea for which you write your book:

ROMAN NIEWODNICZANSKI

that something is done that hasn't existed previously in this form, and that provides a benefit. And to provide a benefit is really a very honourable task. I am happy that I live in a country in which people are free to do that."

For Niewodniczanski, "business virtues, the very classic virtues" are important: "honesty, reliability, passion, enthusiasm, dedication, a certain form of humility. To simply follow a larger goal, as good employees in large companies do. You can summarise all this under the concept of business thinking. I expect, from the smallest employee in my wine market, that he can't imagine anything more beautiful than creating the perfect conditions to create great wines. That's business thinking: long-term, spanning years, and hopefully even generations." And: "Design is very important for me, since aesthetics always has to do quite a lot with quality."

Niewodniczanski explains that he takes business decisions "very intuitively, and in discussion with clever people. By questioning and tapping, but ultimately, even though I learned strategic management, very intuitively; from a feeling, which in turn is the result of moulding and an accumulation of knowledge." If a decision doesn't produce the expected or desired result, Niewodniczanski takes this as an impulse: "Errors, for me, are a prerequisite, to develop new areas. Errors are committed automatically. And contradictions, too, for me are unfortunately a part of intelligent work; there will frequently be contradictions. Contradictions are an unavoidable component." Niewodniczanski appreciates lateral thinkers as "wonderful people, required by any business area to advance", and he is also open to business risks: "I love risks. I believe that great successes also imply great risks that have been taken. Not everybody is aware of that. In retrospect, people don't consider this. But what we know today is that many very successful businesspeople already have gone through a bankruptcy. And you must not founder by one failure. Failures should be used to increase your performance. Failures should motivate."

With respect to his long-term orientation, Niewodniczanski also occupies himself with the evanescence of his own activity: "I occupy myself very intensively with history – I have more historical price lists, manuscripts, Prussian documentation, than anybody else in this business area that I know. If you live on a winery that stands on Roman ruins, and if you manage a company whose business base are 2000 year old vineyards, you'll quickly realise that before you, 40, 50, 60 or 70 generations had the same ideas, at the same place, as you. And then you'll realise how evanescent your life is. If you ask me for the driving force: that's evanescence. The fact that I consider the here and now as simply a blink in a large whole. That I myself am a measly, little worm in a large development, that I might perhaps moult into a larger, fat worm, but one who has a responsibility. I took over a company, I come from a company, I come from a business family. This family has – unintentionally – given me the possibility to build up something extraordinary. The purchase of wine land, the purchase of such a company, is an incredible responsibility for me. I have the obligation to achieve quality, and to guide dedicated employees in such a way, and to provide them with the general conditions, to allow them to achieve great performance. And all this in a very, very short time of a few decades. That's all very, very short. And if you ask me for my motivation – why do I work so much? Because time is incredibly limited! Life is damned short. And in this short time, which is left to me, I want to achieve a lot. Not for the money, but due to the motivation of a great human, personal satisfaction."

With respect to his employees, Niewodniczanski describes his leadership style as "chaotic" and "unfortunately very desire-oriented. I do what is fun for me. That's not always what my office expects from me. I have very good right and left hands which work in my interest and which have to tell me ten times that I have an important appointment, or that an important letter needs to be written or a signature to be placed. Thus, unfortunately, very chaotic. But I am aware of my incompetence." He says that he has "extremely high demands", admits Niewodniczanski, but "unfortunately, I never myself satisfy these demands. And I simply have to live with that, with the fact that I don't manage to do that. Ultimately, this can only be done with humour."

For Niewodniczanski, the optimal employee has "the highest human integrity. Human integrity and value-orientation are the most important things for me." In addition, there is "an inner drive to fulfil a dream. An ideal employee is not financially oriented. An ideal employee must be paid appropriately, preferably lavishly. But he must not be driven by money. He should have an inner drive and a deep conviction, and also transport the greatest human values." As a businessman, Niewodniczanski must create the conditions for this – "every day, day and night", as he emphasises. That which he demands from each of his employees, the employee must also be able to demand from him: "I must provide him with reliability, with a long term, and with security – these are very important things nowadays; and of course also economic satisfaction. But it must be the case that money and economic aspects aren't in the foreground; rather, he must find the general conditions which allow him to work perfectly. I want to have the best people in the area, the very best."

"MANY BUSINESSPEOPLE THINK WITH TOO MUCH FINANCIAL ORIENTATION."

To achieve his goals and produce high-quality wines, Niewodniczanski counts on low yields, a late harvest, gentle grape pressing, and slow fermentation with yeasts from the own vineyard or cellar. "Enjoyment of drinking and light-heartedness are the central characteristics that distinguish my wine", he says. "The region and the vineyards in which I work allow me and my team to produce a wine that differs very delicately from many others. In the sense that it is aromatic, that it got minerality from the slate, that it is great for meals. In its lightness and its aroma richness, it is unique. That's the core: highly aromatic, highly concentrated, dense, expressive white wines, which are very well suited for meals and which are developed drily."

Niewodniczanski goes into more detail: "We follow the idea of natural wine. At the end of the 19th century, one of the reasons for the great success of Mosel wines was the orientation to the natural wine principle. At that time there were different ideas in the wine area, and a small group of top-level winemakers in Germany strongly encouraged a wine left to nature. With 'leaving to nature' at that time they referred to refrain from enriching it. In the current situation, as I consider it, I see the idea of a nature wine as

ROMAN NIEWODNICZANSKI

a development of the terroir idea and of the ecological idea. It's a wine with an origin, in which I can taste its origin, as is the case with all of the world's top-level wines, and which at the same time has an occasion of use, is appetizing and aromatic." Specifically, this principle means refraining from fining, according to Niewodniczanski: In the future, nature wines will be the success, and they result precisely from refraining from fining; from working out lightness in every detail in the vineyard and in the cellar."

The stipulation of leaving it to nature dictates the entire development of the winery, explains Niewodniczanski: "We take this idea of a nature wine so seriously, that the entire new cellar is built around this idea of a nature wine, in every detail. We ask ourselves: What are the colours made of, with which the walls are painted? How does this affect the spontaneous fermentation? What energy fields are there in the cellar? I am neither an esoteric nor a biodynamist, but I believe that there are simply a lot of substances and physical processes that have a considerable influence on my wines. And I want to master them, it's as simple as that."

Niewodniczanski assesses the current developments in this business area in a differentiated way: "I think that all changes offer chances and risks. Each technological innovation, since the wheel or the fire has been invented, has chances and risks. The question is: How do I handle it? And how do I use it for the fulfilment of my dreams, i.e. my business goals? The online business plays an important role. Apart from the fact that I am involved privately as a business angel in different e-commerce companies, I notice that this area is also characterized increasingly by this in the wine business; also in the transmission of knowledge. Just like many others, I see things such Facebook critically, and handle it critically. But I start to open to it, and I try to do it in a serious and very objective way. And I try to eliminate the risks involved. The danger for my branding today is that any market participants can arise within milliseconds as a journalist and do bashing in forums – for instance in a wine forum. That's very dangerous for brands today. Therefore, large company groups take that very seriously – in this case I don't refer to the wine area, I know that this is the case in other companies. I have great hopes from online media and online commerce. However, you really need to be able to handle it."

According to Niewodniczanski's opinion, the wine business consists of different parts: "I believe that you can't talk about the development of the wine area, because there are only the wine areas. I can really only talk about my segment; that's the premium segment of German top wines. A lot is going on here. We are subject to an enormous change. The appearance of structures such as my winery shows how strongly the segment has changed in the last few years. And I believe that this will continue. In the German premium segment, we'll experience a certain consolidation, or perhaps it is already present. Apart from that, branding will surely continue playing a considerable role worldwide." Niewodniczanski estimates that a development as the one that happened in Australia, New Zealand and the USA will "continue even more strongly": "that brands form which supply commerce. That will become stronger in Germany as well. I believe that in Germany we are at a very early stage in the development of this branding for wine names. That is just beginning. We have the large cheap brands, but what about premium brands? They hardly exist. I want to build up a top brand successfully. Branding is just starting."

ROMAN NIEWODNICZANSKI

The key qualifications for the wine businessperson, according to Niewodniczanski, are "quite numerous. I believe that product policy is a very central issue, i.e., it must really occupy itself with products. If he wants to work in the premium area, knowledge of the world's markets and top wines is essential. I can't claim or try to build up a German top brand if I don't know what the top brands in Australia and England and other world-wide markets are, and how they work. That is really very, very important. If one day my children are to take over my winery, I would assuredly send them to an internship into such companies, to allow them to get a feeling for that." Once again, Niewodniczanski considers "classic virtues" to be essential, but the demands go further: "Surely e-commerce is a topic with which you have to deal. New media have a central role; in communication – it is very important to understand how information images are conveyed; it's very important to understand, for example, how a brand even arises." Beyond that, a successful wine businessperson must deal with viral media, to know "how nowadays opinions are formed in the first place".

Opinion leadership is very important for Niewodniczanski: "A wine businessperson is close to the product, and he wants to place products which he must later sell, to pay his work. To achieve that, he must become an opinion leader. Or he must know who the opinion leaders are, and influence them in a way that isn't corrupt, but highly respectable. That isn't entirely simple, since the wine area is, after all, a small area, and we don't have a large marketing budget. Precisely in Germany it's naïve – it's silly, compared to France, compared with the world. Apart from a few large market branders and large cellars, there are hardly any large players. There are many, many, many small players. And here, knowledge about brands has an important role."

A young businessperson in the wine area, according to Niewodniczanski's conviction, needs especially passion: "This area attracts many very enthusiastic people, and that's very dangerous. Enthusiasm, commitment, and passion are the essential conditions for willingness and success. However, it can also cause a disaster, since in this case many enter the area, people who will find out that you can't earn money in this sector. It's an area in which it's very difficult to earn money. And young people must be aware of this from the beginning: fascination for wine – which is often the case – is not enough, by itself, to feed your children. You can get quite unhappy in this area, if you find that at the end of the month you aren't able to pay your heating bill." Young businesspeople "must have a very clear idea of what they do", warns Niewodniczanski. "I believe that today it is very, very important that you deal carefully with marketing. You need to know exactly where, in what market, you want to do what. And to achieve this, you need to burn and fight."

ROMAN NIEWODNICZANSKI

WOLFGANG M. ROSAM
Communications consultant, author, editorial manager and publisher
Vienna, Austria

Wolfgang M. Rosam (born 1957) is the editor of the wine and gourmet magazine Falstaff, founded in Austria in 1980, and which since 2010 also appears in a German edition. Apart from the magazine, the Falstaff publishing house publishes two wine guides a year, as well as a guide to restaurants, hotels and liquors. Rosam joined Falstaff in 2004, and since 2010 he is a majority shareholder. After starting his professional career as a marketing leader at a food company, since the early 1980s he founded and managed several communications agencies, is active as a journalist and author for several Austrian daily papers, and, since 1990, lector for PR conception at the Institute of Journalism of the Vienna University.

The reason for Rosam's entry into the wine area, as he describes it, was "the Austrian wine scandal 1985, where, together with what was at that time a PR agency, the Publico – which today is a Ketchum agency, and at that time was already the greatest agency in Austria – I got the task of re-establishing the image of Austrian wine after the glycol scandal." The Austrian Wine Marketing Board (Österreich Wein Marketing Gesellschaft, ÖWM), which had just been founded at that time, had written out a budget for advertising as well as public relations, "and we won this pitch, that was the entry. For, together with the advertising agency GGK in Austria, at that time we had designed a very spectacular advertising campaign. You might say that that was the first learning campaign in which I participated in my entire marketing and communications career. Really a no-go. Really, in advertising you can't instruct the consumer with your raised finger, etc., but that was what happened. So, that was a learning campaign, in which we tried to teach the Austrian consumers that there was more than just a glass of red wine and a glass of white wine. You had to learn the varieties, you had to learn the vintages, you had to learn the sugar grades."

In this context, he says that is had been his "great task" to get interested for Austrian wines, reports Rosam. There was massive media work, and it became stylish to drink wine." At that time, he says, he had key experiences in training with winemakers: "Of course we also trained the winemakers, how they could better present their wines, etc., and the key experience was the question to a winemaker in Burgenland, a maker of red wine, whom I asked, Well, with what international wines would you compare your blaufränkisch? And he answered: With Lafite-Rothschild. And I must honestly confess that in 1985 I didn't know much about Bordeaux. But of course I immediately purchased a Lafite-Rothschild in a wine shop, and thought, the winemaker must be a bit nutty, he

WOLFGANG M. ROSAM

must not have understood something. At that time I wasn't a great palate, but I was able to distinguish that there were at least two different worlds. However, that challenged me and provoked me to the degree that I started to collect wine – and up to this day, I haven't stopped doing it, and won't stop doing it until the day I die."

Rosam got to Falstaff due to his second passion apart from collecting wine: "I have a second hobby, and that is eating – but unfortunately not cooking", he explains. "So, I am not a cook, but an eater, and I really wanted to purchase the Gourmeo. But that didn't work, so I did my own thing. At that time, it was called 'VIP Gourmet Club'." The goal of this club he founded, he says, was to "democratise restaurant reviews" according to the American model, "where there are not just a few testers from Gourmeo, Michelin, or whatever their name might be, roaming the countryside and, depending on their state of mind, evaluating a restaurant as good or bad, but where we have the population, in other words the visitors, as reviewers. But I also soon recognised that I need a magazine to do this, so I went to Falstaff and offered them my gourmet club, which at that time had 4000 members, and said to them: In return, give me 25% of Falstaff. And I thought that I could then change Falstaff. That's now ten years ago."

However, with the then-owners, that wasn't possible, Rosam tells us, so in 2010 he gave them the choice of either buying back his 25% participation, or instead to sell him their shares of the magazine. He made it clear that he had different ideas about a wine and consumption medium: "That isn't the old fashion wine magazine, what you are doing. After that, there was a long discussion, and in the end, the two founders and former owners agreed to sell me the magazine and the publishing house." As a result, together with his wife he acquired 100% of the Falstaff publishing house. "From the beginning, it was clear that we wanted to make a completely different magazine", says Rosam. "We wanted a luxury magazine, we wanted a lifestyle magazine for gourmets – you might say the 'vogue' of eating and drinking, to say it a bit pompously. We then invested a lot of money into the new Falstaff, and thanks God, the experiment went well. Today, Falstaff is the largest wine and gourmet magazine in the German-language region."

As editor headquartered in Vienna, Rosam watches especially the Austrian wine sector carefully: "During the last two and a half decades, an incredible amount of things have happened. I don't believe that there is a wine market anywhere in the world – except perhaps in China – in which there has been such a radical change and such a rethinking. Really from mass to class, that's a real metamorphosis, one which there has been in hardly any other wine market in the world. That happened in Austria." In the meantime, winegrowing "has also become a generation topic", analyses Rosam. "In 1985, there was hardly a younger generation of winemakers who wanted to get into the winegrowing area. Winegrowing was not very profitable. Winegrowing wasn't stylish, and due to our work after the wine scandal, obviously the winegrowers, too, became stylish." In the course of the advertising campaign at that time, winegrowers were trained to present themselves better in public and to "do media work", and these efforts, he says, were successful. "I called that the 'Miracle of Gols'", explains Rosam. That's a winegrowing place in the Burgenland, where a whole squad, a dozen of young winegrowers, went to their fathers and said, Father, send us to other countries, send us for a year to California, to South Africa, to Germany, to Bordeaux, wherever. We now want to learn, and we want to take over the company." After the gradual image recovery of Austrian wine, he perceived it as "the next wonder, that the generational problem was suddenly solved. That the newer generation was suddenly willing to take over the company, but with their own ideas, their own ways, to make wine, which had nothing to do with pre-1985 wine production in Austria." For this time period, Rosam gives an example: "Anybody who made a blend of red wine was frowned upon, for at that time, people imagined that in Austria wines were only made out of a single variety. There was only the Zweigelt, the Blaufränkisch – and a Cuvée, which of course made up the winemaker's tension in the cellar, and requires all of his winemaking skill, was frowned upon. Getting away from this attitude "was the greatest change that I experienced", says Rosam. "We now experience that in China. There, the world's largest wine market is being revolutionised, so that's the next big thing."

"I AM SUCCESSFUL BECAUSE I ALWAYS QUESTION MYSELF, AND DON'T LOSE MY HUMILITY IN THE FACE OF SUCCESS AND WHAT I HAVE ACHIEVED."

Rosam is convinced that as an entrepreneur in the wine area you need "a large portion of emotion and enthusiasm for the grape juice. You have to be curious. You also have to be willing to invest part of your privately available budget in wine; otherwise you'll get stuck on some level." Rosam leaves no doubt about his own enthusiasm: "For me, wine is a juice of life, which gives me life force. For me, wine drinkers are pure hedonists. The nice thing is that it has no longer remained just a society of old men, as it might have been a few decades ago. In the meantime it has become quite fashionable for young people to find wine. At Falstaff we note that many women, too, find the way to wine. The society of friends of wine has become a very plural society; a bit urban perhaps, in the upper income segment or educational level – which must not needs be the same thing. Many students who are about to graduate become real wine freaks and have a lot of fun trying out new things, including trends such as orange wine and biological-dynamic wine, etc." The wine area and the society are in an extreme movement, "the end of which can't be foreseen", says Rosam. "Wine is not a fad, wine is a phenomenon of a period of life", a period "which, however, you don't leave. I have yet to find a wine drinker who said, I used to drink wine, now I don't drink it any longer. Except if he has a health problem, but otherwise, this doesn't happen."

Rosam returns to the topic of entrepreneurship: "I am an entrepreneur with heart and soul. In 1987 I purchased my first company; that was a management buyout of the PR agency which I managed at that time, the Publico; within a very short time, it became number one in Austria." He then sold this agency to an American agency group, and "half a year later I again founded a communications agency, which I still manage today", the Wolfgang Rosam Change Communications GmbH. Rosam considers Falstaff as his second pillar; he says that he is "extremely happy" with it "and will continue doing that as long as I live", he predicts. "That is to say, to be an entrepreneur for me means freedom, it means self-determination, it means more work as in any employee relationship, but also the chance to earn more money. That's my life, and I couldn't imagine anything else, and you are an entrepreneur for all your life. So, there is no such thing as retirement."

WOLFGANG M. ROSAM

WINE
ENTREPRENEURS

Rosam goes into more details about his personal principles: "Performance, for me, is the irrepressible desire to advance, not to get discouraged by setbacks, to always think about tomorrow and to walk forwards. Motivation for me is the lifeblood – the most important driving force for success. Without motivation you can't be successful." Rosam understands success to consist in "finding the balance between profession and private life". If you isolate business success, "by saying, I now have a great company, and earn a lot of money, but my private life has gone down the drain – in that case, the entrepreneur has failed in his private life. The real success is harmony with private life. I believe that a truly good businessperson will also harmonise his profession and his private life. A good entrepreneur has a good management team which he guides, and that will leave him sufficient free time for hobbies and for his family. I think that that is a work of art that an entrepreneur should strive for, and that's what I try to do for many years. The path is long, but not without success."

"FOR ME, BEING AN ENTREPRENEUR MEANS FREEDOM, IT MEANS SELF-DETERMINATION, IT MEANS MORE WORK FOR ME THAN IN ANY EMPLOYEE RELATIONSHIP, BUT ALSO THE OPPORTUNITY TO EARN MORE MONEY."

Rosam can also define his individual recipe for success: "I am successful, because I always question myself, and don't lose humility in the face of success and that which I have achieved. I am an extremely curious, but also an extremely self-critical person. I constantly question myself. I question whether I could have done something better, whether I should have guided somebody better, how I should have done a job, which perhaps I didn't do very well, better. But I try not to be a masochist about it. I don't want to tear myself to pieces. But I believe that this portion of humility towards those that pay you, that commission you, towards your customers, is important. Also, this considerable portion of self-criticism is necessary, to continue developing. Contradictions for me are necessary and good – precisely to question yourself. The death of entrepreneurship or of a successful manager is complacency. If you are complacent and smug, and no longer question yourself, then you have lost, and then the decline begins."

Entrepreneurial decisions, according to Rosam, are "always a good mix of gut feeling and brain. Of course you shouldn't turn off your brain off, but precisely as an entrepreneur, you should also pay attention to your gut feeling. You have a gut feeling. You also have to be willing to take a risk; you won't always win. Of course sometimes you have flops – that is part of the business. I consider committing errors as something natural. The most important thing is to learn from them, or, as Lao-Tze said, 'If you are lying on the floor, the most important thing is to stand up again quickly'. The important thing is that you don't suffocate from flops, that you learn a lesson, and that next time you do it better."

WOLFGANG M. ROSAM

Risky decisions don't scare Rosam: "I love risks", he emphasises. "But at the same time, I try to keep the risks calculated in a way that it doesn't become a danger for other established businesses which I manage or own. I believe that a risk should be calculable in such a way that you can say: 25% of my income, my profit, or my capital are the bankroll for new companies. But that shouldn't be 50 or 60 percent, or even more. For you always have to include the flop in your calculations, and if you lose 25%, well, you lose 25% - and the next time you win again. I believe that when an entrepreneur has no willingness to assume risks, then he got old and should consider retiring."

Rosam tells us an example from his life: "An extreme entrepreneurial decision was selling my agency when it was at its peak as a business. That was probably the best-earning agency in Central Europe, and I sold it well. And at that time – immediately afterwards – I didn't know whether that was correct. Of course at that time I had withdrawal symptoms, in the sense of: What shall I do now? Though I now have the money, I no longer have a business." He says "well, then I quickly had to found a new company. But in retrospect, that was just the correct thing to do. It is an essential point to perhaps separate from a company at the correct time, start a new one, or perhaps separate from employees and open new doors. I have a sort of motto: 'You first have to close doors well, before the new doors will open well."

Rosam manages changes and flux "very offensively", as he explains specifically with respect to the digital revolution which affects the publishing business in a sensitive way: "Of course I was born before 1982, and thus I am a migrant and not a 'digitally native' person who grew up in this time. But of course that's the present, and the future, no question about that. We currently invest all the money which we have, or which we earn as Falstaff, in online technology. However, we also know that we are in a niche, where people still like to have the magazine, the paper, haptically on the coffee table at home. That sets us apart from the entire print market which is familiar with the news area. That one will change completely", is Rosam's conviction. News "at some point, will no longer be consumed in print, but only online. Simply because news also have a time effect, and because I want to consume news at any moment, when I feel like it, rather than picking up the paper at home."

Falstaff is "something quite different", clarifies Rosam. "If you get home, lie on your couch and stretch – and you'll continue doing that in 20 years – you want to take something into your hand, something that you can enjoy, and that will be magazines such as Falstaff or others." Even so, his publishing company is developing the online area "massively. I see this as a great chance. In business, everything will change, in media everything will change, our entire life will change. 20 years ago we couldn't imagine that we would be able to be reached by phone via cell phone, or permanently via email. At that time, the fax was the silent revolution. Now we live digitally, and we can get accustomed to that very well, and I find this very positive."

Openness also appears in Rosam's dealings with his employees: "I give my employees a lot of flexibility. My employees all have the most modern equipment; each carries his laptop or cell phone around – paid by the company. I don't mind at all where somebody works, whether it is at home, on his couch, or in the swimming pool. What is essential is

WOLFGANG M. ROSAM

WINE
ENTREPRENEURS

that he works, that he is accessible. That's important for me: to be accessible 24 hours, seven days a week, including for our customers. We don't have a time control system or anything similar at our company; I don't need all that. I am only result-oriented, I am only interested in the result. I am not interested in how diligent somebody is and how many hours he spends at the office. I am interested in the results, and I believe that many of my employees like that, since that gives them a maximum of freedom. I also train them a bit as businesspeople."

For this leadership approach, Rosam requires people who fulfil certain requirements. He is definite that "The optimal employee is goal-oriented, is result-oriented, can organise himself, manage himself. The optimal employee simply has a lot of fun and wants to earn money, he wants to advance. Those are my people. I don't want any others." What is crucial is "personality, personality, personality. If somebody has a good personality, he will take care of his education, his betterment, his training. For me, the personal charisma, the personality, the goal to advance in life, to make a career, is much more important than any certificates. I haven't looked at certificates for the last 30 years." Creativity, as Rosam explains, must be connected with competence: "Lateral thinkers for me are an enrichment to society, sometimes too overvalued. Only that lateral thinking by itself is usually just pure provocation, and that should really be matched by experience."

Despite the strong time engagement that he also demands from his employees, Rosam once again draws the connection to his definition of success: "I have an elevated and fairly tight value structure, which I have built up myself. In the first place for me there is really an old-fashioned value, that's the family. I am fortunate to still have small children, six and nine years old. That, for me, is the supreme value. I have sacrificed all my evening appointments for my family. I am at home every evening and take my children to bed. I don't make evening appointments, but my day starts early. My first appointment is at eight, a business breakfast. I have a business lunch every day. Ten appointments a day, which I complete with a driver, to avoid wasting time looking for parking spaces, or in underground car parking, or due to other problems in road traffic. I take a lot of free time for vacations, usually shorter vacations. I can't stand being at some place for three weeks at a time, but I am often somewhere for an extended weekend."

As important as the work-life balance is – Rosam's priorities are clear: "I work hard and intensively, and I love work. If I didn't love it, I wouldn't do it. I am now almost 60, and I have a ten year plan. For the next ten years, every day I look forward to my job. So, I must try to live healthily – that's the most difficult part; for obviously, people who enjoy usually don't live healthily." His biggest challenge is "that a) I shouldn't get too fat, and b) that I don't get any health damage which would shorten my life", admits the pleasure-lover, and describes his life slogan: "La vita è bella – life is beautiful. I want to be able to enjoy every day. You should have moments of enjoyment every day. A day without enjoyment is a wasted day." And he adds an additional dimension: "Design, for me, is among the most beautiful things in life – aesthetics, joy, which you can enjoy every day with a beautiful piece." But in the medium term, Rosam doesn't plan to stop working either: "At age 67, it doesn't end", he states. His plan merely states "that the next ten years imply an intensive expansion and continuous grown of my companies. Of course I must bring in the next generation – both in Falstaff and in my media con-

WOLFGANG M. ROSAM

sulting business. But I am sure there will not be a retirement or something similar. For me, that's a foreign word. Therefore I don't need to worry whether I'll ever get a pension or something similar, for I want to work."

For the future, Rosam estimates "that Europe as a continent, in other words the old world, will primarily develop in the directions that give a large value to leisure time. There is the statement that Asia is the workbench, the USA is the finance market, and Europe is the open air museum. I hope that it won't get so bad, that we only have the character of a museum. But of course here in Europe we have a different life quality than in Asia, you just have to see that, even if we always look with envy to Peking, Shanghai, or Singapore. There, the air is worse, people work longer and more, and are more stressed, and I believe that they enjoy less than we do. So, specifically in the German region, and also here in Vienna where I live, we have an extremely high quality of life. I believe that this is something that I should accept as positive." With respect to the wine area, the Europeans, as Rosam suggests, "should also sell this life quality to the remainder of the world; therefore I also believe that it is nice. After all, China loves everything that comes from Europe – brand articles from Europe. It's no coincidence that precisely our luxury brand articles from Europe, or the cars built in Europe, are in the highest demand worldwide. Therefore I also believe that European wines can provide that, that European foods can provide that, and with it, also the European luxury items and media, such as Falstaff. And therefore I see possibilities for expansion for us in Asia, for example."

"WHEN AN ENTREPRENEUR IS NO LONGER WILLING TO TAKE RISKS, HE HAS GROWN OLD, AND SHOULD CONSIDER RETIRING."

Rosam evaluates the market development within Europe quite critically: "I believe that we have a huge problem with the wine price. Italy as well as Austria, but of course especially France, must carefully consider their price policy for the next few years. I guess that France – especially Bordeaux and Burgundy – will have the greatest problem. For of course the new world crushes in strongly, they have vintages, and precisely here at Falstaff we have published a story – the cover story: the world's 100 best wines." The winner, he says, was a Chilean red wine, sold for a price of €8.90, which got 93 points from the critic Robert Parker. A wine with 93 Parker points – it could also have been 95 Parker points – available for less than ten euros, is of course a challenge. And I must really say that the interior market in Germany, in France, in Italy, but also in Austria, has to ponder a lot. I believe that we have long ago reached the upper end of the price range. A Riesling from Wachau for 30 or 40 euros can no longer be beaten. Or red wine from Austria, for 25 euros or more; here the boys are already playing in a league against wines from the New World – especially from Chile, from South Africa – which cost half the price, but have at least the same quality, or are even quite a bit better." Winemakers will have to react to these developments, admonishes Rosam: "In this case, you have to ponder quite a bit in relation to production methods. Of course there will always be a premium segment, but a medium and low-price segment is also required. If you don't tackle these international challenges, at some moment you'll be left behind."

WOLFGANG M. ROSAM

WINE
ENTREPRENEURS

For Rosam, his own vigour and intrepidity are also the standard from young entrepreneurs who want to enter the wine area: "If I would be able to go back and change something in my professional life, that would be that I would spend more time in other countries", he considers. "Education is essential for me, more important than ever. Especially international education, languages. Today, any young person should spend at least a year outside of his country." His message: "Absolute do, tackle, risk. Life is a challenge, and you have to accept it. You must not be afraid. If you have an idea you are convinced of, you must try it out. And then you must dedicate all your enthusiasm to it, find investors who support you. I just say, to young people: Do! Get out! Look at the world! Come back and start your company! Become independent! I want to intensively recommend anybody, to accept the challenge: Don't be afraid! Tackle it!"

WOLFGANG M. ROSAM

MAX GÄRTNER
Co-founder and manager, Vicampo
Mainz, Germany

Max Gärtner (born 1982; on the right) is one of the three founders and managers of the online wine marketplace Vicampo in Mainz. His two founding and business colleagues are his brother Felix Gärtner (responsible for marketing; on the left) and Daniel Nitz (responsible for technology and design). Vicampo is already the third company founded by the two Gärtner brothers, after the two online wine shops "Weinwelt Rheingau" (for regional wines) and "Wine in Black" (for premium wines); in two of them, Daniel Nitz was also present from the beginning as a partner. Max Gärtner emphasizes that he speaks for all three associates in the following.

The media sciences graduate studied journalism, media sciences, and movie sciences, and also has Master of Business Administration (MBA) degree. Before founding Vicampo, Gärtner was a consultant for four years at the strategy and management consultancy Bain & Company, with emphasis in commerce and consumer goods. He started in the wine business in the year 2009 as he remembers: "After my studies, my brother and I established an online wine business – just for fun. A regional business exclusively for Rheingau wines; an online regional wine shop so to speak. We did that simply because we love wine, because we love Rheingau, and because we consider the subject fun. But without any professional ambition. We wanted to start the project for half a year and then simply continue it as a hobby with one employee."

At that time "the subject of online sales for German wineries wasn't really solved well," says Gärtner. "Many things were not available, and if they were, it was complicated. And relatively bad in comparison. That means: products without a description, without images, without prices. When making a purchase, you couldn't pay by invoice. So, simply everything that people consider important when purchasing online wasn't available." At the same time, he says that he and his brother had "simply fallen in love with this line of business," and "great conversations" with Rheingau wine-growers had encouraged them: "No matter with whom we talked, it was very thrilling. We learned a lot. And we especially saw that this line of business was about to go through a radical change. We started the specialized trade online. An online wine shop, but one that really had its own warehouse," explains Gärtner. Sometimes, customers ordered wines that weren't in stock. "In that case, we called the winery and basically said: 'Please send the order directly.' And the winery did that and said: 'Sure, that's our day-to-day operation. We constantly send out wines to other dealers or to customers or to gastronomy. No problem!'" That happened more and more often with the result "that we said we won't fill up our warehouse too much," said Gärtner, "since money was scarce."

Half of all wineries from which the two brothers order wine for direct shipping agreed to this procedure. "And then we quickly noticed: If we do this with a technical solution for all of Germany, this could become something large, something that lets us work professionally in this area. And after we had contact with entire wineries and with the people behind them, we saw how enthusiastic they were about this. And this somehow stimulated us so we decided to continue with the same passion," describes Gärtner. He says that Daniel Nitz who already took over the Web design for the wine shop "Weinwelt Rheingau", entered as a partner at this stage. "Because we said, you can't sell online if you don't have the basic knowledge of technology, development, and marketing. That's quite critical."

Together, the three young entrepreneurs then founded "Wine in Black", and then Vicampo. "The best for last", smiles Gärtner. "After all the experiences we had from 2009 to 2011, we founded Vicampo in its current form at the beginning of 2012. And there we used everything that we learned. So, in principle: you need to have a good offering, but we have specialized a lot in this area of technology. We said: What we need to be successful online, we have to do ourselves; one hundred percent. And that requires a lot of effort since it takes long at first and you don't see any results. Therefore, at first it took us a while but now, gradually, we have success and I think that we now have an exciting path before us."

"YOU CAN'T REALLY FINANCE SOMETHING THAT DOESN'T WORK YET FROM YOUR DAILY ACTIVITIES."

Gärtner emphasizes "that we only started with our own money – and not much of it. From 2009 to 2011, we financed everything completely on our own – we worked without pay and even added money, 15,000 euros each. But that won't let us advance a lot, quickly." So it was necessary to rethink. "We really wanted to create a system that is relevant, and especially in an online business, that requires being big. Therefore it was clear to us that we needed financial investors. And there are some financial investors who we worked with then." Besides a former professor of Gärtner from the media industry, these are, in particular, two investment funds "which invest strongly in founders who invest in teams. Who, with an idea, have a chance of becoming number one, two, or three in a market. The good thing here is: they are patient. They know that e-commerce models simply require 5-7 years. They are fully professional, and they simply help us get there. We were lucky that we were able to really choose our partners. And that they then told us they will do it. So it was really good, an important path. Without money it doesn't work. You can't really finance something that doesn't work yet from your daily activities."

The objective of founding Vicampo, according to Gärtner, is to leave their own accent, a marking, in the wine business – "to leave a mark". When we are ready, people in Germany will hopefully buy wine differently than they would without it. And better! And now, honestly: when do you have the chance in your life to do something like this? To really help shape an entire line of business. By enabling the wineries to send the wine to the customers themselves, there is no need for middlemen who don't do anything but increase costs. And to give the many small wineries who would have no possibility of selling directly such a chance, that's really amazing." He says that many producers have

MAX GÄRTNER

the problem that the "calling customers" break away. Thus, for large amounts of wine there are middle-term turnover problems because gastronomy and specialized traders are also "fully stocked"; for the large-scale customers, on the other hand, the amounts available are too small. Additionally there are numerous wineries "who make extremely good wines but are too small to hire a professional sales force"; and selling over the Internet is too demanding: "After all, you don't just open a shop and start selling; it really requires a lot of effort until you actually get to the point at which you sell something."

Vicampo wants to "make sure that the wineries that make especially good wines are able to sell beyond their region", and wants to help that customers "don't purchase just any winery rubbish from large industrial plants," but rather "that people actually say: 'I buy my wine from a winery which I got to know via Vicampo. And that's a really excellent wine.' And one that costs six, seven, or eight euros." Therefore, the target group for Vicampo is supermarket customers who are to be introduced to higher-quality wines, and such wines often come from small wineries to which Vicampo offers a distribution platform. The company's approach is "that these things are brought together," summarizes Gärtner. Here we have a unique initial situation and the promise should be, I should say, really solved nationwide. That is cool. Basically we love wine but the skills that we have are very special. The guiding principle is that we want to help drive and really improve the way that people purchase wine online. And of course it is encouraging; after all, we already have a customer base of over 50,000 customers. And there are many among them who discover us and simply say, "Hey, that's cool". And it is really fun. Especially because in many aspects we are only just getting started." He says that often it is said about Internet wine dealers such as Vicampo that customers no longer purchase in specialty shops but change to online wine shops. But Gärtner clarifies: "That's nonsense, really nonsense. According to customer polls, most people who buy from us have never bought in a specialty shop. We reach out to new, relatively young customers. And we are confident that we are going to grow precisely with these customers."

Gärtner explains that the fundamental decision for entrepreneurship was a very targeted one: "All three of us have consciously said that we would like to resign our job – or not accept a job, in the case of Felix; my brother had just completed the European Business School. – We wanted to become entrepreneurs because we had the impression that the chances were good enough, that we could contribute something. And that we could do something that was really fun for us, in a business area that we simply like a lot." He says that the novelty of the idea was important, "the way how we approached the topic, namely with decentralized shipping, including the wineries in logistics. That is to say the customer orders and the winery ships directly to the customer. Previously, that wasn't available on a large scale. It simply didn't exist when we started to deal with this topic." Gärtner outlines the vision: "Once we are ready, customers – wherever they live in Germany – can purchase directly from the winery on site. And thus in a first step we can make the online retrieval business ready for the 21st century. And that really is something new, something that actually represents a strong technical competency. Vicampo is a type of market for wine, highly specialised." Once again, it is about "leaving a mark, so simple that what we have done should really represent a change. Simply to open a wine shop; well, at that time there were already twenty, and now there are over a hundred. But that wouldn't be innovative in this sense."

MAX GÄRTNER

The decisions in the company itself occur on two different levels, as Gärtner explains: "On a strategic level, company decisions are always made by the three of us. This has a lot to do with common sense, for here, planning is often also guessing. On an operational level, where we have to make lots of company decisions every day, these decisions are – quite on the contrary – based on data to an enormous extent; so in each marketing decision, each purchasing decision, portfolio decision; we work a lot with data. So this means: at the strategic level the gut feeling and common sense; at the operative level it's data-driven."

Gärtner and his associates are aware of the risks for the company, but they no longer see an existential risk for their company: the worry "that Vicampo ceases to exist, that's a stage we left behind. There is enough business now," says Gärtner. "The greatest risk that I see in general is that we don't manage to become the company that we could become. If we were to be a company with 15 employees, we would already be profitable and everything would be OK. The question is: can we really manage to make a company such as Vicampo grow to 40, 50 or 100 employees? The risk where you say that with this one decision we risk the entire company is something we don't have. The most important thing to limit the risk, I believe, is to concentrate strongly on our core competencies and really leave out everything else." He says that it is also important "not to go into an ivory tower, but to consciously involve people with whom you then mirror certain things." In case of uncertainty the associates get "external opinions from people who may already have more experience in a specialised area." What allows an entrepreneur to sleep well at the end of the day is "a lot of work invested and the feeling of having done your best."

"A LEADERSHIP STYLE REALLY MEANS THAT YOU YOURSELF HAVE A STYLE AND IMPOSE IT ON OTHERS."

After Vicampo itself is an online platform now, technological change and digital media in the company play an important role. According to Gärtner, "In our office, we have four times as many monitors than employees. We practically have a paperless office with very few areas in which we still use it. We are completely in the cloud with respect to the subject of service. We use relatively many tools in every area that helps in automation. And that is part of the business. That is very technical but it is important that we are well-established in this area." For when a new company is being built up, "you can create very efficient structures if you use the corresponding tools. Of course there are always some things that put you back, for example, some tax issues because, in part, the state is not yet ready. But that is the case everywhere. After all, we work digitally and have no catalogue; nothing that is printed in any way. I believe that Felix and Daniel don't even have a business card since everything is done digitally. In that sense, the new media is everywhere. The good thing is that when a new company is built up, on the one hand you always lack some experience. On the other hand, there are no fossilized structures which must first be broken up. In that case, workflows are very simple and very efficient which, in turn, is very good since it lets you process many things quickly."

MAX GÄRTNER

The organizational structure at Vicampo has several layers but "the hierarchy is flat," explains Gärtner. Under the three associates and the manager there is the position of a COO (chief operations officer), "and below that are the corresponding chiefs of area: marketing, longtail portfolio, shorttail portfolio, etc. And below that there may be others – other full-time employees, trainees, working students, etc. Each person is attached to another person." The leadership in the company is done situationally: "After all, a leadership style really means that you yourself have a style and that you impose it upon others," explains Gärtner. "We have the opinion that you have to look at the person sitting in front of you and then decide how to guide this person in the most sensible and efficient way. We use the skill-will-matrix to do this." With this instrument, the capabilities and motivations of each employee are analysed. "A person who is a high performer, top-motivated, and top-enabled, has the highest value here. And everybody has to get there. Leadership gets especially important when somebody doesn't perform well; then the question arises: why doesn't he perform? And depending on the answer to this question, you have to adapt your leadership style. But on the other hand, there are people who you motivate or initially build up by clearly telling them what they have to do. Therefore, we don't have a leadership style. We try to adapt to the person that is to be led. Of course, the objective is that everybody has fun with one another but, at the same time, performance is also very important at Vicampo. Every employee is evaluated, a large portion of the salary is dependent on the performance, and individual goals are agreed upon. There are sometimes fierce conversations here. For me, performance is strongly based on results. And in my opinion, motivation can only be related to content. That is to say, you like to do what you do, and you have the feeling that you are good for it. And from that, you draw strength to continue. As a result motivation arises when you can contribute something. Therefore, we try very much to bind people to us who have the same urge as us."

"THE WINE BUSINESS HAS COOL PEOPLE WHO DO THEIR THING WITH A LOT OF PASSION; ALL OF THEM SMALL ENTREPRENEURS."

To create the most optimal possible conditions for performance for such employees, there needs to be infrastructure first, explains Gärtner: "First of all, the technical part is very important, that everything really works seamlessly, that everything is fast, etc., in other words, everything has to be perfectly equipped. That is not always entirely easy." In addition, "clear job descriptions" are important: "You have to clearly think, what are the goals? And what happens if the goal is reached or if there is a discrepancy from the goal? Of course, that is always an iterative process. But at the end of the day, I think it is very important to agree on goals together and then also to get the employees to think: How do we achieve the goal? And that you should be available to help. And it can often happen that we consult external help as I have already mentioned before. For example, if we have a problem in a specific area, if we aren't very sure internally, we try to consult and involve one of the specialists for such an area when it is really related to a know-how topic. However, that seldom occurs; this is more likely to happen when new topics are set up." Another important prerequisite for a positive work environment, he says, is "to assign responsibility and also to give a chance to commit mistakes. Eve-

MAX GÄRTNER

rybody commits mistakes; afterwards you get smarter. Mistakes are part of the process. If you imagine something, it always happens that you initially believe it to be simpler than it actually turns out to be." Thus, mistakes are "part of the day-to-day operations." Gärtner considers lateral thinkers as "in part useful, in part annoying, in part amusing". Contradictions, for him, are "necessary, often necessary for the debate, and often also part of the solution. The world is not black and white." According to Gärtner, you get successful "if you achieve the goals you set yourself."

"For the employees we are basically a mix of being fair and being demanding," defines Gärtner. "We try to be open and transparent, but that also means that there has to be some straight talking. The dealings are respectful of course but also demanding, really demanding. It is very important for new employees that they show a certain openness towards very direct feedback. Knowing that the intention is always positive since it is a matter of developing. And that doesn't always happen by using satin gloves all the time. If we hire somebody it basically means, first of all, that we like this person or that we like something about them. The entire topic is strongly driven by personal development. Everybody gets his personal development plan if you will. How to continue developing oneself with goals; that you somehow get more efficient, etc." The internal information policy, too, is based on transparency: "All employees know where our business is, how the business is working, how it might continue, etc. They are involved in a very open way, and that, too, is very important for us."

According to Gärtner's understanding, the employees are one of Vicampo's four stakeholder groups: "For us, it is important that we have a company that somehow has a positive influence on all the people with whom we relate," he says. "That is to say, we have associates, we have partners, we have employees and we have customers. Those are four stakeholders that are important for us. And at the end of the day, we don't want to have a unilateral optimization; we rather want to have a company that we can proudly look back to 20 years from now, for which we might even still be working at that time. So, customers should be able to say: 'Vicampo is a great thing; it is great to buy my wines there. I get wines directly from the winery which I wouldn't get otherwise.' Wineries say: 'Without Vicampo, I couldn't sell the wines that way.' Employees say: 'Vicampo is a fair working place.' And the investors, perhaps also the associates, say: 'Vicampo is a good investment'. For us, it is important to find a fair balance here for everyone involved."

Gärtner and his colleagues consciously entered the wine business. "For me, wine is a passion. It is very fun for all of us," he admits. "That's the reason we wanted to go into the wine business. We had the feeling that we could contribute something. But we also actively said that we would like to work in this area. Not because it is important for us to earn money – of course we somehow do need to earn our money. But we simply find this line of business cool. So, entrepreneurship in the wine line of business is the coolest thing that we can imagine for us. Because we simply love the product. And the people who participate in it. The wine line of business has cool people who somewhere do their thing with a lot of passion; all of them small entrepreneurs themselves. There are a few headstrong people there, who, let's say, have their own character. But all-in-all, it is interesting and exciting to a high degree. And they especially love what

MAX GÄRTNER

they do, and that radiates an incredibly positive energy. And especially on the producer side, the wineries – that is impressive when you see the work they carry out and when you also understand that there is really an actual philosophy behind the products. That simply is the fascination with the entire subject."

According to Gärtner, to be successful in the wine business you need to have "a very strong technical competence. That is the alpha and the omega. We have not yet spent a single cent externally for design or development. We have done that 100% on our own. If you want to be successful, you first have to know and understand how to sell things online. And then, in a second step, you also have to specialise in the wine topic. Basically we have a strong love for the product itself, it is fun for us. But of course this is not a hobby; we do this professionally. And the thing that makes up professional success in the wine business – in the online wine business – is technical know-how and understanding so that you can then also do online marketing which would otherwise not be feasible."

Even if the Internet wine business has a strong growth, Gärtner estimates "that good specialty stores will continue operating. I know some good specialty stores myself. The experience of tasting right in the shop won't die out. As a specialty store, you simply have to be really active. Just opening the store in the morning won't work. You really have to get involved, do great things. There will surely continue to be a certain consolidation on the producer's side because when the quality is not correct, the situation for the winery will be difficult. Obviously, quality is decisive." Wine sold in discount markets must not taste better than the one that the winery itself tries to sell, otherwise "you have a problem," according to Gärtner. But, he says, the wine quality has clearly improved. "There are hardly any more wineries that make really bad wine. Therefore, I believe that there will be a certain consolidation. However, there will also be an additional professionalization. The online area will be professionalized. There will be no new startup in the online wine business. That much is for sure. Perhaps in the area of mobile business a bit more, but not any more on the Internet. The concepts are now there, people have tried out a bit, some survive, some don't. Since the beginning of 2013, no more money went from professional investors to a wine startup in Germany. The niches are all occupied. And there are professionals who have been in the business for a long time. There are state niches, there are shopping clubs, there are market places that are occupied. All the players are well-defined. There are some concepts that are promising and some that won't work."

In general, Gärtner considers that in the future there will certainly be "many, many possibilities in the wine business to find your path with innovative ideas. But no longer in the area of commerce. So, a thousand good ideas, but you must really start to think outside the box. Just saying that I will somehow purchase and sell wine won't be enough. You have to somehow make sure that you add your seal, your competence, to generate an extra value. All the structures are now so occupied that 20 million euros in capital have already gone into them. With which sort of idea do you have to go to an investor for him to say that really changes everything? There are clubs, there are those that have recommendations, there are market places, there are the traditional commerce models, and in all these startups, many man-years as well as millions of euros have been invested. That

MAX GÄRTNER

means that you really need to have a really extreme concept for an investor to say that's something really new. Perhaps something really sophisticated, an innovation in partial areas of the whole, something that people need. The logistics chain still allows for many, many innovations. I think there are many points at which you can somehow add your competences to the area of wine. But not in e-commerce anymore."

MAX GÄRTNER

GERD RINDCHEN
Managing partner, Rindchen's Weinkontor
Bönningstedt, Germany

G erd Rindchen is managing partner of the wine import business Rindchen's Weinkontor in Bönningstedt near Hamburg. The wine company, founded in 1977, has 12 offices in northern Germany, Berlin, and Munich; the major customers and gastronomy business make up a large part of the turnover. In his branch offices, Rindchen also organises numerous events such as tastings, seminars, culinary evenings, and wine trips.

Rindchen, who studied as an insurance salesman, grew up in Bremerhaven, and he dealt with wine even before his insurance training. However, he earned his first money at the age of 16 in yet another area: in a pub on Sylt, as a fast poet he sold verses that he himself rhymed, to the customers. "Even as a child I read a lot; my nickname was Professor Rindchen", Rindchen says. "At the age of seven, I published my first poem in the Nordsee-Zeitung. I just need a few keywords, and within minutes I can convert them into a poem." Writing poems was quite profitable: "Per poem, I asked for 5 Deutsche Mark; thus, in one evening, I earned over 100 Mark." One day, one of his spontaneous clients was an insurance broker from Hamburg. "He was so pleased with my poems that he immediately wanted to have me as an apprentice", describes Rindchen.

"FOR ME, INDEPENDENCE IS A MEASURE OF SELF-PROTECTION."

Thus, instead of the originally planned study in business administration, he decided to start in the insurance area, and with his old VW bus, which he called Traugott, he moved to Hamburg. Ultimately, the vehicle had also been a key for the wine trading, says Rindchen: at the age of 18, he had started to sell wine, "but at that time not as a goal in life, nor because I somehow drank wine, since as a youth in Bremerhaven people don't socialise with wine, but with beer. It was just the idea to drive a car, to drive the VW bus – Traugott, which I bought with the credit from my father. And I simply wanted to earn money on my own – by delivering newspapers, with moves, and also by taking wine from the south to the north. That's when it really started."

However, Rindchen did realise quickly that his heart tended more towards language arts and enjoyment than for the world of numbers in the insurance companies. "The very first week I knew that that wasn't for me", he admits, but he still completed his apprenticeship. "Education for me is essential, to be able to move things with a certain depth", he comments. After ending his daily work he went after his hobbies: he appeared as a poet and sold wines, which he brought with his VW bus from tours in the Palatinate, to his parents' friends. The first invoice in his archive is from 1977 – "so since then I have been independent", says Rindchen. He then noticed "that I have quite early gathered quite a ragbag, and that I started to really have fun with this topic. For me, wine is a lot of enjoyment, a lot of enthusiasm, and an important part of my life content. Thus, during my apprenticeship and during my civil service I did that in parallel. And then I slipped into it full time."

In 1979 – at the age of 20 – together with his cousin he started to import wine part-time from France to Hamburg, according to Rindchen. In 1983, then, "the jump to the first shop, to independence" occurred. The first office was in the Hamburg City North and was at first rather cumbersome: "A horror: nobody came in, until I got a license to serve beverages, and offered lunch", Rindchen remembers. For the wine selection, he quickly found his own style: "Quite quickly, several things crystallised: a lack of respect for great names, a lack of reverence, no barons and counts of this world, but unknown wineries, great discoveries right around the corner". Then, as now, Rindchens Weinkontor stands for small, quality-oriented producers, as well as own bottling and creations. Rindchen explains his success "from the fact that, from the very beginning, I concentrated on forcing unknown discoveries, but then also to have them exclusively. That was an early characterisation, and I believe that in today's era of the Internet and transparency, it pays for itself, and makes us viable. I am successful because I have a clear idea of what I want and what I don't want. Because I have built up everything myself, and I still myself choose the wines that we sell."

Independence, for Rindchen, is the preferred way of being, having said of himself that he is "completely incompatible with hierarchies". Creativity is his strong point: "Contradictions, for me, are delightful and challenging, and lateral thinkers for me are people like myself." In the company, he is responsible for purchases, marketing, and communications, while his wife Christine is in charge of organisation and human resources. His motivation, to live as a businessperson, is "fun in self-design", explains Rindchen. "During my apprenticeship, there have been a few times when I was subject to extreme arbitrariness, when somebody had to decide about me. I couldn't stand that. For me, independence is a measure of self-defence. I can't stand having the feeling that I know or can do something better, and someone else is practically entitled to throttle that." Rindchen has his own approach "how I imagine a business culture, how I imagine communicating with one another, as well as communication wines to the customers. The selection of wines for the customers, the unknown discoveries, the best price-enjoyment ratio of producing, and this self-determination to a great extent, to be able to carry this through and communicate it in such a way, that's something I only get with independence", he clarifies.

Rindchen perceives entrepreneurship in the wine area as "very different", as he says. "I know many people who are also a bit embittered. Who cling to old times, when people still looked for their exclusivities, when there was a Italian winemaker who happened to have a distributor in Berlin, one in Hamburg, one in Munich, and one in Düsseldorf; in other words, the pre-Internet era. I see many who haven't adapted to the changes, who mourn the old times, and don't really realise why their markets escape from them. And I know others who start into the new world, the Internet, with great hopes. Who set up new sales concepts with venture capital, perhaps even without having an affinity with wine." He also notices "a great uncertainty", explains Rindchen: "Where are we headed? What chance, what future, does the wine specialty trade have? If it has one, will it be stationary or over the Internet? I see many people, as I have always seen, who participate with lots of joy and enthusiasm. But I also see a lot of uncertainty."

THE WINE DEALER HAS CONTACT WITH INTERNET USERS AND WITH SUPERMARKETS; ALSO, HE HAS NO GLAMOUR FACTOR THAT PROTECTS HIM. HE MUST BE SO GOOD IN PURCHASING AND MARKETING THAT HE CAN ASSERT HIMSELF WITH HIS PRODUCTS, IN COMPETITION WITH THE OTHER FORMS OF DISTRIBUTION."

Rindchen looks back: "The seventies were surely a chaotic time, a time when many started to set up alternative wine corner shops – with wine from the barrel and rustic stories and delicatessen specialties added. Then came the time of the professionalization of the eighties and nineties. And starting in the two-thousands we now have a) a threat by the Internet, and b) – something that I consider to be a very important factor – an upgrading of the wine area at sophisticated foot retail companies, who now have an assortment of wares which makes quite a few specialty shops really green with envy. I believe that the stationary, classic wine dealer must think something up, and that he is under pressure from different sides – on the one hand, simply from the Internet, and on the other, from the regional food retail companies, who have discovered wine as a contract model for themselves and in part also handle it as a hobby." The food retail markets also have a clearly higher customer supply than the specialty shops, Rindchen analyses. He wants to cut back the initial fears from the wine specialty shops: "Anybody has a right to enjoy, and we, too, offer good wines starting at four euros."

To be successful, according to Rindchen a wine dealer needs "attentiveness – in other words, the capacity to communicate." He must "be open towards people, and give them the feeling of not being excluded. Many wine dealers commit the error of treating people condescendingly, of giving them the feeling of ignorance, of being a bit maggoty. That shouldn't happen in any case. The wine dealer must be eloquent, he may not be lifted, and he must face the people. He must also take along a person who wants to get a good bottle of wine for five euros and show him full respect; I consider that to be very important. And many colleagues don't do that." In addition, the dealer must "be in love with the product and go along a clear course", for "the first bottle is sold due to marketing reasons; starting with the second bottle, he sells quality", is Rindchen's conviction.

GERD RINDCHEN

A successful wine dealer must "try to maintain a good price-enjoyment ratio in his corresponding niche – however small or large it might be", demands Rindchen. What's important is "to make people an offer, with which they open a bottle at their homes and say: 'I haven't been screwed with this one. This bottle is worth, or more than worth, its price.'" Rindchen describes three scenarios that can result if a customer buys a bottle of wine from him for seven euros: "Either the customer says: 'OK, that's appropriate.' In that case we played a draw. Or he says: 'Recently I bought a wine in the supermarket that cost 5.99 euros and which was at least as tasty.' In that case I lost. Or the customer says: 'The wine is so great that I would even be willing to pay one or two euros more for it.' In that case I won. And my goal is that with every wine, I score with the customer in such a way that they say, at the least, 'The price which I paid for it was worth paying.' That is to say, the customer is not in a shelter; rather he is in contact with Internet users and with supermarkets; also, he has no glamour factor that protects him. He must be so good in purchasing and marketing – in communications – that he can assert himself in the competition against other forms of distribution."

Success, for Rindchen, means "to be content, to live in harmony with your surroundings." He says that his drive is "mainly this desire for harmony, to live in harmony with your surroundings. I say: 'Treat everybody as if you will be broke tomorrow.' Performance, for me, is to be faithful to yourself and thus to be successful." In this sense, for Rindchen, success is also "Rest – for I didn't have that for many years now. I do this for over 35 years. At least 32 of those years were with my back against the wall. We never had enough money, no material security; also, we always had a little bit of latent insolvency risk, since after all I come more from the communicational than from business. Now – touching wood – we have a fairly good phase."

Rindchen differentiates: Business success for me is certainly connected to economic safety – i.e., earn money and set up a pension for old age – but also with confirmation through praise, to have people tell you: 'What you do is good, the people in the shops are friendly, I like your assortments, the wines are tasty.' That, I think, are classical things, nothing extraordinary; confirmation through normal things. To have people tell you 'What you do, you do well, that's fun for us, we like to purchase from you.' To have employees say: 'We like to work for you and to be in your shop.' And that, ideally, all this eventually gets reflected in the bank account."

Rindchen doesn't find it easy to name a recipe for success – "considering that I have worked in such a volatile way for the last years, i.e., not strictly successful, but with clear highs and lows". However, his basic principle can still also be understood as a recommendation: "in any case, remain faithful to your own line." Rindchen outlines his approach as "an almost autistic work: don't look left or right, rather have an own idea which you follow. I was never seriously interested in what my colleagues do. I always had an idea in my head and a plan, how I imagine things, how I interpret wine, how I want to implement wine, how I want to communicate wine, how I want to calculate, how I want to sell it. I always tried to implement this, and I did it regardless of what happens around me. That way I have surely slept through a lot of trends, and perhaps left back quite a lot of potential and money. But on the other hand, we have a completely authentic line, a honed profile. That represents unknown discoveries and the best price-enjoyment ratio. We stand for what we say: 'People who drink names won't find what they want with us. People who buy and drink to rise above his friends or business partners won't find much with us. But somebody who goes out on discoveries with relish, who doesn't care so much about prestige, will be happy with us!'"

Rindchen takes decisions "on the basis of the autistic attitude", as he says. "I have an ideal in mind, and everything is subordinated to that. Motivation, for me, is to stand up in the morning and ask myself: What can I improve? And ideally, to be able to reply to the question successfully." The wine businessman deals with risks "in a fatalistic way: for me, errors are things from which ideally you learn, but sometimes you need a second or third start. For me, that's part of it. I have experienced many situations in which we weren't successful, and we surmounted so many low points that for me, in the end, the situation of economic success almost represented a pleasant surprise. Of course the will is there, to finally be so successful that a dignified retirement is possible. But the possibility of failure is always present, always in the back of my head, since our business area is not very sexy, if you consider it just as earnings potential. There aren't many commercially successful wine merchants, and there are reasons for that." He also considers the future of his company in a detached way, and points out "that we don't have a succession within the family, since our son wants to do something else. The goal is to actually get out of the work life at some moment and to say that we may still have a few nice years ahead of us, and to be covered in this sense. Whether in 20 or 30 years there will still be a Rindchen's Weinkontor or not is, quite frankly, secondary. There is no classic goal in this sense."

The "slightly autistic variation, not to look left or right but to rely on your own compass" is, for Rindchen, also a value principle of his business activity, "so, not to measure yourself a lot and compare yourself with others". Another important value he names is "respect for the taste of the customers, the people. I believe that most people simply have a much, much better inner feeling for taste than what they trust themselves to. I have dealt with an enormous number of people who make themselves small, saying: 'I really have no idea about wine.' And I tell them: 'You don't need to have an idea about wine.' If you go to a car dealer, he doesn't expect from you, either, that you be able to take the engine apart and then assemble it back again."

Rindchen complains: "The wine topic is contaminated by prestige, and I try to get us down from that, to get more roots, to simply say, wine has to do with enjoyment and sensuality. And anybody who feels like it also has a right to conquer this enjoyment for himself and to live it out. I try to make the topic less elitist, to throw it from its pedestal, and to pull down this enjoyment level – pull it up, really. I say: 'Please trust yourself and seek out what tastes good for you and what doesn't; then we can advise you optimally. Forget about prestige!'"

Yet another saying by Rindchen is "to treat everybody transparently – customers, employees, and suppliers. For you always see one another two or three times in your life, and I always treat people as if I were to become insolvent tomorrow. With every wine-grower and every customer that I meet, I ask myself: How would he treat me now, how would he – in retrospect – deal with me, if I lose my job and go broke tomorrow? And

GERD RINDCHEN

GERD RINDCHEN

since I am a person who desires harmony, I desire that people continue liking me and that they like to drink a glass of wine with me. 'This hasn't worked at all today, but you are still quite nice, and you always treated me fairly.' That might be a weird approach, but I have met lots of people who, when they were high on top, and I was very small, treated me like shit. We then also experienced how it was the other way – in other words, I being in a somewhat better position, and they somehow broken. They often had a problem with that, for of course they still knew how they had treated me. I didn't use this against them. You can notice it in the people." For Rindchen, personal integrity is important: "Nowadays there is no safety. If something goes back, at least I don't want to be looked down upon tomorrow by the people with which I deal every day – those are basically the customers, employees, and suppliers."

Rindchen considers that his leadership style towards his employees is "not good – in the sense that I am not myself very structured and wouldn't be able to provide a lot of structure. I believe that I am quite good with soft factors, in the sense that I can motivate people. But I can hardly tell them what I really want or expect from them, and where I see them. For that, I have Christine, my wife, who complements me and is much more consistent. She is much more empathic for the people who work for us, and worries about how they will well cared for and motivated. And she is also clearer in the specifications, what they are to do. Thus, I would say that my leadership style is chaotic."

Correspondingly, an optimal employee is "one who can read my thoughts, so to speak, without me communicating them", says Rindchen. "However, that doesn't work quite well. For the people who work with us, we look for friendliness, human attentiveness, and enthusiasm, rather than professional knowledge. Professional knowledge is something we can transmit, and our assortment is great, really great. I believe that I am a sensational buyer and that the assortment is unequalled with respect to precision, clarity, and price-enjoyment ratio. We can then also get people who work for us enthusiastic for it, that's not the problem. The problem is to find people who can really get enthusiastic, who carry our message outwards with a shine in their eyes. Ultimately, this of course also applies to the office staff, i.e., the people who are at the phone."

"THE POSSIBILITY OF FAILURE IS ALWAYS PRESENT, SINCE OUR AREA IS NOT SEXY ENOUGH, IF YOU SIMPLY CONSIDER THE EARNINGS POTENTIAL."

Rindchen summarises: "I really look for self-determined people, who get motivated from the inside, to do a good job, for the immediately daily pressure which comes from us as the company management is not very pronounced. It isn't as if we go there in the morning and start shitting around. We depend on people who are able to motivate themselves by themselves. That's what we look for. And they, in turn, have a working environment with a relatively large amount of freedom and relatively few restrictions." As a businessperson he must show "respect for the personality, respect for the own taste, for the own preferences" of the employees, and "provide an environment in which, first of all, employees have the feeling of being taken seriously and accepted as people, and to be able to develop on this basis."

From digitalisation and new media, Rindchen expects "more chances" and more direct contact to new customers: "A very, very small niche – we do a lot in this respect. We make the wine shop of the Süddeutsche Zeitung, we cooperate with Amazon, with brands4friends, with Channel21, with all sorts of distribution methods, with magazines such as the Fokus, with newspapers such as the Rheinische Post, the Berliner Morgenpost or the Hamburger Abendblatt. We provide publishing houses with revenue models, how they can refinance themselves with successful merchandise sales. We really work with all channels you can imagine – with respect to both classic media and new media. But all this is based, for us, on an enormous procurement competence. That only works because we simply buy incredibly good wares, in part at incredibly cheap prices, through our path of special companies, unknown discoveries, young wineries – otherwise all this wouldn't be possible. We take all this with us, with the full pot."

In this context, marketing cooperation is very important for Rindchen: If I were to insist on the classic, stationary specialty trade, I think I would be condemned. We are successful in the medium term if we include these media. You can also be successful in the medium term if you try to create exclusivities and thus raise the added value potential. Someone who focuses on the known wines – whether they are brand wines at the entry level, brand champagne or the amply known Bordeaux – one who only deals with marketing these products is at the end of the food chain, because he is comparable. And something that is comparable is either too expensive or it doesn't contribute to the profit margin. That's the equation. You can only try to get away from this by having your own exclusivities, your own special bottlings, things with which you simply set up a market that didn't exist before, and then you can actively deal in that."

For the future, Rindchen expects a certain consolidation in the wine business. Among the market actors who don't need to earn their livelihood from selling wine, there will be "many fragmented ones who remain". With this, Rindchen refers to the so-called garage dealers: "The classic teacher couple who can deduct the vacations in the Toscana from their taxes because they declared a wine business as a side-line income will survive in any case. Those are the garage dealers – I have been one of those as well, it's interesting. There will always be niches. Apart from that, I believe that in the stationary area the high-class food retail merchants will continue scoring points in the next few years." These merchants are well-known, have a large customer base, and the capital required to "finance that throughout", explains Rindchen. In the specialty trade, there will "be a few niche providers who survive"; those are "high-grade specialists" with an exquisite offer. "But those who will have a difficult time will be the second-class merchants, the corner wine dealers, who in part have an overlapped assortment, in part are too expensive, and actually don't have much special to offer, not much profile", warns Rindchen. "It will be very difficult for them in the next few years. Merchants come increasingly from all parts, from the Internet, from the food retail, from specialists."

A significant future key qualification in the wine area identified by Rindchen is impartiality. As a dealer, to concentrate exclusively on large, well-known brand names won't bring a dealer to success, for "those are indeed exactly the things which are transparent, and sold via the price". In this area, the profit margins will decrease, predicts Rindchen: "There will always be someone, somewhere, who gets it for less." Therefore he relies

GERD RINDCHEN

on "impartiality, experimentation, the capacity to put your own accents, and openness towards the new media" as success factors in the next few years.

Young businesspeople in the wine sector should "keep the costs low, go their own paths, and make sure that the type isn't comparable", advises Rindchen. Once again he emphasises independence, "that's a very important factor. You can only provide added value if you aren't compatible. To be incompatible, you must create or discover something that's your own. That means discovery rather than traditional sommelier knowledge: 'I will now get myself free from everything, and only decide according to my own taste.' That's what I have done." Instead of the wines, according to Rindchen it is the merchant himself who must become a brand: "Due to the fact that we have so many unknown wines, a person can indeed not decorate themselves by saying 'We buy the Frescobaldi, or the Rothschild, or something like that.' Rather, in Hamburg it happens indeed that people say: 'We buy from Rindchen.' And that stands for a certain statement. A statement that in part even angers me, for we stand for good and inexpensive wines. When our wines are expensive, then they are really, really good. If we sell a wine for 18 euros, that is of course the Mega-Granate. In part, people won't purchase that, since they don't think far enough. I believe that for the people we are indeed, basically, a good and inexpensive wine dealer. But that's more and more a niche in which we currently survive, with economic success. In that sense, I can live with that – even if that is unfair against our competitors in the premium segment."

GERD RINDCHEN

MARTIN KÖSSLER
Co-founder and manager,
K&U Weinhalle
Nuremberg, Germany

For over 30 years, Martin Kössler is the manager of the wine business K&U Weinhalle in Nuremberg. The "K" in the company name stands for his family name; the "U" is for his business colleague, Dunja Ulbricht. K&U was founded in 1982 by a total of four partners. At that time, "from a dedicated group of wine tasters, a small wine business arose, which provided a growing number of wine enthusiasts with 'stuff'", says Kössler. At first, the offering only included Italian wines, but it soon expanded all over Europe and finally overseas. "The demands grew, so did the turnover; the number of employees increased continuously", says Kössler. "When the turnover increased to several times what it used to be, K&U became what is today GmbH & Co KG with silent partners, foreign subsidiaries, and millions in turnover."

Kössler started off in the scientific area. Kössler, who got a diploma in material engineering, studied chemistry and physics, and shortly before graduating he changed to the wine area. A decisive factor for this was a stay in the United States, as he narrates: "We always vacationed in wine-growing areas, and that fascinated me. The most important station was surely California, since there I met something that is virtually unknown in our own country; namely, technical wine tasting. That was like a flash. So, people taste a wine, and they don't say that's a good wine, but rather it is about immediately knowing how it is manufactured, what defects it has, and why." When tasting with Californian winegrowers, he "noticed clearly that all these people had committed these errors themselves. Not because they studied, but because they practically made wine in their garage." Thus, he learned "to understand wine in a different way. So far I had always understood it with my senses, and then suddenly I understood it technically." By tasting with the winegrowers in California he experienced "a completely different approach to wine", says Kössler, "suddenly making the wine come alive. That is no longer a construct; rather, suddenly it starts to live, and you notice that they really can find, and taste, the errors they committed in the wine. And that was really the greatest influence that I ever had in my entire wine life. This is a topic that occupies me. In this sense, this is really a rigorous development from technology back to the senses."

Kössler remembers that there had not been a conscious decision to become an entrepreneur: "That just came out that way. You get into youthful madness." However, he appreciates his life as an entrepreneur and considers it to be fun: "The fascinating thing in our line of business is that you have lots of enthusiastic people. And to make a profit out of this enthusiasm is very difficult; for then you suddenly get the parameters: to pay

MARTIN KÖSSLER

employees on time, to keep the business working, to be able to pay the winegrowers – that's a really difficult process." As a wine dealer, Kössler points out to different motivations for founding and managing a business: "Nowadays, modern businesses only result from marketing and sales. They just took a brief look at wine and said, we can make some money here, and come up with some concept. The other part of the market resulted from enthusiasm, but not from proficiency in the sense of entrepreneurship. And bringing the two things together is not entirely simple."

For Kössler himself, the motivation as an entrepreneur is "the immediate feedback for doing", as he states it. "Entrepreneurship has a positive and a negative aspect. The positive aspect is that you remain fresh and young, since you are constantly challenged; you always have a thorn in the flesh. That's the competition, that's the market, that's all sort of things. The other aspect is: It is a treadmill in which you can't stand still. You run and run and run, and there is no possibility to stand still. Nowadays, standing still means death, and that also applies to entrepreneurship. You can't indulge in a minute of rest; you really have to watch out for the market, plan ahead. But that's precisely what I find to be fun." This became clear to him when before his planned graduation he worked as an engineer in the automotive industry, describes Kössler. He could have "easily" stayed there; however, "Today I am happy that I didn't do that, because I need this challenge. I believe that you are born as an entrepreneur. It isn't something you can learn; you have to have it in your blood."

According to Kössler, to be an entrepreneur is "always a tightrope walk. There are sleepless nights, and there are nights in which you sleep great. Specifically when you are successful. But now in our line of business there are so many tempests and structural changes. That wasn't easy. But in the end we managed – or I managed – to always foresee trends, to foresee developments. And that's what I consider to be fun." The "wine itself" isn't what gives him the greatest pleasure in his activity today, admits Kössler. "Of course wine still has a charm, and it goes through incredible changes. But what makes is much more fun for me today as an entrepreneur is the challenge, to recognize markets, analyse them, and use the information to make decisions. That's really the driving force for me today."

That also means "to communicate wine; that's much more exciting". In this sense, Kössler considered entrepreneurship in a differentiated way: "One part of entrepreneurship is the numbers, and the other part is the philosophy behind it. And I see a task there for us as businessmen. You might say, as communicators of the market – to make market, consult winegrowers in the sense of bringing the market close to them. And indeed also to shape the market in small areas, as we do it. After all, our function has changed quite a lot. Our entrepreneurship changed from selling bottles to become an essential communicator. And that's what I find so much fun today."

Kössler explains that as a wine dealer, author and consultant he researches the question "why wine tastes as it does". He wants to "make quality and taste understandable through information about the product", and he laments, "that the business area continues indulging in inflationary cheers and stupid evaluation citations, instead of achieving more interest in good wine through profound, critical and self-critical information".

Good wine, according to Kössler, is "a naturally pure, sensually sophisticated foodstuff, which free from ideologies and dogmas is an expression of natural and cultural variety". According to Kössler, K&U buy their wines all over the world directly from the producer, without exceptions. "Thus, we really know our providers personally. We don't just act as if, we really know them", he emphasizes. "During our regular onsite visits, our exclusively artisanal winegrowers not only open barrels and bottles for tasting, they also disclose their work procedures on the vineyard and cellar. For us, the type of wine cultivar, bio-logic or biodynamic cultivation, soil and leafage preparation, harvesting and selection procedures, as well as development and fermentation methods – together with the chemical control analysis – are essential quality criteria". Thus, K&U includes in its portfolio its own taste and quality concept, which "doesn't submit to conventions or to the point and evaluation dictates of the market", but rather follows its own style "both self-consciously and independently".

Kössler sees the objective of his entrepreneurial activity in "successfully setting up a business", but that must not be understood to have just a single dimension: "Being successful doesn't mean that the sales increase all the time. I think that here, too, as a society we are in the midst of a massive change, that we no longer have the growth that we had for the last 30 years". Kössler says that his endeavour is "to create jobs that are fun for employees, that are fun for me personally. I have the great luxury of having a profession which earns money through its nose, and I don't go to the company every day with a stomach-ache; rather, I like going there. My personal goal is that everybody be able to do this. And it would be nice if this also has an effect on the customers."

Kössler doesn't make decisions clearly just in his head or just out of a gut feeling; he says: "There is surely some of both. After 32 years, that naturally includes an extreme knowledge of the market." As an example, he cites the developments in champagne, where "12, 15 years ago" a group of about 25 young winegrowers started to produce champagne in a new style. "Those are business decisions; where you say: 'I am married with a successful house; should I change that? Should I add something new?' And those are decisions, for those you have your gut feeling." He says that these circumstances have been favoured by the fact that he "had always had an international orientation" and "always was able to travel a lot. And therefore, I think, I simply have a sort of inter-national horizon for our business area which helps me in such business decisions, since I believe that I am able to see markets. Quite simply, what happens in Japan, in America, in England, will eventually also happen here. Those are aids that obviously have a si-gnificant influence on my company decision", says Kössler.

When dealing with risks, you "certainly need some perseverance", Kössler assures. He identifies two types of companies; on the one hand, "today's modern companies: here, I need to turn over the entire inventory within 14 days. Everything that I don't turn over, everything that hasn't been turned over, is kicked out." On the other hand, he himself at K&U has an approach in which the emphasis is not on the capability of quickly selling the wines, but rather their individuality: "We see that in quite different perspectives. And that, I think, is simply a very old-fashioned entrepreneurial point of view. If today I believe something different, I go through with it. Of course, if it doesn't work and we have to drink it all up ourselves it becomes embarrassing. That is painful, and in that

MARTIN KÖSSLER

case we change something. But on the other hand, as a result of an analysis of the market and its changes, ultimately we are forced to act in a niche, and I have to communicate this niche and develop it. And as a result, such decisions arise, and you stand by them." According to Kössler's conviction, that also includes mistakes and contradictions: "Mistakes are extremely important for me; it is only through them that I learn. And for me, contradictions are an elementary driving force for my activity."

Individuality is also an explicit part of Kössler's definition of success: "Success is when you survive", he laughs. "With a concept that others consider to be unnecessary." But it's about much more than this. "For me, success is when your occupation is fun. And I am successful because I find my occupation to be fun. Success is when you can pay your employees on time. Success is when something is left over, when the separation between private life and company is not too strong, and when you ultimate have a fulfilled life. I believe that that is the greatest success that you can have. And this is something that affects us entrepreneurs quite positively, since we have an immediate result from what we do. If we do something successful it comes back to us, and it is something that you can immediately measure. And that is feels good for the soul."

"YOU ARE BORN AS AN ENTREPRENEUR. THAT ISN'T SOMETHING YOU CAN LEARN."

The highest rank in Kössler's personal value system is credibility – for him, it is "the most important thing. A guiding principle for all actions. We want to be credible. For me, that's what it's all really about." And Kössler graphically shows us this credibility by formulating his two most essential beliefs quite drastically: "First, I don't want to work with assholes all the time. That's a real belief. And second, I don't want to screw others; rather, we really want to do what we stand for, and want to act in a credible way. And in this occupation we are able to do that." Another important value in his capacity as entrepreneur named by Kössler is humaneness, "the human dimension. The word 'sustainability' is spent; we would rather not use that, but we really want to be credible, authentic. That's the company's goal."

Kössler clarifies that he doesn't have a concrete recipe for success: "It just goes on and on." In his opinion however, his employees are an elementary part of the business's success model. With a wink, however, he describes his leadership style as "catastrophic". He never "learned to guide employees in this sense. You grow into it, and the employees come due to the wine; they are enthusiastic about this. Now, to really put that into practice, so that it affects everybody in the company and to let everybody participate, isn't simple. You have to learn that laboriously. It is a leadership style which, in my opinion, affects the employees strongly, in the sense of 'I will take it with me on this trip'. And therefore we hardly ever have serious staff problems, because these are all people who stand behind this idea. However, I think this is due in part to the fact that we are a company with a clear idea. People come to use because they follow this idea."

MARTIN KÖSSLER

The ideal employee for Kössler's company "must of course have a private interest for this topic – enjoyment, challenge, communication, etc. And they really all do that." The only suitable employee is one "who doesn't just come and sits out his job; rather, it must be a vocation. That, I think, is the great difference, that we have a profession and not just a job. And the employee must also understand this as his vocation. That's the great thing about this business area: it's something that can get people enthusiastic." The hierarchy at K&U is flat; Kössler explains that there is a medium-level leadership layer mainly due to technical reasons: "Just think about the Internet; it has to be constantly maintained, etc. Therefore obviously there are some people at a higher level. Also because they need to make independent decisions about technology."

The entrepreneur can and must also himself create the conditions to enable his employees to achieve what he demands from them. Kössler names this as an essential requirement: "to fulfil the notions". Here, however, the wine business is in a special situation: That isn't really a professional profile that you take out of a drawer. This is a professional profile that arises de facto. And that is the great challenge. For this profession, you can't just look for somebody by announcing: 'Looking for a wine dealer.' After all, in Germany we don't have that. Rather, those are professions you grow in to, and which you have to fill in according to your personality. And that is really something exciting for somebody who is willing and able to do that." However, according to Kössler this means that many of his colleagues are overwhelmed by this: "Therefore you have so many crutches in the wine business, and unfortunately only a few who really know how to do it", he judges.

In general, Kössler assigns considerable deficits to the wine business and specifically to wine commerce: "I consider my area of business as one that is incredibly unprofessional. Most people don't have criteria for what they do. Wine sellers for example have virtually no concepts. I consider this wine area a very, very unprofessional area, and also, if you allow me to say this, one that has no vision. I don't consider it to be innovative. The fascinating part is that it is an archaic area of business. Very archaic. There are no contracts; things are agreed upon by handshakes. The entire area is incredibly transparent. That is really fascinating, because it is really archaic, that isn't progressive." Kössler also names what, in his opinion, is missing the most: "Vision. Vision and knowledge. Competence. There is no competence. There is no professional competence. Hardly anybody can corroborate that. There is a lot of rambling, a lot about taste. That happens to the entire business area." Kössler complains that "there is a lot of mixing", and that "there is really no professional honour, no professional ethics". This is a really weird story. A wine dealer must have international connections, he must be able to talk technically at the level of a winegrower. Actually he must be better than the winegrowers, for after all, winegrowers are no tasters. And actually he should be the communicator of an area of business, not just a seller of bottles. That's what I consider to be entrepreneurship today, in the wine business."

Kössler sees the wine dealer as confronted with at least the same challenges as the winegrower: "The winegrower has three professions: to grow the wine, to make the wine, and to sell the stuff. And we must be good merchants – at least we should be – and here, too, only very few actually are. Finally, we should be visionaries with respect to the market. We should make the market and not just amble behind it. In this sense, we should be

MARTIN KÖSSLER

networked in marketing, and we should be good wine people. Thus, we should also have visions, concepts, a programme; not just offer some wines. That is the key qualification for an entrepreneur in the wine area. To stand for something, to have a profile."

Due to the dynamic market environment, the progress in information technology and social media, the challenges get even greater. According to Kössler, "Of course, that's an incredible structural change, and we have it all over the place. In the past, businesses worked with catalogues; nowadays, nobody reads them anymore." He says that he had foreseen the effects of globalisation early and positioned himself accordingly. He closely followed "how this development arose, that wineries get disconnected, that they say, 'We individualise, we go back to the vineyards, we go biological, we want to maximally individualise the wines.' After all, we reflect this, we might say that this was our entrepreneurial decision to participate in this step. Entirely against the market, since there wasn't yet a market for it; we had to create it in the first place. But that was a huge challenge, and that is precisely what interests me today." Once again, it is about the issue how wines are communicated nowadays and how they should be: "After all, nowadays wine is an entirely different medium than it was in the past. It used to be elitist; there were high barriers to get into the wine business at all. Nowadays – you just have to take a look at Facebook, what people talk about – wine is a commonplace product, and many people can participate in the talk about it. And of course that also makes the entire issue exciting, since I have different possibilities of influence, to intervene here."

Thus, in the technological and social development Kössler recognizes "more of a chance than a risk. After all, it's an old-fashioned area of business, which never knew how to properly communicate. The contents of the wines, of course, would also be quite different. I need to understand wine in a different way than I did so far. I have to do that every day. I don't yet have a recipe to do that. But that is surely the greatest challenge that confronts us. It is not the quality. On the side of the wineries, there is the quality of the distribution, and on the side of the business, there is the quality of communication: How do I continue getting to my customers in this historical change? That's the challenge that we have to confront. And there is a lot, really a lot, to be done there."

Kössler explains that after the turn of the millennium, for five or six years he had been "completely unsettled" – "there were the wineries; the entire market was uncertain. Nobody knew what would happen. Today, I think, we can more or less channel that. You can see it in the numbers: 80% of all wines sold in Germany pass through the self-service shelf. That means that the specialized shops, the classic wine sale, is simply pushed into a niche. And now we might say that it has to get out of there and must try to define itself in a new way, or else it will go even further into the niche. And it must redefine itself; we must reinvent ourselves. As I already mentioned, we also have a different role. Much more than in the past, we are suddenly communicators. That, I think, is the result of this digital revolution."

In the long term, Kössler believes that the wine market will separate into two parts: "One is the area that we have now – more or less since the year 2000. What we might call the industrial wines, the inexpensive everyday wines as a drink for an effect. That is to say, it is technologically more and more improved. Quite drinkable, but relatively normed." However, that is not his world and his market, for "That which will emerge – and I work hard for that – is the greatest challenge for us: to communicate wine as a manufactured product, an authentic artisanal product, so that the steep slope makes sense, that the manufacturing makes sense, and that the client can resolve this. And that the reason he drinks wine is because it is such a fascinating natural product with all the challenges confronted by the winery. Thus, I really believe that we will have these two directions. On the one hand, the technical product wine as a design product, and on the other hand, the cultural product that you follow even in your spare time because it is something valuable. That, I think, is also important for the customer."

"IN OUR LINE OF BUSINESS, THERE ARE A VARIETY OF PROFESSIONS THAT REALLY AREN'T PROFESSIONS, SINCE I CAN'T DESCRIBE THEM IN FIVE SENTENCES."

Kössler is not afraid from young, progressive start-ups in the wine business, which get on the market more and more thanks to the assistance of financial investors, and which usually specialise exclusively on online and shipment sales: "They only cook with water. And when I look at it – there is not a single model that acts according to contents. Rather, they are re-cooked old soups, where wine is sold by price, or by points. A lot of money has been invested there, and we can't compete against that, but the content is missing – no matter who you consider." In view of this background, Kössler's forecast for the future sounds determined: "That will work for a while, and then it will peter out, if they don't invent anything new. Because we continue developing, because we have to react to that, and we do it. And because we – the few who are left – ultimately have the contents and the experience to transmit that. They can't do that. They only think about the price, the pressure of money, by stupidly reserving over Google." However, he thinks that this threatens to overtax the wine consumer. "The customer will more and more move in one direction or in the other. And then there will be a clearing up of the market; on the one hand, the strongest and largest will win, and on the other hand there will indeed be special niches, but these must be filled up with content, not just with gimmicks."

In this context, Kössler considers the price to be unusable as a competition factor: "Sorry, but the price discussion is from before-yesterday. It's time that we forget about it. If we don't manage to do that, we have screwed it up in this business area – and quite badly so. For this won't help us advance. Rather, we must transmit values; we must say why the wine from steep slopes can't cost three euros. Why it has to cost seven euros, or perhaps eight, nine, or ten. That's the challenge for the future! To convey wine as fun, as content, as a cultural heritage. And none of these startups is able to do that. Not one of them. I follow this quite closely. Nor does any of them try it – they don't even begin to try it."

According to Kössler's assessment, the wine business of the future will have large and complex tasks: "It has to be extremely well-prepared, precisely in our current time. So, it must be well-prepared with respect to the Internet, to technology, and it must get involved with marketing. That's quite a lot. And of course with respect to wine, it will have to be capable of quite a lot more than what we are currently capable of. Also

MARTIN KÖSSLER

what we currently do. So I think that the challenge is especially of a technical nature. It must really be able to speak eye-to-eye with the companies and have international connections; otherwise it has no chance whatsoever." Lateral thinkers would have an advantage: "I consider lateral thinkers to be visionaries. I believe that people who don't think laterally will hardly be successful in the modern world. There are many modern managers; none of them is a lateral thinker."

Kössler summarizes in one word what makes an entrepreneur in the wine area of business successful – including young newcomers – today and in the near future: "Profile, profile, profile. Don't look. The great thing is: when you get started, you are naive. You have an idea in your head and follow it strictly. And that's precisely what all these start-ups are missing. They are incredibly calculating. A clear concept is given, one that has already worked hundreds of times elsewhere, on other markets. They didn't have any new idea. 'What works with shoes also ought to work with wine', is their reasoning. And that's precisely the mistake, that's why they are so soulless. What counts in our area of business is a company's credibility, its soul. And I would try to come from the side, from the enthusiasm. However, I would implement that with competence, technology, know-how, and networking."

Despite his criticism towards start-up companies in the wine business, Kössler concedes: "There are some that are great, greatly done. But the content isn't new. That's all the same brew. And I think that the few people who are now successful, for example among bloggers, where there are some that are really great, those are the niches. There you have people who have developed an incredible competence. And they will continue being successful with this competence. But only just using a bio stamp, that won't work any long. Or only natural wine, or orange wine. That's past. There must be more. Today there is more. There is a completely different challenge for a company. And this challenge is characterized especially by communication. Therefore it is all about enthusiasm and not about calculation."

"A WINE DEALER MUST BE THE COMMUNICATOR OF A LINE OF BUSINESS, NOT JUST A SELLER OF BOTTLES. THAT'S WHAT I CONSIDER, NOWADAYS, TO BE ENTREPRENEURSHIP IN WINE COMMERCE."

Kössler points out once again that one of the peculiarities in the wine area of business is the fuzziness in specific job descriptions, and that younger professionals should perceive this as an opportunity: "There are professions that come out of the drawer. They are clearly outlined, and therefore they are studied so successfully: business administration, law, medicine, etc. In our line of business there is an incredible amount of professions that really aren't professions, because I can't describe them in five sentences. But if somebody is interested in this area – savouring, wine, manufacture, marketing, etc. – there is an incredible variety of possible professions that only become a profession by the fact that I fill them out. That would be my message to all the young people who are interested in wine. That you don't see yourself as powerless against this, but that you get interested in it, that you tackle it. It should be tackled with a vision,

MARTIN KÖSSLER

WINE
ENTREPRENEURS

with respect to quality, and I am one hundred percent certain that wine also provides a future in this sense. We also need that. We need a new wine business. We need a wine business that has a vision, a concept, that is slick in a technical sense – and not the sleepy bottle dealers from the past, who are more retarding than visionary. And that is a very important issue that is dear to me."

MARTIN KÖSSLER

Founder, Vom Fass
Waldburg, Germany

Johannes Kiderlen is the founder and previous chairman of the board of Vom Fass AG in Waldshut, which uses a franchise system to sell wines, beverages, vinegars and oils, and fills bottles in different sizes in the shop for customers. Kiderlen, who studied as a cooper and beverage engineer, initially took over, from his father, an import business for wine and grape juice, which he continued, and then at first established a beverage market chain.

Kiderlen says that he had been a businessperson from the start. "My parents had a wine shop, and when I was still young they always said: Eventually, you'll take over the business. That was quite clear, I wasn't really asked. My father was sick; he was in the war for 10 years. At that time, I wanted to do an apprenticeship as a cooper and go to Geisenheim. But when I had my engineering title and was finished in Geisenheim, I immediately had to start with the shop." The trading company at that time had been "a shop that wasn't worth anything", for it "only traded in cheap wines from Italy" which they bottled themselves. "I could see when I would go broke", Kiderlen comments drily. "We already had a retail shop in Ravensburg, and then I also took over a retail shop in Biberach. That was a wine shop which had already sold open wines, and then we also started to sell a few things open."

"CHANGE IS IMPORTANT, BUT IT MUST BE LONG-TERM."

At that time, he had also provided the largest supermarket chain with wine – "there, you always have to be the cheapest one, otherwise there is no deal", describes Kiderlen. But then he concentrated more on wine sales in his own shops, "and when I had sufficient turnover in the retail business, I relinquished the wholesale trade. I told them, from one day to the other: Well, no more wine from me. They were thunderstruck. At that time I knew that that was enough to live from. So, I had always been a businessperson. I was born into that. Nor could I get out of it, for when you take over a business from the parents, you also have debts! At that time, when my wife and I took over the company, we owed two million Mark." If Kiderlen had had the choice after his studies, "I would probably never have stayed in Germany. I was always a person who liked to get out. I even had a position available in Taiwan, to build plants. I would never have gotten into the parents' business, if I hadn't been under pressure. But that way, I developed out of the necessity, and was also able to build up a successful business", the Vom Fass founder recounts.

JOHANNES KIDERLEN

The initial impulse for the sale of loose wines and liquor started from a large sherry delivery for his shops. Instead of the two pallets he had ordered, he got a truckload of them – "that was a very good quality in bottles, but it didn't work, since it had no brand name", Kiderlen remembers. Then he had an idea: "People repeatedly came to my shop and told us how things are done in Italy, that you can buy wine directly, openly, in a can, or oil from the oil farmer. I thought about it, that people always liked that, when they were on vacations, and that's really how the Vom Fass (German for "from the barrel") concept started. I simply did that: We opened the bottles and decanted it into barrels, and we sold sherry from the barrel. People could have a taste, and suddenly the sherry was sold in a short time." Thus he noticed that customers get confident "if you can first taste when it is dispensed from the barrel. And that's how the idea developed. Quite early, we expanded our shops in Ravensburg and Biberach with these open products."

However, it wasn't possible to transfer the concept to Kiderlen's beverage market chain. He also tried to introduce the open offer there, "but that failed", the businessman admits frankly. "In a beverage market, people want to quickly buy beer or mineral water, and don't want to spend time there. There it didn't work, but we then simply virtually outsourced this idea, with which we started in Biberach and Ravensburg." In 1994, Kiderlen provided a young man, who showed interest in his sales concept, with a shop, at his own expense, in Aalen, and the same year two more shops followed in Landshut and Nuremberg. "That worked very well", he summarizes, "and in just a year, it was clear to us that it works very well as a franchise system. Thus, it developed almost explosively."

In 1995, Kiderlen founded the Vom Fass AG in Ravensburg as a franchising central, which later changed its headquarters to Waldburg. He sold the beverage market chain – his wife was initially not enthusiastic about it, as he recounts: "We had two small children, and we were well-positioned at that time. She didn't like giving up this security and starting again from scratch." But Kiderlen had recognised: "There are more and more single households, and they prefer to buy in small quantities." And he names additional favourable conditions for his plan, after the possibility of multiplying the business concept had already shown to be feasible: "After all, I travel a lot – whether it is in France or in Italy – and at that time, I was around quite a lot among providers. The knowledge about retail trade, since I was always in the shop", was also important and advantageous. Through this personal experience as a merchant, he learned soon "to do what the customer wants, not what I want", says Kiderlen. "Listening to the customer was the most important thing for me, so I said: We have to do what the people want. The Vom Fass idea hit the spot about certain requirements – this also applies to wine, etc., if you can first taste it and then get the exact quality."

In the first two years after founding it, the franchise system grew by almost 70 shops a year. Now there are over 280 franchisees in over 30 countries all over the world, even in Asia. "Of course you can't just go ahead and copy a German concept one-to-one", explains Kiderlen. "You need to adapt to the local conditions and always be open for something new."

On the wine market, Kiderlen has a special position with his trade concept. He outlines the market situation: "Today we have these discounters, which get stronger and stronger, which take away market shares. But of course in this case the wine has a certain anonymity. Even if it has "Selection Franz Keller" written on it, the wine doesn't really come from Franz Keller; rather, many wineries somewhere deliver their grapes or their surpluses, and the wine is produced there." Kiderlen refers to scale effects and grape purchases. For other customers, it's important to know where a wine comes from. These people link wine with an experience; they travel to the winegrowers and purchase wine directly from the producer. This philosophy is taken up by Vom Fass, explains Kiderlen: "There simply is a certain type of customers who go to Bardolino, purchase at a nice winery, and fill their trunk." However, when they finish their wine, these customers "don't go back down to Bardolino, but rather they go to Vom Fass or order from us in the Internet shop", says Kiderlen. "However, the price must be right, so that we don't charge twice as much as the winery – whether it is in Italy, Spain, or southern France."

"AT SOME MOMENT YOU ARE DRIVEN BY THE MARKET, THE MARKET DRIVES YOU, AND THAT IS FUN."

According to Kiderlen, a clear offer is important: Wine dealers "with a thousand types of wine and a confusing assortment will lose market shares. In the next few years, a lot will change here, I think. The typical specialty shop, which has an all-round assortment and covers everything, will have a hard time. I am sure that only one who limits his assortment and really stands behind it has a certain chance." Kiderlen also considers it essential to have an online shop: "Online – that can no longer be avoided; the customer simply wants to get informed. The young people all get informed online. You would also do it that way, you would also get into the Internet and take a look, what does that one offer, and what does he do."

Professional competence in the wine business, according to Kiderlen's opinion, is not limited "to be able to describe the wine nicely and say, that one is good, and to add nice word images"; rather, the dealer "also needs the knowledge. Today, a wine dealer should have worked at some point in the vineyards, he should have knowledge about the topic of biological wines, he should know how it is produced, how it is sprayed, how the soil conditions are. What type of soil does a Riesling need? Those are all things that he should know, not just by reading about them, but also by getting informed on-site and then also by setting up a relationship with his producers." Formerly, when he was in the shop himself, he had "always sold the wines from wineries which I know. That provides a conviction, in that case something shines within, and that goes over, like a spark, to the customer." A dealer who sells wine from 50 or 60 wineries, but doesn't know the companies, "has no advantage compared to discounters or supermarkets. The sales girl in the food retail doesn't know the wineries either, but as soon as you make an effort and deal with it, you have a certain chance. Still, it will get more and more difficult for the wine specialty shops."

JOHANNES KIDERLEN

In this context, Vom Fass benefits from a certain spread in the offer, explains Kiderlen: "Of course we earn money from wine, we have to earn money from wine, but we have the advantage that we also have vinegar and oil, as it were as a supplement, which help us with our gross margin. Liquors provide us with a good gross margin, especially whisky, as well as cognac, etc." Wine on its own is "difficult", due to the price policy: "You just saw some beautiful wine from the Rheingau at the wine specialty shop, and then you access the Internet and see that you can get it for three euros cheaper, in Rheingau at the winery. Either the wine specialty shops reduce the price, to become credible once more, or the winery gives the wine dealer a significant discount – and he doesn't really like to do that. The discounts which the wineries give the wine dealers simply get smaller." Thus, Kiderlen expects the customers to increasingly buy directly from the producer: "Nowadays, wineries have 40, 50, or 60 percent of private customers. A winery in Germany, who might have three, four or five hectares of vineyards, and has to live off that, is not necessarily able to provide the wine shops – he can't survive that way. He has to make sure that he establishes a private clientele. He must make sure that he also provides a few specialty shops regionally, but he won't give him the percentages that he used to give in the past." Therefore the dealers will change to cheaper foreign wines, according to Kiderlen. However, he also observes that meanwhile German wines once again increase in popularity among the customers, since thanks to a reduction in yields the wine quality has clearly improved.

The joy with your own activity, according to Kiderlen, is an important motivation and success factor. He comes back once more to the topic of his parents' company: "That which I took over was fun for me – selling cheap wines. If you do something and sell something that isn't fun for you, you won't have business success either. At that time, when we made these wine markets, I was more content. Today at Vom Fass I can choose the best, no matter where it is, and we can sell that. Quality is the only criterion. And that is fun, when you can sell a product that is also perfect."

Business success, for Kiderlen, is dual: "On the one hand, of course the financial aspect, that has to work. The bottom line is that it's no good if you say, that's fun, I sell the best wares, etc., but at the end of the year nothing is left. Thus, financial success is an important aspect. But you must also sell a product that you consider fun. Motivation, for me, is the quality – and satisfied customers, and satisfied employees. We also train many young people, and that is fun for us, if we see: those used to be with us as trainees or as vocational academy students, and they advance, they get on, they get out into the world."

His personal success, according to Kiderlen, is "to be healthy, and to simply be satisfied at the end of the year or after some stage. Satisfaction. For me, performance is to be ready to do everything and not to shy away from any work – from the simple area upwards. I am successful because I simply like to work a lot, that's fun for me. And when I always advance. I have a great team, a great business, and of course that's a lot of fun. I also consider this to be a business success: to be economically successful, to also have a great relationship with the employees and have them cooperate with one another, and to sell wares that continue working afterwards. When you have these factors you need nothing better", is Kiderlen's conviction.

Not only as a wine dealer, but also as a franchise dealer, Kiderlen values quality highly – of his partners, his franchisees. He makes it clear that "we don't sell hot air". "Vom Fass is a franchise concept, and you have to pay a certain fee, which in our case is about 6000 euros. If somebody applies to us, there is a certain application procedure that we go through. It doesn't cost him anything, he is trained, we do on-site analyses, and out of every 100 requests which come in, one or to become franchise partners with us. We also do the starting advertisement onsite, the partner doesn't need to print letterheads, he needs nothing at all, he gets everything from us. He has his customers, and that practically costs him an amount of 6000 or 6500 euros. We don't want to have expensive licenses; rather we want to have partners who get enjoyment from their products and their business onsite."

With almost 300 franchise partners "you will get a few grumblers, that can't be avoided", admits Kiderlen. At the beginning of the 2000s, Vom Fass was sued for restitution due to an alleged bogus self-employment, and the case went to the federal court. In the highest instance, Kiderlen won. At that time he could have lost his entire livelihood, but only a few shops were closed. Today, he analyses: "At first, we accepted many franchisees which really didn't go along with us. Then we got the invoice, and we learned: It is important that you are faithful to yourself." Survey results of the Münster University confirm that Vom Fass currently is among the franchise companies with the highest partner satisfaction in Europe, Kiderlen is happy to report. "The bottom line is that we now have extremely satisfied partners."

The franchise and company businessman manages risks level-headed and self-consciously: "Of course we know that our system works in any country. People find that great. But it isn't the case that we just have to be on every corner. In Germany, we once thought that we will open 1000 shops. Then we reduced that, and I believe that if we have 200, the market is saturated. We don't want to cannibalise ourselves." Due to the nature of the franchise concept, in any case there is a certain risk spread, according to Kiderlen: "In the end effect, the risk is always for the franchise partner. Of course, if he doesn't stand behind it, and doesn't do it well, and his shop is dirty, that would be bad. Therefore the people are clearly trained by us from the beginning, and usually fall through. Thus, the risk for us is limited."

Financially, Kiderlen – now, because he is able to – acts conservatively: "Here in Waldburg we have of course invested a lot, and now once again we invest, in a new oil mill which we are building, and in new storerooms, etc. That does cost millions, but the bottom line is that this is calculable for us today, for we only invest what we earn. That is to say, we don't want to have bank debts. If we earn more money, we invest, and if we don't earn money, we don't. This is the current way of thinking, with respect to debt." To "just pick up a few millions" and to embark on new projects with the attitude "I hope that that works", is something that "thanks God, we don't have that anymore." Now the investments at Vom Fass "are from the cash flow, but that has to be reinvested too."

JOHANNES KIDERLEN

Kiderlen thinks in the long term: "We don't do anything in the short term, we only think in long time periods. We have a tremendously long-term way of thinking, as well as constant marketing. And yet, we have to think every day: How can we change? Change is important, but it has to be in the long term. Lateral thinkers are very important for me; every day. Contradictions are also important for me. You have to know how to manage them, you have to learn from them." In the team, they discuss "what will endure and what won't. For after all, the franchise partners invest as well. Those are also people who get independent. They come to us and set up a contract for ten years, and when the contract expires in ten years, they want to continue being with us. They want to continue having success, therefore we can't make short-term decisions."

When Kiderlen sold his beverage market chain in the mid-90s, he was 44 years old, and "started completely from scratch, from zero, with Vom Fass", he emphasises, and goes into more details about the topic of changes. His goal was to create livelihoods, and to expand the system: "We have lots of livelihoods of young people who at some time finished their school or their studies, then came to us, and nowadays have a good business. That gives me pleasure. People said, first the German market, then eventually Europe was added, and now the world. That's fun, when something grows healthily; you can't say that we'll give this up. That's also an important topic for a company: standing still means going backwards. Competitors will get on the market, and they will try to copy you – so you always need to be better than them. At some moment you are driven by the market, the market drives you, and that's fun."

In the course of his long-term orientation, regulating the succession in the family business is also important for Kiderlen: "After all, the many franchise partners all are somehow dependent on the company's success. You have to make sure there is a succession." This is ensured through Kiderlen's son Thomas, who is currently chairman of the board. "He was four years in Hong Kong, and achieved a successful position there", reports the father. "But eventually I said: 'either you come, or I make a management buyout, i.e., give it to the employees.' I have some strong people there – but he came. I can't be the boss until I am 80, as many great businesspeople do it, and then they die and the company goes down the drain, that doesn't work. I have a responsibility towards my franchise partners, towards my employees in the company and that's the task." His son, too, had initiated innovations and changes. That is simply important, and the company must continue. My goal is that I would like to continue with the company and continue working with it for many years, and to see that the company is healthy and grows, nothing more." Kiderlen doesn't see a definitive goal – for instance, "to say, once I have 1000 shops I'll stop".

Also in view of new media and digitalisation, Kiderlen trusts his son as successor. He himself, "when I consider this from the point of view of age, I am somewhat neutral. But there is my son, who took over the company today, and I am behind him, he is completely immersed, and I also see this in our Internet shop, with the access rates that we get." Dealing with online marketing, according to Kiderlen's conviction, is essential: "After all, we now train young people. They don't get around it. That's the future – whether it's the cash system which they have today, the entire networking via Facebook and Twitter, or whatever. I also have an iPad and an iPhone, and work with it. I used to say, I don't accept this type of crap, but people who are a bit fit can't avoid it. I have acquaintances who say: 'I don't buy anything over the Internet; I buy from a dealer onsite. Then I say, 'Great, I do that too, but first I get informed over the Internet, and if the dealer has that, it's OK.' Even if it's only through information, the market is canalised and mapped. They can't avoid it at all. If today we look for people, we hardly do that anymore through newspaper ads, but through Internet portals. There we get more inquiries and better people than if we set up a newspaper ad."

Kiderlen has clear expectations from new employees: "The person who introduces himself to us must think about Vom Fass, must look at Vom Fass on the Internet, must visit a shop. Either he is ablaze or he isn't, and we have no use for those that aren't. We won't convince anybody how great Vom Fass is; people should make up their own mind about that. The person who is ablaze for us will do what we do, because he is directed by the way that we go. We already notice this in the presentation talks, if somebody doesn't orient himself with our philosophy, if he doesn't know how we think. I don't convert anybody, and that works well." The appropriate employee for Vom Fass is one "who is ablaze for this idea, who wants to come to us, who walks our path, to sell quality rather than hot air", summarises Kiderlen. Employees must walk "slim paths, decide quickly, and always be flexible", and they must "show honesty. It is really quite easy, the way things work at our company." The optimal employee, however, "the egg-laying wool and milk sow, doesn't exist", knows Kiderlen. "You must simply get, out of each employee, whatever strengths he has, recognise his strengths and use him accordingly. We have people in our company who are great, we recognise that. It is interesting what people have inside them, and how they advance more and more. In the past, I unloaded many trucks by hand, in other words, I worked a lot physically. And I have a problem with people who believe that they can do everything with their head. I always say: 'First of all, go into a shop and learn what the customer wants.' We don't need to see what somebody has studied and learned; rather, he must know the market itself." Kiderlen gives the example of a new marketing leader, whom he sought. "It's quite interesting, the type of people that come, who actually learned quite a lot, who have a lot in their head, but who don't know how the market ticks. They got everything from books and who knows where else, but then I ask: 'Were you ever in a shop for half a year, and showed that you can do it?' And the answer I get is: 'Well, no, I don't need to do that.' That's difficult. We don't have secretaries or something like that, everybody in the company writes his own letters. We have well-trained people, but in our company there are very, very flat hierarchies, and everybody must be capable of communicating with others."

"I DON'T MANAGE UNDER PRESSURE, BY BEING THE BOSS; RATHER, I MANAGE WITH A VACUUM."

The type of employees also corresponds to Kiderlen's leadership style: "I have a lot of trust. When I have good people, I have them on a long leash. I have laid out my philosophy." When an employee commits a mistake, there are bosses who say, "if you do that again, if that ever happens again, you're fired!' That's not the way I handle things. Errors must be committed. I say, 'Man, now you did some crap, but I am sure you won't do that again.' That is to say, I give the people responsibility, and I have them make a promise.

JOHANNES KIDERLEN

We go together, not I in the front and the other behind me. If I go into the warehouse, and pallets have to go onto the truck, I help. I don't say that I don't need that. I don't lead with pressure, by being the boss; rather I lead with a vacuum. There are always two possibilities; pressure produces counterpressure."

A strict leadership style – "do this and that, and if you don't have it finished until this evening, there'll be trouble" – results in resistance or flight tendencies among the employees, explains Kiderlen. Leading with a vacuum, on the other hand, means messages such as "I believe that you can do that", or "I am curious whether you can manage that", and the employees must then fill this vacuum. That results in much more force – this is also the case in physics. With a vacuum, you can do much more. The same happens on the market: if you buy a wine and know there are a million litres of it, you have to sell under pressure. That is to say, you have to start a marketing action, you must have cheap prices, you must do something." In the case of a wine which is available in a limited amount, "people develop energy, to get this wine. And that, too, is my leadership style; in other words, not through pressure, but through a vacuum, and that works great. I have a cell phone, but no matter where I am, I don't get called from the company. My people are so good that they don't need me. We have our meetings, and the issue is done."

For the future, Kiderlen expects some dynamism for the wine area: "People will continue to like drinking wine, and among my acquaintances I see lots of young people who like to drink wine." For the wineries, Internet commerce is indispensable: wine sales "will be more and more online, and that includes friends getting together and placing collective orders." Kiderlen predicts a spread of the market: "The good qualities which you get everywhere nowadays will increase. The large cellars in the middle area, which only produce cheaply, as there were many in the past, will be less and less. The middle level will go more in the direction of discounters and supermarkets. They do have great wine sections and good marketing. There are more and more large bottlers, and the middle level will have to fight. You can see that with the cooperatives: if the local cooperative is really good and makes good deals regionally, they endure." The large regional winery associations, on the other hand, "are hard pressed, they join together, and thus get even larger." Somebody who, as a winemaker or merchant, does quality work, "must move in the upper segment", concludes Kiderlen; in the middle segment, the price will determine the competition.

A young businessperson in the wine sector must "be good", as Kiderlen formulates laconically: "In the past, the winemaker delivered his grapes to his cooperative. Today, such a young man must not just be able to grow wine, he must also understand the development, he must be able to do marketing – the result onsite is important. And when he is ready to do that, he will be successful." Somebody who instead of producing wine wants to trade wine "must also consider that he doesn't just open a store, but that he must organise events; lots of events, and that requires a lot of work." Events, for Kiderlen, go way beyond wine tasting; they can be wine menus in cooperation with one or more gastronomers. "And there you must do a lot, quite a lot, you must be ready to stand in the shop during the day, and then to continue moving around in the evening, in the event area. Then you will have success. But you must be ready for that; that's difficult. If somebody asks me whether he should do that, I say: 'I don't know that either.'"

JOHANNES KIDERLEN

Kiderlen quotes an aphorism: "Never wait until you have time. In other words, don't postpone it indefinitely, for if you say, I want to do that eventually, then usually you never will. I get to the company at seven in the morning, even though I have nothing more to say in the company, but I am still fully recognised, since my performance is right, and thanks God my knowledge is still appropriate. Since I am simply willing to get involved. If I once again had my professional life in front of me, I would do the same things again – only in that case, I might have started the Vom Fass idea earlier."

JOHANNES KIDERLEN

HENDRIK THOMA

Wine consultant, moderator, author, and wine importer
Hamburg, Germany

Hendrik Thoma (born 1967) is an independent wine consultant, and since 2011 he moderates the Internet wine show "Wine am Limit" ("Wine at the Limit"). Born in Westphalia, after his education Koch first worked for a few years in the profession he learned – among other things as a saucier in the "Landhaus Scherrer" in Hamburg and as a trainee in the "Auberge du Soleil" in Rutherford, California – before he completed an internship in a Rheingau winery. In 1994, he completed training for a state-certified sommelier, and in 1999 he obtained the "master sommelier diploma" as the highest international diploma for wine experts in the hospitality business. From 1994 to 1995, Thoma was chef sommelier in the "Intercontinental" hotel in Leipzig, and later occupied the same position for ten years in the hotel "Louis C. Jacob" in Hamburg. From 1999 to 2009, he moderated cooking and wine programmes at VOX and NDR, and for the last 15 years or so he writes contributions for daily papers and magazines ("Die Welt", "Welt am Sonntag", "Der Feinschmecker", "Living at Home", "Playboy"). In 2008 he got independent and consults wine investment funds, wine collectors, large wine suppliers and top-level restaurants. He also organizes wine tasting events, wine trips, and other events, and he has set up his own wine import business.

"THE MOST IMPORTANT INVESTMENT IN THE LIFE OF A WINE ENTHUSIAST IS PURCHASING A CORKSCREW."

The change from cooking to wine as his main profession was related to his stop in California, tells Thoma: With his studies as a cook, he "was really always interested in wine, and also found that very exciting." However, "there wasn't much in my environment where I could have furthered my training." Even though his parents had, among their friends, "a few people who had a great wine cellar", and during his military service time he worked in a restaurant that already had wines from the "established" German winegrowers on its card, describes Thoma. "I thought they were a bit ahead of their time. But the most important step was surely in Napa Valley, simply to learn handling wine. Especially with an international clientele as well as international players, be they French, Italians, or Germans, who after all are active in wine-growing there. I was fortunate to get in relatively well and quickly due to family relationships, and to look at a lot. After all, I also worked in the 'Auberge du Soleil', here too in part in the kitchen, but

HENDRIK THOMA

WINE
ENTREPRENEURS

I had already started to work in the winery. And the decision became clear for me: 'Now I'll get into the wine business!'"

Another influential stage in his career was then the "Louis C. Jacob" in Hamburg, says Thoma. Initially he hadn't planned to remain for 13 years in one business, "but you grow so much into a task, and the shoes you put on are at first a bit larger." At the hotel inauguration in 1996, the media had a lot of interest in the new house, while the team still had to be "shaped", he says. He then went along and experienced the team over the years, "just like the first little plants start to grow and at the end they even bear fruits. That, of course, is very decisive. In my opinion, many sommeliers as well as many people in the wine business don't stay long enough in their positions to really see the fruit of their work – for after all, the entire business – at least in the high end – is based on the long term. Create trust and credibility, and observe a market. Hence, the Jacob was surely the pivotal and crucial point for me."

His time in the Hamburger Hotel also coincided with his further training as a master sommelier, which Thoma also considers to be important for his career. "My employers didn't handcuff me; rather, they gave me quite a lot of freedom. So, while doing the job, I was also able to prepare for the examination", he remembers. "When you do this in parallel with your profession, it's really good to have an employer who gives you some freedom; after all, you do need to cram and learn. I mean, at the end you take the exam yourself, but it's also good to have someone in the background who approves that."

Freedom, or more accurately "creative freedom", was the motivation for him to become active as an entrepreneur after being for some years in an employee relationship, Thoma explains. "I noticed that there was an opening for me, left by some companies. Let's put it this way: the large ones are really not capable of giving an individual speech, and also have a huge problem with respect to personal branding. After all, large companies only live from the brand, not from the people. And I am clearly selling my person. I sell my know-how, my standing, and my opinion. When you have worked for some time as a salary slave or employee, that's really like jumping into cold water. I was lucky that due to my media presence and also due to my connections, which I had established, while I worked at Jacob I was pretty well cushioned. So I continued getting tasks from large companies, who reserve me for events; for example, for wine trips I had a large, large amount of regular private customers, who remained loyal to me. Those were all things that I had started while I was at Jacob. And now, of course, I had more time and freedom to do this. I could simply dedicate more time to it. And therefore, the jump was not so freezing, because I knew who my contacts were, and thank God, I already had customers who booked me." Thoma owes his media presence to the relevant television programmes in which he appeared as moderator or as guest, as well as the wine columns in transregional print media. "There I had already had a perception", he summarises. "Somebody who wants to get from zero to one-hundred must think it over very well. That's isn't really simple. I therefore now say that this was not a jump into cold water, but only into warm water."

Thoma defines his greatest incentive as "seeing something grow", and "for the next years, I had already planned something, precisely with 'Wein am Limit'." After he "hadn't extended, after two years" the cooperation with the wine trading company Hawekso for the wine video format TVINO, he decided: "I would like to go along my own paths. And I really started off by founding 'Wein am Limit', to be able to see what is possible or what I want; and in parallel, I continued working on my wine import. In the meantime there are 20 wineries which I represent, most of them exclusively. I want to expand that, and this year I managed to do so quite well." For his wine importing business area, Thoma "is actually quite confident. However, in this case it's a real advantage for me that I have been in this area for a long time and that I have subconsciously already done a lot of 'homework', simply by having set up a very, very good network. Of course that currently helps me in marketing and sales. That is, I get into many houses, not as petitioner or salesman, but rather as a friend or colleague talking eye-to-eye. And that's also how I consider my colleagues or customers: not as people whom I absolutely have to sell something, but as people whom I try to help find the correct assortment, and who have fun with the things that I sell them."

"PERSONALITY IS IN DEMAND ONCE AGAIN. AND ALSO, ESPECIALLY, REAL KNOW-HOW."

Thoma names his essential goal and a motivation for his activity to be responsibility: "If you list a winery, you buy their wines and must market them. However, I also know that there are families related to it, who live from it. Just as I and my family want to live from it. In other words: responsibility. However, that's not the most important reason. The most important reason for me, really, is that I have wines in my collection, wines that I want my customers in Germany to be able to experience at some moment. I dared to import things which not just any dealer dares to handle. If, like me, you have the luck to really drink all over the wine world, and to experience and see what the wine world really offers nowadays – there are many great and exciting things going on. But the customers must first be taken out of their shell, to avoid them from getting always into the same behaviour pattern. I know that many companies want their customers to always drink the same shit, and preferably that it always looks the same. But thank goodness there are small market parts – a niche, in which I participate – who are happy about variety. They have the background, and they know that in Australia you can eat very, very well and that you can drink not just thick and heavy wines, but also super elegant and fine wines." Individual wineries produce wines which are consciously opposed to "that which is otherwise on the market", says Thoma. And for this there is a small market, but that's enough for us. Thus it is large enough after all – there are not many market participants."

In general, in the wine area there are "very different approaches", judges Thoma. He acknowledges that large wine business groups do have professionalism in their area: "Those, of course, are people who know their stuff. They have a strong background in sales, they have marketing knowledge, and they are very, very good in collecting addresses. So, in other words: They don't differ from other industrial companies. However, that's precisely the gap which such companies often leave behind, namely for small entrepreneurs whose approach is to have a very targeted assortment and a much more personal appeal, and perhaps even more sophistication. Of course they, too, have their justification on the market." Thoma considers entrepreneurship in the wine business as "partially sluggish",

HENDRIK THOMA

as he admits, "but of course there is also a dynamic part of this area; however it is small. The German market is basically very conservative, and nowadays many customers buy not because they want to have the wine, but because the advertising appeals to them, because they want to get six glasses, or because they get a crossed-out price. That, I think, is something that is not conscious for many who want to approach the subject with passion and fervour. They find such things hard to handle. Thus, in other words: it certainly is a tough market, many move in it. But not everybody can swim in this type of water."

To be successful as an entrepreneur in the wine area, according to Thoma you "should be progressive" and "use the Internet, Social Media, YouTube, and whatever it is all called for yourself. But I am a bit old school in this sense. I believe that personality is in demand once again. And especially, also, real know-how." People who sell wines should "consider their wineries a bit as their sheep. In other words, those are people whom they must place on the market. A big problem which many dealers have nowadays is this tremendously tough price competition on the Internet, which results in competition distortion. After all, in Germany more or less anybody can import any wine. Unfortunately that has resulted in the fact that this area is professional only in some cases. We have a lot of what I tend to call garage dealers. They were on vacations, purchased two palettes of wine, and somehow peddle it over the Internet. And they do it at prices which don't allow doing a qualitatively good work. That is to say, they put the prices on the Internet. But what really matters if you want to sell really good wine is that you know the people, that you know your customers, that you know their wine card, that you know their needs, that you don't oversell, that you also sell the people a good feeling." Thoma describes this approach as the old-school. "But I also claim: Nowadays you must also be capable of knocking; you must be able to bang on the table, you must be able to show that you are there. For this, I claim, there is once again the Internet with all its possibilities, like what I do with 'Wein am Limit', for example. But there are also other countries, for example the USA, in which Gary Vaynerchuk has shown that you can thus shake an entire business area in its foundations. In Germany we'll have to wait a few years for that to happen, but I am convinced that this will happen here as well. That is, part of the business area must really wake up."

Another factor for success, according to Thoma, is a certain specialisation in the offer: "Exclusivity is important. The market has become fast, has become rapid." German Internet dealers, he says, not only sell their wines in Austria, where they speak the same language, but they also sell it "quickly in Holland or in Denmark, by making their website bilingual." Therefore it has become even more important to concentrate; and Thoma means "that you clearly choose the segment in which you want to work, and that you don't just manage a vendor tray, as many wine dealers used to do in the past. That is to say, they sold all sorts of stuff, because there was somehow a customer for every article. Nowadays people buy everything they need for their daily needs from a specialist or from a generalist."

Thoma defines success as "the sum of all parts", and performance, for him, is "the willingness to give everything. Ultimately, of course, you also have to take a look at the bank account; there is no way to avoid that. But I think that the most important success that you can have is that an idea starts to grow and that you can duplicate the idea.

HENDRIK THOMA

Considering this, entrepreneurial success, on the one hand, can of course be measured in numbers, but on the other hand it is the recognition that you get – from outside, but also from within, from friends, etc. Success means that you find your place in society." Thoma identifies his personal recipe for success "the fact that I stayed consistently with one topic." After an "interlude at Metro, which not everybody understood" and that "failed due to many small as well as some large things", he recognized: "That won't be the path that I go. So, I remain consistently with one topic. I believe that many people try to tackle too much. So either you go high-end, or you make a discount, and you can do that very well. But I consider having a vendor tray not to be credible. You can't sell Aldi wine and guzzle Mouton Rothschild."

According to Thoma's opinion, entrepreneurial decisions are taken "with the heart and a gut feeling. However, your intellect must of course always be awake, and you have to recognize your opportunities. You have to be careful that you don't somehow make a fool of yourself. Mistakes are unavoidable, and especially, they are quite wonderful since you can learn from them. Contradictions, too, if they are well-presented, are something that you will always have to think about; sometimes they are even the greater part of recognition. And lateral thinkers are extremely important, for otherwise we would have no innovation." With this background, Thoma advocates "rather the art of small and conscious steps"; a successful entrepreneur, he says, "must always be able to take a look at his environment and ponder it." He considers it as a fact that decisions also imply risks: "Nobody knows what tomorrow will be like. Currently, thank goodness, we have a business boom, which also favours the area of wine sales a bit. That is to say, people have more money, feel secure, and are willing to spend more money for wine. I also notice this in the situation of my orders: there is a budget available for bookings, events, what agencies do and plan." He "hasn't planned" for economically more difficult times, Thoma admits. "Of course I have reserves. After all, the topic of high-end wines, which I mainly represent, has a lot to do with a functioning economy. And with the topic of wine, we are not on place number one of people's needs."

Thoma's favourite quote is from Antoine de Saint-Exupéry: "You can only see well with the heart; the essential things are hidden from the eyes.' That touches me again and again. That, I think, is a very nice story, that you shouldn't let yourself be guided by superficialities, but rather – and very importantly – from the things that really mean something." He himself is successful, he says, "because I want to be it. The important thing for me is that I like to do what I do. And that radiates unconsciously to my surroundings." He understands motivation in this way. "I don't vie it; I simply do what I think is right, but I always find the customers. I always said that to my people at Jacob: 'If you really want to become a good waiter or sommelier, you have to behave as the customers would like you to.' A waiter should have the same demands as a customer, but he should fulfil his customer and not himself. That is, of course he should go into a restaurant at some time and let it affect him. What do you want? Do you want a sommelier, do you want consultation? Thus, you should go ahead and develop needs, for only from such needs you can consider what you can give to others. Many people are quite afraid of their customers, because they don't assess their needs at all; because they simply want to continue doing their job, and think that it's enough to carry the dish out or to serve the wine. But the difference is always made by those who are capable of seeing or

HENDRIK THOMA

reading their customer. That's what I claim." This property, emphasizes Thoma, is also relevant in telephone marketing and wine sales: "You must be able to listen to your customer, to know what he likes to drink. That won't work any other way. The moment you are not able to do that, you simply sell by formula, and off the shelf. And the customer will notice that; in which case he will only buy according to the price, or because he absolutely wants to have the product. But in the long term, you can't achieve customer loyalty that way. You only achieve that if you really manage to read your customer."

For Thoma, "It is important to transmit enjoyment, and snobbishness has no place there." For him, openness and reliability are the basis for getting along with employees. After all, I am only a small entrepreneur, more or less a one-man-show; now I have hired two ladies who help me in the daily business", he recounts. He describes his leadership style as "open and also dynamic. That is, I do specify a pace, and people who work with me must be able to keep up with that pace. In this I am uncompromising; I do expect this. We are a super small team; in this case there may not be much between the people, you have to be very open with one another. Of course, for the front I am the Capo, but it is much more important that the processes work in the back. After all, you can make a lot of wind; of course you have to beat the drums. But others must work well, and especially, it must be fun for them. In other words, the guy who beats the drums must motivate the people and not oppress them."

For his activity in the wine area, Thoma considers it important "that an employee should not only have a passion for technical processes, but wine should also be fun for him. In that case it is much simpler. I believe that every bookkeeper who also likes to drink a glass of wine can do his bookkeeping much better and understand much more about the relationships than if he just stupidly does his job. Passion for a product is very important; it can, or it must, go through the people in a company. For in that case, it isn't service according to prescription. You might say that wine is, for me, the liquid in which I like to swim." On the other hand, in the case of a high wine affinity by the employees, Thoma warns "that everybody thinks that he knows things better than others. So, if you gather a bunch of such know-it-all's around you, of course there is a risk that the leadership style is affected by that. But for me, the optimal employee is one who understands himself as a brand. This almost takes us, again, to the topic of social media: nowadays, it is very important for me that an employee has his own history on the Internet, that he communicates with the people or with the customers there. And that he stands up consciously, saying 'That's my opinion.' There are already enough yes-men. You also need people who have a personality."

The prerequisite to have motivated and successful employees "must of course first be, that a company continues progressing", demands Thoma. "After all, many companies stagnate or like to continue with that which they know. In other words, the employees are then pressed into a mould. You have to provide dynamism, for people to feel well. I claim that this is as in the zoo: The animals also need good caretakers, and the optimal leadership style, I think, takes into account each employee's very different needs. And a leadership style must really include that, the fact that it recognizes that. In every company you have to observe what the employees want, and of course you must also be able to judge whether they are capable of it."

For a company to survive on the market, Thoma considers a sovereign dealing with digital technology and social media to be essential. "In this sense, I must say that Germany is still somewhat sluggish", he laments. Young customers have already grown up with the Internet; "for them, there is nothing new. But of course those are not necessarily those who have a fat purse. The customers of tomorrow will know more than today's customers. They can compare prices and quickly get information online in different places. Mobile, too, in other words is at the shelf in the point of sale. That means that not only the price will matter, but of course also a liking for a specific brand. And social media can help load a brand with emotions. I believe that here social media are completely misunderstood as a sales tool. With social media you can show how a company works from inside, how well it is positioned, and how interested it really is in a true dialogue with its customers. Many companies nowadays have a person in charge of social media, but that is usually the trainee. I think that many people who are in management and in the boardroom nowadays don't fancy the idea at all; they recognize or acknowledge that they have to work on it, but they really only do it half-heartedly. After all, many companies don't really want to expose a lot about their internal structures." Thoma laments that hardly a wine dealer offers video interviews with its wineries on their website: "Precisely in the wine topic there are so many nice stories which they could tell. They might stop right now with the wine lyricism and instead show the people, the techniques, behind it, but especially also the effort, which people make in artisanal work."

Thoma assumes that the market "will become independent anyway". The companies "that then dominate such a market are not necessarily the fast ones; those will be especially the fast ones. I claim that in the long term, the fast ones will eat up the slow ones, and not necessarily only the large ones will eat up the small ones. And that is surely stimulated by the digital revolution and the social media", he is convinced. Many Internet presences "are only powered by processes", he analyses, "but we must not forget: We really have the technology to simplify things for us. We shouldn't become slaves to technology. Nowadays many companies only use crossed-out prices, and cheaper, and minus 60%, and then they add six glasses to the offer, just to grab the addresses. But I think that that doesn't necessarily make a brand more credible. And in the long term it doesn't give it any lustre, either; on the contrary, it is more likely to take away from its glamour. And people ask themselves, if you get 60% off on a wine – what was it worth before that? That gets quite dangerous."

On the Internet, you need to "have a good content for there to be relevance at all", explains Thoma. "There are many people who get into the business and do anything, but that is so insignificant or uninteresting for the customer that there is no demand whatsoever. But more important than the traffic is that you start a dialogue with the customer. And social media are good for that, to keep the customers interested and to provide them with information. Nowadays, if a customer lives in Nuremberg you can very well consult him very well from Hamburg, and serve him personally; at least, that's the feeling he gets. This closeness is achieved with social media. That's the really revolutionary thing about it. But as I said before, here in Germany I have the feeling that in many boardrooms there are control freaks who are afraid of social media. They know that they must do it, but they also know that on the other hand they are sitting on the

HENDRIK THOMA

powder keg. For if they once publish a bad post, there is a damn big storm, that's what they are most afraid of. They are afraid of transparency. In this case, social media are once again counterproductive, or a few cuddle up in it." And yet, the presence in social media is a considerable success factor, according to Thoma. He got the largest learning effect from an Internet video, in the creation of which he participated as a guest of Gary Vaynerchuk in his "Wine Library": "What I really found to be great is that you suddenly have a huge feedback rate. I didn't have that in printing, nor in television; I got that through the Internet. For me, that was an influential experience, this direct contact with the customer. And there I noticed: it's better to work with a small community, but in an effective way, than for example with a large community. Here a video channel is extremely good, since whatever I do on my side is uncut, raw; I want it to be handmade. The people should simply see that I like to do that, that I find that to be fun, and that basically anybody can do that."

Thoma clarifies that social media also includes the fact that a customer that has a question gets a reply, even if he doesn't purchase anything. Here the phrase of the "thank-you economy" has a role. I believe that if somebody feels good on a website and notices that he is a welcome guest, that he is expected to comment and that he is noticed, that's the same as when he goes into a good shop, where he might not always purchase something, or not purchase a lot, but where he continues constantly being a good customers, because he notices that he isn't anonymous and that the people who are sitting on the other side do their job with fun and enjoyment and love."

"THE FAST ONES WILL EAT UP THE SLOW ONES; IT IS NOT NECESSARILY JUST THE LARGE ONES WHO WILL EAT UP THE SMALL ONES."

HENDRIK THOMA

Thomas's forecast for the future development of the wine market is ambivalent: "If the economic situation continues being stable, then it will continue looking good for the wine area, I think. I believe that the market will continue diversifying, the Internet will have a large participation, the price war will get tougher, and wineries who today don't think clearly to whom they give their ware may founder with their brand. For today there are lots of dealers who only want to define themselves via the price, and who don't care what they trade. A winery can no longer rely on producing the wine and simply giving it to the market and that somebody sells it in his interest. For here it is very important – precisely if you produce high-quality wines – that you establish long-term partnerships. For the next ten years, I think it will become tougher, but there are also other possibilities." If anybody wants to survive successfully as a wine entrepreneur in this market, he must be able to reflect and have a relevant product assortment, according to Thoma. "If it has no relevance, he needs to create it, and then he must use all the possibilities which the market provides today. And there I am, once again, in my favourite topic of the Internet and social media: if you don't have a large budget, those are precisely the correct tools. For social media doesn't cost me much, other than time. And those are things with which you have to occupy yourself and which you have to confront. If you don't do that, you may lose out during the next few years, for the customer base that is growing up now has quite a different understanding in the digital area. That doesn't mean that they are completely in bondage, but for them, it's nothing unusual. For the older clientele, who are quite solvent nowadays, that really doesn't make a difference. They have their interests looked after, and they might perhaps look into the Internet now and then, but they purchase at quite different conditions. The market will continue to grow, and if you need qualifications, it is precisely to generate the required traffic for yourself."

For an entrepreneur who wants to enter the wine area today, Thoma advises that he must have "gone through all the different aspects": "He should have the qualifications as well as the passion for the product. Sometimes I have the feeling that some are only driven by processes, and that precisely people such as business administrators or computer scientists know perfectly well how to set up a business. But a business must be filled up by contents – at least in the wine area – and I would say, especially when wine gets personal. Therefore I would advise the people to start off by doing their homework, perhaps on the basis that they do an internship at a winery, that they perhaps get a bloody nose and really do acquisitions in a door-to-door business. That way, they know how their customer looks; many of them don't know how the customer looks."

HENDRIK THOMA

MIGUEL A. TORRES
President, Bodegas Torres
Vilafranca del Penedès, Spain

Miguel A. Torres (born 1941), together with his siblings Juan M. and Marimar Torres, is co-owner of the winery Bodegas Torres in Vilafranca del Penedès near Barcelona, which was founded in 1870 by Jaime Torres, and with over 1800 hectares of vine area is currently one of Spain's most important producers. The family business also includes the wineries Jean León in Penedès, Miguel Torres Chile in South America, and Marimar Torres Estate in California. Torres studies Chemistry in Barcelona since 1957, Oenology and Winegrowing since 1959 in Dijon, and joined the Bodega in 1962.

"YOU CAN ONLY PURSUE THE WINE BUSINESS IF YOU HAVE LOVE FOR NATURE AND FOR THE PRODUCT WINE, BUT NOT OUT OF PURE COMMERCIAL REASONS."

Today, the fourth family generation – Miguel A. Torres as president, as well as Juan M. Torres and Marimar Torres as vice presidents – manage the business jointly with the fifth generation, represented by Miguel Torres Maczassek (manager of the Torres Group since September 2012), Mireia Torres Maczassek (manager of the winery in Priorat, of Jean Leon, and responsible for the new Cava Project), Arnaud Torres Rosselló and Cristina Torres. In addition, Anna Torres Maczassek and Marta Torres Rosselló also belong to the fifth generation; they are part of the company's board of directors. Miguel A Torres's German wife Waltraud is the president of the Miguel Torres Foundation.

For his success in the world of wine, he received numerous international awards.

Torres introduced international vine varieties of French origin such as Cabernet Sauvignon and Chardonnay to the winery and relied early on increasing quality through yield reduction and through the use of modern cellar technology. To put these innovations into practice, he had to struggle a lot with his father, as he recounts: "It was very, very difficult. Perhaps I didn't have enough patience. I wanted too many changes all at once. The situation in 1981 was not entirely simple, and therefore I decided to do a sabbatical. So I left the company for a year. My father accepted that. At that time he was still chairman, I was director, so for a year, that was feasible." Torres was attracted to neighbouring countries: "My journey took me to the University of Montpellier. There I had time to think and to expand my capabilities. But after my return, I also had to learn to continue having patience, and to ring in changes only slowly." Despite the differences with his father, "we had a harmonic relationship until his death in 1991", says Torres. But his own experiences ware a lesson for him: "Today, with my children, I do this differently. I don't need to commit the same error", he observes. "Today my son works as the manager, and I only care about the areas of environment, legal, and public relations. But even at interview I refer to my children and seldom make exceptions – for example when the topics are environment and climate change. As a result, my son has full authority, and I no longer give instructions. But I do inquire and get informed, for instance about what happens on the German market, etc. But I don't say what should be done as a result."

"IF YOU THINK ABOUT SUCCESS, FIRST THINK ABOUT YOUR FAMILY. FOR YOU'LL HAVE NO SUCCESS IF YOU FORGET YOUR FAMILY."

Apart from his involvement in the company, Torres is active in two charitable organisations which he founded: the Miguel Torres Foundation, which is involved in social projects such as building schools, and the Torres & Earth Initiative, which combats climate change and supports reforestation measures. Bodegas Torres itself deals with ecological winegrowing since the mid-70s, and refrains completely from using insecticides and herbicides. The architecture of the current winery fulfils all environmental and energy standards – the wastewaters are processed, renewable energies from solar and wind power are used exclusively, a biomass power station is operated, and the company fleet consists of environmentally friendly vehicles with hybrid drive. "Protecting nature is one of our most important priorities, and one of our most important goals is to reduce the carbon dioxide emission per manufactured bottle by 30% until the year 2020", explains Torres.

"Wine is my life", he expresses with great pleasure: "My favourite wine is the one of my friends. In 1991, together with Robert Drouhin, I founded the Primum Familiae Vini Foundation, in which the world's leading wineries come together: Marchesi Antinori, Château Mouton-Rothschild, Maison Joseph Drouhin, Egon Müller Scharzhof, Hugel et Fils, Champagne Pol Roger, Famille Perrin, Symington Family Estates, Tenuta San Guido and Vega Sicilia. Of course I prefer to drink my friends' wine – and of course my Mas la Plana." The Mas la Plana location is also the origin of the Torreswine, which in the 1979 "Wine Olympics" of the Gault & Millau Leader, as a Spanish Cabernet Sauvignon, beat the famous Bordeaux. Torres appears self-conscious, but also sensitive: "I believe that the victory in 1979 was good and important. Perhaps it was a bit too much of a good thing – too much success? The wine Olympics has made it clear and visible – precisely in European and American markets – that Spain can produce wine in premium quality. Perhaps we weren't prepared for this great success. In the past, Robert Parker had given our Mas La Plana good grades, but after that, the situation was once again different, and we increased prices by 50%. Perhaps that wasn't so good, for many journalists, as well as Robert Parker, didn't necessarily agree with that. Perhaps that was an error. Today it is clear: Success doesn't necessarily mean to be able to charge higher prices."

MIGUEL A. TORRES

Torres is also self-critical with respect to the wine business: "You have to note that the wine business area is certainly not something for intelligent businesspeople. You can only handle the wine business if you have love for nature and for the product wine, but not for purely commercial reasons", he clarifies. "The structure as a family business keeps us stable and independent. 95% of the profit stays in the company, and 1% of the turnover is invested in research projects – for products, packaging, experimental vineyards, and quality increase."

For him, becoming a businessperson wasn't a deliberate decision, reports Torres: "I didn't think about this when I started. In 1962 I came back to the company and worked there. And after all, I wasn't manager from the beginning. This continued in small steps, starting with the product development, and passing through other sections. Then I gradually took over more responsibility, until I became the general director. I didn't decide consciously to become a businessperson, since after all it was more or less clear that that's what I would be when my father was no longer among us. I don't believe that as a young person I had a specific idea about this. When you are 25 or 30 years old, you simply do, and want to achieve something. But you don't have these clear ideas and goals, to become a businessperson one day. I have to say that I have also always thought with a strong product orientation. I was strongly influenced by the chemical and technical part – especially after I returned from Montpellier. And when my father died, I continued my training in business administration in Lausanne, for until then I didn't know much about that."

"COMPANIES WANT FORECASTS FOR A LARGE TIME PERIOD – THEY SET UP GOALS AND WRITE BUSINESS PLANS. BUT THAT DOESN'T WORK! YOU HAVE TO BE WELL-PREPARED AND BE FLEXIBLE."

Torres's driving force is striving for quality, as he explains: "For me, motivation is challenge. Performance for me is hard work and self-confidence, if you start something; to always have a goal. It's important to work really hard and to always motivate your people. For many, success is equated to wealth. I want to be among the absolute worldwide top of quality wineries." Torres gives an example: "I was just in Tokyo, and there we did a blind tasting – Mas la Plana with Japanese journalists and professionals. There we were certainly very convincing. But bottles that cost around 600 Euros also participated, and Mas la Plana just costs one-tenth of that. But you have to approach this development thoughtfully and not commit the same error as in 1979. We have to do this slowly." Torres also evaluates the concept of success in a similarly differentiated and careful way: "I am not sure at all whether we are successful. In general, of course, you might say that we are somewhat successful. But still there is so much to do, such an incredibly large amount. We are still very far from our goal. The final goal is our vision, as I said before, to be along the world's top ten quality wineries. Also, that the continuation of our business in the fifth generation continues being so successful. That's very important. I get older, and the younger generation has to take over completely."

MIGUEL A. TORRES

Torres is happy about small events that confirm his success: "I just came back from To-kyo, and we flew from Dubai to Barcelona – with the large airbus and in the business class. That has a bar, one where you can go and take a drink together with the other people. And after 20 minutes, there were a lot of people there who came to me and said: 'Hey, aren't you Mr. Torres? I like your wines.' That's nice. People know the brand. And the same happened to me in China. And I believe that that's the reason that we won the prize 'The World's Most Admired Wine Brand 2014', and got selected the world's favourite wine brand – ahead of Casillero del Diablo, Château Latour, Penfolds, Château d'Yquem or Château Margaux. Many people know the brand and trust it. You know that if it says Torres, it contains a good wine. That's success for me. Good wine and good results among consumers and professionals."

For Torres, the brand is the centre of his success considerations, for the issue is "a constant search for added value for the brand. I am no longer the wine maker, in this sense I can't do much there, but I recognise Japan as a market, so I sit down and learn Japanese. That way I can help my brand, even if I am 73 years old. And anyway, that's also good for the head." Torres urges to consider success integrally: "Success for me is progress. Some can be measured. Many people believe they are successful because they are active in 150 countries and received several international awards. But true success – that's very difficult to reply for me. Are you successful because you were on the front page of New York Times? Or because you have a lot of money? The only small recom-mendation that I want to give is that if you think about success, first think about your family. For you have no success if you forget your family."

When dealing with risks, according to Torres's opinion life experience plays a role: "Er-rors, for me, are possibilities to learn. With age, you get more conscious of risks and perhaps you take fewer risks. Still, you must take decisions over and over. With the risks it is perhaps as with mountaineering: A young man can quickly climb the mountain; on the other hand, an older man has a larger and more complex overview, and due to his experience, he can think through different scenarios. That is possibly an advantage."

Torres recommends farsighted thinking and acting, and with an example, he once again refers to the central importance of brand and image: "What happens with a manager in publicly listed company who spends 300,000 euros to renovate a school in China, after it was destroyed by an earthquake? What do you think? Yes, he'll probably be fired, for his purpose is to get profit for the company. But in a family business it is possible to take such decisions. For our manager, who did precisely that, has taken a video of the school before and after, and if we show that to our customers today, they are very impressed by our commitment, which they don't necessarily expect from a Spanish company. People can hardly believe that. And so, it turns out that money often comes back somewhere else. If you give money to society, it often comes back by itself; not always, but quite often. And in any case it's good for the brand."

For Torres, values are very important in his company. He calls the company model in which they are summarised the brand DNA. "The most important thing at Torres are the people", he emphasises. "And the people are not just our own employees, but also the customers, providers, and everybody who participates in the value chain. Fair trade is the keyword. We pay fair prices. That applies to the 900 winegrowers in Spain, as well as their colleagues in Chile. We expect our employees to identify with this DNA and that at any time they consider what they can do for Torres and how they can create added value. Here it's especially important for us that our employees enjoy their work. We want them to come happily to Torres every day."

Torres has a high opinion of situational leading, as he explains: "If I had the time or the possibility once again, I would study psychology. I believe that today a manager needs psychological knowledge. I always read every edition of the Harvard Business Review, and at least half of the articles are about the topic of psychology and applied management. Perhaps I should have done that. In management courses, books, and from gurus, I heard and read that there is a certain type of managers and these types of leadership styles; the cooperative one, the democratic one, etc. Perhaps six or seven types in total. But I also read – and I believe that that's the truth – that in your leadership style, you have to adapt to the situation and the person. For example, if an emergency occurs – and in my times, we had several of those – then I am the captain, and I have to take the decisions. At that moment you have to take the steering wheel and be the captain – precisely when you don't have much time and options. In other cases, as an executive you have to always give your best, and have your managers participate; you must give them the chance to unfold. It depends a lot on the specific situation."

However, the employees, too, must bring the correct attitude, clarifies Torres: "Of course we have clear job descriptions. Even so, everybody here must be willing to do everything in each position, and must not be too good for anything. Even if it isn't your job, you shouldn't be too elegant to go into no-man's land somewhere in the world and give a customer presentation, or to stand in a shop somewhere in the tropics at 40 degrees Celsius, on a beer crate, and sell wine. I would say that we have a 'low key profile'. If, for example, I hear from a customer that somebody from the sales team has announced his visit for nine and then he only arrives at ten, I must say quite clearly that that's no man for Torres, or that we are no company for him. I know that here in the company everybody is very busy and that the workload due to meetings and conferences is very high, but I have the opinion that every manager must always be very near to the customer."

Closeness to the customer also results from digital change and social networks, but "to that, I must say that it isn't my world", admits Torres. "Sometimes I ask my managers how many fans we have on Facebook, and I am always very impressed when I hear that it's now close to 300,000. That always sounds fantastic for me, and I hope that it's true. But I don't use it myself. I don't have a profile at Facebook or other networks. I do work with emails, but I don't like to do that with a PC, rather with my smartphone. In Japan, too, I checked my emails every day, that isn't difficult. But the other digital media, that's not my world."

For the future, Torres hopes "that the wine topic continues developing. Companies want to make forecasts for long periods of time – they set up goals and write business plans. But that doesn't work! How are you supposed to know all that? Everything changes so quickly – precisely in politics. So what should you do? I have learned that at the university: You must be well prepared, and flexible. Take a look at the Russia crisis. Would

MIGUEL A. TORRES

somebody have thought a year ago that that would happen? That was a very interesting market, and as a result of the Ukraine crisis, and the devaluation of the rouble, now the situation is suddenly quite different, and we sell less there. Things can change that quickly. Everybody concentrates on the emerging markets such as Russia, Brazil, China, and India, but there are additional interesting markets, which so far had a shadowy existence, for instance Poland, the Philippines, Korea, and the growing middle class in Africa. Wine increases the qualitative standard of living, and I hope that that continues being so."

For the next generation in business, Torres first of all has a general message: "Many young people go to the University, at some moment they get their degree as an engineer or something similar, and then they hang their certificate on the wall in their office. But that's not enough. Nowadays you need to learn permanently, all your life – that's education." Someone who wants to get started in the wine business should first of all ask himself "whether he has analysed all the options for himself", recommends Torres. "Only if he is really in love with the product and is into nature, if that satisfies him and not just the big money, he should try it. This is no easy business; you can see that every day, in Germany as well as in Spain; more and more companies want to get into the wine business area."

MIGUEL A. TORRES

CREDITS & MENTIONS

Photo Heinz Kammerer	Wein & Co	© Susanne Sellinger
Photo Friedrich-Wilhelm Dauphin	Allée Bleue Estate	© Allée Bleue Estate
Photo François Perrin	Château de Beaucastel	© Famille Perrin
Photo Eduardo Chadwick	Viña Errázuriz	© Viña Errázuriz
Photo Christian Ress	Balthasar Ress winery	© Balthasar Ress
Photo Roland Köhler	Publisher Vinum	© kömedia ag
Photo Sir George Fistonich	Villa Maria Estate	© Villa Maria Estate
Photo Doug Shafer	Shafer Vineyards	© Shafer Vineyards
Photo Christoph Mack	Mack & Schühle	© Mack & Schühle
Photo Frédéric Drouhin	Maison Joseph Drouhin	© Maison Joseph Drouhin
Photo Gary Vaynerchuk	Wine communicator	© VaynerMedia
Photo Wilhelm Klinger	AWMB	© Monika Saulich
Photo Utz Graafmann	Wein-Plus	© Karoline Glasow
Photo Leo Hillinger	Leo Hillinger winery	© Weingut Leo Hillinger
Photo Angelo Gaja	Az. Agr. Gaja	© Az. Agr. Gaja
Photo Stuart Pigott	Wine journalist	© Robin Schwartz
Photo Gerhard Eichelmann	Wine critic	© Verlag Mondo Heidelberg
Photo Roman Niewodniczanski	Van Volxem winery	© Van Volxem
Photo Wolfgang M. Rosam	Publisher Falstaff	© Rosam GmbH
Photo Max Gärtner	Vicampo	© Vicampo
Photo Gerd Rindchen	Rindchen's Weinkontor	© Marcus Vogel
Photo Martin Kössler	K&U Weinhalle	© K&U Weinhalle
Photo Johannes Kiderlen	Vom Fass	© Vom Fass
Photo Hendrik Thoma	Wine consultant	© Michael Holz
Photo Miguel A. Torres	Bodegas Torres	© Miguel Torres S.A.
Photo Prof. Dr. Ruth Fleuchaus	Heilbronn University	© Hochschule Heilbronn
Photo Alexander Schreck	Editor	© Armin Dörr Photography
Photo Carsten M. Stammen	Editor	© Dirk Beichert BusinessPhoto
Cover design	Medienagenten Bad Dürkheim	medienagenten.de
Transcriptions	TranskriptionsSpezialist Augsburg	transkriptionsspezialist.de
Translations	Giuseppe Tricarico Berlin	dadatranslation.de
Photos inner part	Misha Sokolnikov, Dinuraj K.	
Layout inner part	photowebhouse Nicole Effendy	photowebhouse.de

Zeitfracht Medien GmbH
Ferdinand-Jühlke-Straße 7
99095 Erfurt, Deutschland
produktsicherheit@kolibri360.de